THE CAMBRIDGE COMPANION TO
THOMAS PYNCHON

The most celebrated American novelist of the past half-century, an indispensable figure of postmodernism worldwide, Thomas Pynchon notoriously challenges his readers. This *Companion* provides tools for meeting that challenge. Comprehensive, accessible, lively, up-to-date and reliable, it approaches Pynchon's fiction from various angles, calling on the expertise of an international roster of scholars at the cutting edge of Pynchon studies. Part I covers Pynchon's fiction novel by novel from the sixties to the present, including such indisputable classics as *The Crying of Lot 49* and *Gravity's Rainbow*. Part II zooms out to give a bird's-eye view of Pynchon's novelistic practice across his entire career. Part III surveys major topics of Pynchon's fiction: history, politics, alterity ("otherness"), and science and technology. Designed for students, scholars and fans alike, the *Companion* begins with a biography of the elusive author and ends with a coda on how to read Pynchon and a bibliography for further reading.

INGER H. DALSGAARD is Associate Professor of American Studies, Department of English, University of Aarhus, Denmark.

LUC HERMAN is Professor of American Literature and Narrative Theory at the University of Antwerp.

BRIAN MCHALE is Distinguished Arts and Humanities Professor of English at the Ohio State University.

A complete list of books in the series is at the end of this book

T0318290

THE CAMBRIDGE
COMPANION TO
THOMAS
PYNCHON

EDITED BY
INGER H. DALSGAARD
LUC HERMAN
BRIAN MCHALE

CAMBRIDGE
UNIVERSITY PRESS

CAMBRIDGE
UNIVERSITY PRESS

University Printing House, Cambridge CB2 8BS, United Kingdom

Cambridge University Press is part of the University of Cambridge.

It furthers the University's mission by disseminating knowledge in the pursuit of education, learning and research at the highest international levels of excellence.

www.cambridge.org
Information on this title: www.cambridge.org/9780521173049

© Cambridge University Press 2012

First published 2012
Reprinted 2012

A catalogue record for this publication is available from the British Library

Library of Congress Cataloguing in Publication data
The Cambridge companion to Thomas Pynchon / [edited by]
Inger H. Dalsgaard, Luc Herman, Brian McHale.
p.   cm. – (Cambridge companions to literature)
Includes bibliographical references and index.
ISBN 978-0-521-76974-7 (hardback) – ISBN 978-0-521-17304-9 (paperback)
1. Pynchon, Thomas–Criticism and interpretation.
I. Dalsgaard, Inger H.   II. Herman, Luc.   III. McHale, Brian.
PS3566.Y55Z5766 2011
813´.54–dc23
2011037730

ISBN 978-0-521-76974-7 Hardback
ISBN 978-0-521-17304-9 Paperback

CONTENTS

CONTENTS

CONTRIBUTORS

JEFF BAKER teaches at Moorpark College in Moorpark, California. He lives in the San Fernando Valley with his wife, poet Kim Young, and their daughter, Annie Blue. He continues to be interested in and has published various essays on what John Krafft calls "the strangely neglected subject of Pynchon's quintessential Americanness."

HANJO BERRESSEM teaches American Literature at the University of Cologne, Germany. His publications include *Pynchon's Poetics: Interfacing Theory and Text* (1993) and *Lines of Desire: Reading Gombrowicz's Fiction with Lacan* (1998). He has edited, together with Leyla Haferkamp, *Site-Specific: Pynchon\Germany*, *Pynchon Notes*, 54–55 (2008) and *Deleuzian Events: Writing\History* (2009). Currently, he is completing a book on the work of Gilles Deleuze: *"Crystal Philosophy": Radical Constructivism and the Deleuzian Event*.

DAVID COWART, Louise Fry Scudder Professor at the University of South Carolina, is the author of *Thomas Pynchon: The Art of Allusion* (1980) and numerous articles on Pynchon and contemporary American fiction. His most recent books are *Don DeLillo: The Physics of Language*, which won the SAMLA Literary Studies Award in 2003, and *Trailing Clouds: Immigrant Writing in Contemporary America* (2006). A consulting editor for the journal *Critique*, Professor Cowart has been an NEH fellow and has held Fulbright chairs in Finland and Denmark.

INGER H. DALSGAARD is Associate Professor in American Studies at the University of Aarhus, Denmark, and holds a doctoral degree from King's College, University of London, and MIT. Her work on Thomas Pynchon, science and technology has been published in a number of collections and journals, including *Pynchon Notes*.

BERNARD DUYFHUIZEN is Associate Dean of Arts and Sciences and Professor of English at the University of Wisconsin-Eau Claire. His research interests include Thomas Pynchon, the novel and narrative theory. He is the author of *Narratives of Transmission* (1992), and he is completing a study of the reader in *Gravity's*

Rainbow. Duyfhuizen is also a member of the musical group Eggplant Heroes, whose first CD, *After This Time*, was released in 2010.

AMY J. ELIAS teaches contemporary literature and culture, narrative theory and digital humanities at the University of Tennessee. She is the author of *Sublime Desire: History and Post-1960s Fiction* (2001), which won the ISSN's Perkins Prize, has published numerous articles and book chapters concerning contemporary narrative, media arts and historiography, and is completing a book on dialogics. She is creator and past president of ASAP: The Association for the Study of the Arts of the Present and organized its 2009 launch conference.

LUC HERMAN teaches at the University of Antwerp. He is the author of *Concepts of Realism* (1996), the co-author of *Handbook of Narrative Analysis* (2005), the editor of *Approach and Avoid: Essays on* Gravity's Rainbow (1998) and the co-editor of *(Dis)continuities: Essays on Paul de Man* (1988). His research interests in narrative theory and the work of Thomas Pynchon have led to co-authored essays in *Contemporary Literature, Critique, Mosaic, Narrative, Pynchon Notes, Style* and *Texas Studies in Literature and Language*.

KATHRYN HUME is Edwin Erle Sparks Professor of English at Pennsylvania State University. She has written numerous articles on Thomas Pynchon's novels, and her books include *Fantasy and Mimesis: Responses to Reality in Western Literature* (1984); *Pynchon's Mythography: An Approach to* Gravity's Rainbow (1987); *Calvino's Fictions: Cogito and Cosmos* (1992); *American Dream, American Nightmare: Fiction since 1960* (2000); and *Surviving your Academic Job Hunt: Advice for Humanities PhDs* (2005; 2nd edn., 2011).

JOHN M. KRAFFT teaches English at the Hamilton campus of Miami University. He co-founded *Pynchon Notes* in 1979 and served as an editor of the journal until 2009. He has co-authored several recent essays on Pynchon with Luc Herman.

BRIAN MCHALE is Distinguished Arts and Humanities Professor of English at the Ohio State University. He is the author of *Postmodernist Fiction* (1987), *Constructing Postmodernism* (1992) and *The Obligation toward the Difficult Whole: Postmodernist Long Poems* (2004), and co-editor, with Randall Stevenson, of *The Edinburgh Companion to Twentieth-Century Literatures in English* (2006) and, with David Herman and James Phelan, of *Teaching Narrative Theory* (2010).

DEBORAH L. MADSEN is Professor of American Literature and Culture at the University of Geneva. Her research focuses on cultural articulations of American Exceptionalism. She has published on Thomas Pynchon, his colonial ancestor William Pynchon, and literary representations of the Pynchon family. Her most recent editing project is *Native Authenticity: Transatlantic Approaches to Native American Literature* (2010), and her most recent monograph is *Understanding Gerald Vizenor* (2009).

THOMAS HILL SCHAUB is Professor of Literature at the University of Wisconsin, Madison, and author of *Pynchon: The Voice of Ambiguity* (1981), *American Fiction in The Cold War* (1991) and *Approaches To Teaching Thomas Pynchon's The Crying Of Lot 49 and Other Works* (2008). He has published essays on James Fenimore Cooper, Ralph Ellison, Cormac McCarthy, Marilynne Robinson and Don DeLillo, among others. He has been editor of the journal *Contemporary Literature* since 1989.

DAVID SEED holds a chair in American Literature at Liverpool University and published *The Fictional Labyrinths of Thomas Pynchon* in 1988. Since then he has published studies of other American novelists and brought out *American Science Fiction and the Cold War* (1999). His main research areas have been Cold War culture, the relation of fiction to film, and different aspects of science fiction. He is currently working on a study of Ray Bradbury.

STEVEN WEISENBURGER is the Mossiker Chair in Humanities at Southern Methodist University, where he teaches American studies courses. Author of *A Gravity's Rainbow Companion* (2nd edn., 2006), *Modern Medea* (1998) and *Fables of Subversion* (1995), he has published extensively on American literature and topics in American history. He is completing a book on the cultural history of American white supremacy and, with Luc Herman, working on a co-authored study entitled Gravity's Rainbow, *Domination, & Freedom*.

CHRONOLOGY OF PYNCHON'S LIFE AND WORK

1937   Thomas Pynchon is born on May 8 in Glen Cove, on Long Island, New York.

1945   The Second World War in Europe ends on Pynchon's eighth birthday, VE Day.

1952   Pynchon's earliest known stories begin appearing, anonymously, in his high school newspaper, *Purple and Gold*.

1953   Pynchon graduates from Oyster Bay High School and enters Cornell University as an Engineering Physics major.

1955   Pynchon joins the US Navy.

1956   During the Suez Crisis, Pynchon serves aboard the USS *Hank* in the Mediterranean.

1957   Pynchon returns to Cornell as an English major.

1958   Pynchon collaborates with Kirkpatrick Sale on a musical, "Minstrel Island" (unfinished).

1959   Pynchon's first two mature short stories, "The Small Rain" and "Mortality and Mercy in Vienna," are published. He receives his BA and moves to Greenwich Village. He applies, unsuccessfully, for a Ford Foundation Fellowship to work with an opera company.

1960   Pynchon moves to Seattle to work as a staff writer for Boeing Airplane Company's in-house newsletter *Bomarc Service News*. Two more short stories, "Low-lands" and "Entropy," and the technical article "Togetherness" appear.

1961   "Under the Rose" appears. It will receive an O. Henry Award.

1962   Pynchon leaves his job at Boeing, his last known salaried employment, and moves to Mexico.

1963   Pynchon's first novel, *V.* (J. B. Lippincott), is published. It will receive the Faulkner Foundation Award for best first novel of the year and also be a National Book Award finalist.

1964   Pynchon tells friends he has recently been denied admission to an undergraduate program in mathematics at the University of California at Berkeley. His last short story, "The Secret Integration," appears.

1965   Pynchon turns down an opportunity to teach at Bennington College. In "A Gift of Books," in *Holiday* magazine, he praises Oakley Hall's western novel *Warlock*.

1966   Pynchon's second novel, *The Crying of Lot 49* (J. B. Lippincott), is published. It will win the Rosenthal Foundation Award. The essay "A Journey Into the Mind of Watts" appears in the *New York Times*. By now Pynchon is apparently living mostly in California.

1968   Pynchon's name appears, along with more than 400 others, in an advertisement protesting the US war in Vietnam.

1973   *Gravity's Rainbow* (Viking) is published. It will share the National Book Award with Isaac Bashevis Singer's *Crown of Feathers*, be a runner-up for the Nebula Award, and be recommended for but denied a Pulitzer Prize.

1975   The American Academy of Arts and Letters awards Pynchon the Howells Medal for *Gravity's Rainbow*. He refuses it.

1983   Pynchon writes an introduction for the reissue of his late friend Richard Fariña's *Been Down So Long It Looks Like Up to Me*.

1984   Pynchon collects five of his early short stories, with a reflective introduction, in *Slow Learner* (Little, Brown), and publishes "Is It O.K. to Be a Luddite?" in the *New York Times*.

1988   Pynchon receives a five-year MacArthur Foundation Fellowship. "The Heart's Eternal Vow," his review of Gabriel García Márquez's novel *Love in the Time of Cholera*, appears in the *New York Times*.

1990   Pynchon's fourth novel, *Vineland* (Little, Brown), is published. Pynchon is now married and living in New York City.

1992   Pynchon writes an introduction for the collection *The Teachings of Don B.*, by his late friend Donald Barthelme.

1993   Pynchon's essay on sloth, "Nearer, My Couch, to Thee," appears in the *New York Times* as part of a series on the deadly sins.

1994   Pynchon writes liner notes for the retrospective CD *Spiked!: The Music of Spike Jones*.

1995   Pynchon writes jacket notes for the band Lotion's CD *Nobody's Cool*.

1996   "Lunch with Lotion," an interview conducted by Pynchon, appears in *Esquire*.

1997   Pynchon's fifth novel, *Mason & Dixon* (Henry Holt), is published. Pynchon also writes an introduction for the reissue of Jim Dodge's novel *Stone Junction*.

1999   Pynchon writes "Hallowe'en? Over Already?" for the *Cathedral School Newsletter*.

2002   *Playboy Japan* publishes sarcastic remarks attributed to Pynchon about reactions to the 9/11 attacks on the World Trade Center. Pynchon's agent quickly disavows them.

2003   Pynchon writes a foreword for the George Orwell Centenary edition of *Nineteen Eighty-Four*.

2004   Pynchon lends his voice to the character "Thomas Pynchon" in two episodes of *The Simpsons*.

2006   Pynchon's sixth novel, *Against the Day* (Penguin Press), is published. Pynchon also writes a program note, "The Evolution of *The Daily Show*," for a tenth-anniversary celebration.

2009   Pynchon's seventh novel, *Inherent Vice* (Penguin Press), is published. Pynchon narrates a promotional video for the book. The American Academy of Arts and Sciences names him a Fellow.

Compiled by JOHN M. KRAFFT

INGER H. DALSGAARD, LUC HERMAN AND BRIAN MCHALE

Introduction

"A screaming ...

... comes across the sky": certainly the most celebrated opening sentence in twentieth-century US fiction, probably surpassed, in the whole of American literary history, only by its nineteenth-century counterpart, the opening of Herman Melville's *Moby-Dick* (1850) – "Call me Ishmael." What screams across the sky in this signature sentence is a V-2 rocket – or a nightmare of one – falling on London in 1944, and the novel that it opens is of course Thomas Pynchon's *Gravity's Rainbow* (1973), generally acknowledged to be a masterpiece of American and world literature. The author of seven novels to date – four of them of gigantic proportions, the other three more conventionally scaled – as well as a volume of short stories, Pynchon is a major figure of postwar American literature despite (or because of) his formidable difficulty, polymathic range of reference, personal elusiveness and reputation for outrage and obscenity.

It is impossible to conceive of postmodernism in literature without reference to Pynchon's fiction. Canonized in the 1980s as the foremost American postmodernist mainly on the strength of his two most celebrated novels – *The Crying of Lot 49* (1966) and *Gravity's Rainbow* – he has become a staple of academic reading lists dealing with the period. Indeed, while his works are all complex, and some of them are massive, his indispensable position in the literary canon has ensured that he is widely taught on all university levels in the US and Europe, and that he remains a popular topic of advanced research at colleges and universities around the world. Academic publishing on Pynchon has proliferated to the point that scholars speak self-deprecatingly of a Pynchon industry, or "Pyndustry," analogous to the Joyce industry. Yet at the same time Pynchon has also attracted a devoted readership of non-academic fans, earning him a "cult" status comparable in some ways to that of (say) Kurt Vonnegut Jr. or Charles Bukowski.

Despite the sheer volume of published scholarship on Pynchon, the editors of the Companion that you hold in your hands believe that it addresses a definite need, and fills a particular niche. While the academic Pyndustry is booming, there are relatively few books aimed specifically at those who study and teach Pynchon as part of the many courses devoted either to his works in particular or to their place in the postmodern canon more generally. There are even fewer books about Pynchon that the non-academic fan could pick up and read with pleasure and profit. We hope that the present Companion satisfies the needs of all these (overlapping) constituencies – teachers, students, fans and, yes, scholarly specialists too.

There are a few notable exceptions to the norm of specialist literature aimed at the research community, including Patrick O'Donnell's edited volume, *New Essays on "The Crying of Lot 49"* (1991), the Chelsea House books edited by Harold Bloom, on *Gravity's Rainbow* in 1986 and on Pynchon's oeuvre as a whole in 2003, Steven Weisenburger's invaluable companion to *Gravity's Rainbow* (1988; 2nd edn., 2006), J. Kerry Grant's similar companions to *The Crying of Lot 49* (1994) and *V.* (2001), and the volume of essays specifically devoted to the teaching of Pynchon's novels, edited by Thomas Schaub (2008). Line-by-line explanations of terms and references in Pynchon's texts are increasingly available online, where readers can look up explanations for slang terms, technical references and historical and literary allusions in co-created wikis. These and other more specialized works can be found in the bibliography to the present Companion. An earlier bibliography of work by and about Pynchon, compiled by Clifford Mead (1989), is so comprehensive for the earlier decades of Pynchon scholarship that we have opted to skew our own selection of secondary sources toward the present, retaining only a few of the older works, those that still seem most relevant today. In the interests of capturing as wide a range as possible of notable books and essays, we have generally refrained from listing individual essays from collections of Pynchon scholarship or those that have appeared in *Pynchon Notes*, the pre-eminent journal in Pynchon studies. So central is this journal to the field that any kind of Pynchon research should always start there, not least because each issue contains a bibliography of recent publications by and on Pynchon. We also list important websites, among which the wikis for each of the novels, curated by Tim Ware, are particularly useful.

By contrast with most of the items on our selected bibliography, which either take the form of very close textual guides or are exclusively aimed at the community of advanced researchers, the present Companion comprises essays which give a broader overview than textual companions and wikis can provide, while also making accessible advanced specialist insights, reflecting the state of the art in the field. Unlike various online resources, whose contributors' reliability and expertise may be inconsistent or questionable, our Companion showcases the work of proven Pynchon experts capable of formulating cutting-edge ideas while introducing fundamental issues in ways that are stimulating and accessible for teachers, students and fans alike.

"Shall I project a world?"

Who *is* Thomas Pynchon, anyway? We know relatively little about his private life, hardly more (or so it sometime seems) than we do about Shakespeare's, some four hundred years earlier; and evidently Pynchon himself prefers it that way. In any case, the little that we do know is summarized by John Krafft in the chronology and biographical note included in the present volume. While the chronology that launches our Companion is relatively extensive, Pynchon's decision early in his career to avoid personal publicity has meant that his life could only be put in the proper perspective in a separate biographical note. John Krafft enhances the record by integrating all the available material into an essay that respects Pynchon's privacy but does not hesitate to consult early letters or to venture the occasional guess as to his whereabouts in the 1960s. The latest developments are included as well. With his guest "appearance" on *The Simpsons* in 2004 and his voice-over for a YouTube video to promote his latest novel, *Inherent Vice* (2009), Pynchon has started playing around with his own media status as a reclusive author.

The chapters that follow Krafft's biography are organized into three sections. First comes a series of chapters specifically focused on the novels and short stories of the Pynchon canon, beginning with the earliest (the short stories and *V.*) and proceeding chronologically to the more recent novels, apart from one chapter that groups together the three shorter novels set in California, *The Crying of Lot 49*, *Vineland* (1990) and *Inherent Vice* (2009). The second section is devoted to aspects of Pynchon's artistic practice, or poetics, that can be found right across the Pynchon canon, in all of his novels. A third section addresses some of the largest issues engaged by Pynchon's writing, including history, politics, otherness (or alterity), and science and technology. A coda asks how one is supposed to go about reading a novelist as challenging as Pynchon, and ventures some answers.

Canon. Pynchon's canonization in the 1980s as the iconic author of American postmodernism has produced at least two accepted masterpieces, *The Crying of Lot 49* and *Gravity's Rainbow*. The status of Pynchon's first novel, *V.* (1963), is less clear, which may well be due to the fact that it still carries many signs of his apprenticeship as an author. Tracing the start of Pynchon's literary career from its inauspicious beginnings in a high school newspaper to the early 1960s, Luc Herman in Chapter 1 highlights the importance of the *V.* typescript at the Harry Ransom Center in Austin, Texas, as an important clue for an understanding of Pynchon's artistic development, and especially of the central role the historical imagination would come to play in his subsequent work.

Thomas Hill Schaub's topic in Chapter 2 is a trilogy of novels published at wide intervals across Pynchon's career – *The Crying of Lot 49, Vineland* and *Inherent Vice*, published in 1966, 1990 and 2009 respectively – which are all set in the same place and time, Southern California in the late sixties, and which together trace a trajectory of late twentieth-century American culture from its high-water mark of social experimentation and utopian hopes to the conservative reaction of the Nixon and Reagan years. Where *Lot 49*, Pynchon's most widely taught novel, is forward-looking, bursting with subcultural alternatives and subversive energies, *Vineland* and *Inherent Vice* are retrospective and reflective, focused less on utopian possibilities than on exposing the apparatus that maintains the status quo.

The highpoint of Pynchon's career, by almost universal consensus, is *Gravity's Rainbow* (1973). Though he had originally intended to entitle it "Mindless Pleasures," it is hardly escapist entertainment, for all its humor and carnivalesque extravagance; rather, as Steven Weisenburger shows in Chapter 3, it is a supremely mind*ful* moral fiction. A historical novel about the roots of the Cold War and the military-industry complex, *Gravity's Rainbow* explores our collective complicity – including its author's own personal complicity – with bureaucracies of terror and mass destruction. If some of the novel's characters imagine a postwar condition ripe with possibilities for freedom, Pynchon counterbalances their euphoric vision with a darker, ironic alternative in which history's arc terminates in the death camps.

In her chapter on *Mason & Dixon* (1997), Pynchon's massive re-imagining of one of the formative episodes of American history, Kathryn Hume develops a reading method derived from central metaphors in the novel itself. By visualizing the text both as layers of material and as networks of connected points – two structural images Pynchon himself develops throughout, for instance when he identifies the sandwich as an example of lamination – readers can relate to Pynchon's speculation about the existence of alternative realities. Hume proposes the archetypal American plot of two men going into the wilderness as the chief layer in such a reading, and science and power – but also less weighty matters such as beavers and the Black Hole of Calcutta – as some of the nodes that facilitate connections with other layers of the novel.

A gargantuan work over 1,000 pages long, *Against the Day* (2009), according to Bernard Duyhuizen in Chapter 5, is based on the genre of Menippean satire, which mixes multiple genres, blending them into a heteroglossic narrative containing a multitude of voices and discourses. The early chapters featuring the Chums of Chance evoke dime-novel boys' adventure novels and science fiction. Later chapters display traces of such genres as the espionage thriller, adventure travel writing, the anarchist novel, the multigenerational novel, the revenge plot, noir detective fiction, and various types of film, theater and popular song, all woven together into a dense fabric of genres, voices, allusions and parodies.

Poetics. In order to place Pynchon in literary history, the topic of Chapter 6, David Cowart first turns to the period of his apprenticeship, when the premises of modernism were being reframed to suit mid-century needs. Not satisfied with the work of Norman Mailer, the Beats and other contemporaries and predecessors, Pynchon forged a new poetics in which pastiche became central. Cowart goes on to suggest that Pynchon's work not only satisfies the traditional demands of literary permanence (not least because of his deep engagement with history) but also displays great sensitivity to contemporary questions of class, race and gender. Pynchon's greatest achievement, however, is his superb evocation of the encyclopedic vision, which he consistently undermines so as to expose our insistent but futile desire to understand the world. In a final section, Cowart briefly considers the contemporary authors who have been inspired by the master.

Pynchon's fiction is literally the paradigmatic case of postmodernism, Brian McHale argues in Chapter 7. Pynchon's novels exemplify various theories of postmoder*nity* – the historical and cultural conditions of the postmodern period – including those of Lyotard, Baudrillard, Haraway and others. They also illustrate various theories of postmoder*nism* – the period's characteristic aesthetic forms and practices – including those that characterize postmodernism in terms of double-coding (Huyssen, Jencks), suspensive irony and pastiche (Wilde, Jameson), the ontological dominant (McHale) and cognitive mapping (Jameson). Pynchon's novels exhibit the full range of typical postmodern narrative strategies, including strange loops and *mise-en-abyme*, narration under erasure and gardens of forking paths.

Pynchon is a above all a historical novelist, and his evocation of the past relies, as David Seed demonstrates in Chapter 8, on his practice of intertextuality, that is, on gleaning textual material from a diversity of historical sources. *V.*, for instance, draws heavily on Baedeker guidebooks for travelers. *The Crying of Lot 49* makes telling use of Marshall McLuhan's *Understanding Media*, just as *Gravity's Rainbow* does of Pavlov's *Lectures on Conditioned Reflexes*, counterpointed against the Freudian writings of

Norman O. Brown. Charles Mason's and Jeremiah Dixon's journals are a source for the novel bearing their names, while *Against the Day* articulates its history of the early twentieth century through references to the popular fiction that flourished in that period.

Issues. In Chapter 9, on the issue of history, Amy Elias contends that Pynchon shares three assumptions in common with the contemporary philosophy of history, namely the assumptions that history always features a medley of voices, that it is produced by events reconfiguring the social landscape, and that it is determined by the tropes available for the telling of stories. The notion of polyvocal history leads Pynchon to offer paranoia as an instance of the "cognitive mapping" that Fredric Jameson has described as meaningful resistance against the disorientation of the individual in late capitalism. History as event entails Pynchon's construction of history as sublime. The notion of history as tropological narrative, finally, turns Pynchon's fictional historiography into explanatory myth, a legend about the values grounding society.

Jeff Baker, in Chapter 10, locates Pynchon's fiction within an American political tradition derived from Ralph Waldo Emerson, entailing a notion of "self-reliance" that can be understood in starkly opposed ways, as either the rugged individualism of laissez-faire capitalism or as democratic communitarianism. From novel to novel across his whole career, Pynchon reflects on the political differences between these two versions of the Emersonian self, and explores how each in turn might define the nature of American exceptionalism. Averse as he is to direct political statement, Pynchon in his novels nevertheless insists that responsibility for cultural resistance begins with the self-reliant, community-minded Emersonian individual.

Deborah Madsen defines "alterity" in Chapter 11 as the process that constructs an "Other." She documents Pynchon's engagement with this process by showing how his work has simultaneously undermined and legitimized various examples of such construction. Zooming in on Slothrop's disintegration in *Gravity's Rainbow*, Madsen establishes the fundamental uncertainty affecting both characters and narrators in Pynchon's fictional worlds. Devoid of the innate selves imagined by liberal humanism, these figures appear determined and even kept in check by agents such as corporations or popular culture. The pervasive presence of colonialism in Pynchon's work is no coincidence, since it provides the author with a metaphor that reveals both individual alienation and complicity with the powers that be.

In Chapter 12, Inger H. Dalsgaard surveys key features of Pynchon's wide-ranging use of science and technology, and representative approaches to this distinctive aspect of his writing. Pynchon, she finds, interrogates through science and technology many aspects of Western industrial civilization, from the nature of power to the powers of nature. This aspect is explored by critics primarily interested in his treatment of engineering, material or human, as subject matter. At once critical and reflexive, however, Pynchon also enacts the premises and methods of science and technology *within* his own work. Science and technology, Dalsgaard suggests, fuel both Pynchon's experimental poetics and the deeper issues raised by his novels.

Coda. Reading Pynchon is not easy. In a coda to this Companion, Hanjo Berressem surveys the history of Pynchon criticism to highlight the main solutions to this problem so far. From early views of Pynchon as a prophet of doom, through a poststructuralist phase, and continuing on to an approach informed by New Historicism, critical takes on Pynchon have developed a logic of multiplicity that is suited to the exuberance and variety of his work. In the second part of his coda, Berressem considers the communal dimension of every creation of meaning. Pynchon looks for this sense of community and resonance with his readers, but the will to resonance is repeatedly overridden by forces outside one's, or for that matter the community's, control. Berressem concludes that the production of complex narratives may help to resist that (sometimes violent) determinism.

"They fly toward grace"

The creation of meaning is communal, Hanjo Berressem tells us, and Pynchon seeks community with his readers. Yet how can this be? His books are notoriously difficult, sometimes to the point of hermeticism, demanding kinds and degrees of attention that casual readers may not be willing to grant. Some readers may be alienated by Pynchon's irresponsible frivolity, by his obscenity, by what sometimes appear to be displays of sexism, misogyny and homophobia, or even aggression or resentment toward the reader; he does *not* always appear to be reader-friendly. Moreover, don't his reclusiveness and his refusal to do interviews or to make media appearances – even the paper bag that his animated surrogate wears to disguise his features on that famous episode from *The Simpsons* – don't these all indicate the *opposite* of seeking community with readers? And what about the cultishness of Pynchon fans, and of academics who labor in the Pynchon industry – their tendency toward obsessiveness, their circulation of choice details and phrases from the books like magic talismans, their delight in gossip about Pynchon sightings, their in-jokes – aren't these all ways of flaunting a special "insider" status, and of turning one's back on the larger community of readers? A case in point: the subheadings of the three sections of this very introduction, each drawn from a different Pynchon novel – "A screaming ..." from the beginning of *Gravity's Rainbow*, "Shall I project a world?" from near the middle of *The Crying of Lot 49*, "They fly toward grace" from the very end of *Against the Day* – all immediately recognizable by Pynchon "insiders," but no doubt cryptic and opaque to everyone else.

That's one side of the Pynchon problem – the dark side; but there's another side as well. The very difficulty and apparent unfriendliness of Pynchon's novels create a sense of solidarity and, yes, community among Pynchon's readers – a sense that we are all participating in a collective enterprise of reading wherein no one of us could succeed without the help of the others. Pynchon's refusal to make himself publicly available – which only means, really, his refusal to cooperate with the apparatus of celebrity – has the effect of clearing a space in which we, his readers, can make up our own minds, free of "authoritative" pronouncements and directives (apart from rare exceptions such as the introduction to *Slow Learner* [1984]). Pynchon, it appears, has decided to *leave us to our own devices*. It is this sense of having been left to our own devices, and of needing to help each other out, that animates such collective enterprises as the co-created online Pynchon wikis, or a journal like *Pynchon Notes*, or for that matter the very Companion that you are holding in your hands. Our Companion has been a communal effort from start to finish, involving not only close collaboration among the three editors and eleven other contributors, but also the support and assistance of others both inside and outside the Pynchon community, among whom the editors want especially to acknowledge Dale Carter and Toon Staes.

It is the sense of sharing in a collective enterprise of reading that transforms a cult of insiders into a community. We invite you to join the community of Pynchon readers. We are all in it together.

JOHN M. KRAFFT

Biographical note

Thomas Pynchon has so carefully guarded his privacy that relatively little is known about his personal life. He evidently prefers to have readers focus on his fiction. His principled determination to avoid personal publicity has led to his routinely, and inaccurately, being described as a recluse, has sparked some bizarre rumors – that he was J. D. Salinger, or the Unabomber – and has provoked some spiteful and some self-serving revelations.[1] Now in his seventies, Pynchon seems to have let down his guard a bit, perhaps as the effect of being a family man with a teenage son. In 2004, he mocked his own reputation as a "reclusive author" by allowing himself to be represented in two episodes of *The Simpsons* as a figure with a brown paper bag over his head, voicing the caricature himself. In 2009, he even narrated a short promotional video for his latest novel, *Inherent Vice*.[2]

Pynchon's ancestors can be traced back nearly a millennium, to the time of the Norman Conquest of England.[3] His earliest ancestor in America, William Pynchon (1590–1662), born into the modestly landed English gentry, joined the Great Migration of Puritans to New England in 1630. A member of the Massachusetts Bay Company and treasurer of the Bay Colony, William Pynchon was a founder of both Roxbury and Springfield in Massachusetts. He was a successful merchant and fur trader, a magistrate and an amateur theologian. But he returned to England in 1652 after stirring up controversy by writing *The Meritorious Price of Our Redemption* (1650), a book which Massachusetts authorities judged heretical and ordered burned in the Boston marketplace because of its subversive political, as well as theological, implications. William's son John (1625–1703) was also a prosperous New England merchant, trader and landowner. The rest of the Pynchon family tree includes politicians, clergymen, educators, scientists, physicians, inventors and financiers. One wrote a chemistry textbook; another wrote a Gothic tale about a ghostly dog; one patented both an instrument for performing nasal surgery and an airship propelled by dynamite, and wrote a pamphlet on enemas; one was a stock broker and noted yachtsman. The family tree does not include the "Pyncheons" so fiercely satirized in Hawthorne's *House of the Seven Gables* (1851); they were actually modeled on Hawthorne's own ancestors.[4] The novelist's father, Thomas R. Pynchon, Sr. (1907–95), was an industrial surveyor, highway engineer and local Republican politician. His mother, Catherine Bennett Pynchon (1909–96), was a registered nurse and volunteer librarian.

The eldest of three children, Pynchon was born on May 8, 1937, in Glen Cove, Long Island, New York, and grew up in nearby East Norwich. This scion of New England Puritans was raised a Roman Catholic. A half-dozen of his earliest known stories appeared anonymously in the Oyster Bay High School newspaper, *Purple and Gold*, in 1952–53. These satirical, irreverent juvenilia feature issues and techniques central also to Pynchon's mature fiction.[5] After graduating at sixteen from Oyster Bay High School as class salutatorian and a prize-winning English student, Pynchon entered Cornell University with a scholarship as an Engineering Physics major. He remained in that program for only one year, then switched to Arts and Sciences.[6] As summer employment, he may have done the kind of roadwork recalled by his characters Profane and Slothrop.[7] After his sophomore year, he enlisted for a two-year tour of duty in the US Navy. During the Suez crisis of 1956, he served aboard the destroyer USS *Hank* in the Mediterranean, possibly as a communications specialist. He returned to Cornell in 1957 and graduated with a Bachelor's degree in English in June 1959. Offered a Woodrow Wilson Graduate Fellowship and the opportunity to teach creative writing at Cornell, Pynchon reportedly preferred to concentrate on his own creative writing.[8]

At Cornell Pynchon became close friends with other aspiring writers, notably folk singer and novelist Richard Fariña, and editor, historian and activist Kirkpatrick Sale. Sale and Pynchon collaborated in 1958 on a never-finished dystopian musical, "Minstrel Island." Faith Apfelbaum Sale would have editorial responsibility at J. B. Lippincott for Pynchon's first novel, *V.*, shortly before its publication. Other Cornell friends included the freelance writer Jules Siegel and the future fiction-editor of the *Atlantic Monthly* C. Michael Curtis. No reliable evidence available to date supports the persistent rumor that Pynchon took a course taught by Vladimir Nabokov, the author of *Lolita* (1955), although he may have audited Nabokov's classes, known him personally or worked with him informally. Pynchon's most famous instructor of record was M. H. Abrams, later the founding editor of *The Norton Anthology of English Literature*.

The year 1959 saw publication of Pynchon's first two mature short stories, "The Small Rain" and "Mortality and Mercy in Vienna." Pynchon was already being represented by Candida Donadio, who would remain his agent for twenty-three years. "Low-lands" appeared in 1960 – despite a publishing executive's prediction that its author would "be selling used cars within a year."[9] Pynchon's best-known story, "Entropy," also appeared that year, and was chosen for inclusion in the next year's annual *Best American Short Stories*. "Under the Rose," published in 1961, won an O. Henry Award.

Pynchon spent the last half of 1959 living in Greenwich Village, where he and Fariña "would … listen a lot" to jazz in nightclubs, and working on *V.*[10] He applied for a Ford Foundation Fellowship to work with an opera company, proposing to write an original libretto or else an adaptation of either Ray Bradbury's *Martian Chronicles* or Alfred Bester's *Demolished Man*.[11] His application was unsuccessful. So from February 1960 to September 1962, he worked as a technical writer on the staff of a house organ, *Bomarc Service News*, at the Boeing Airplane Co. in Seattle.[12] While there, he completed writing and extensively revising *V.* (1963), which received the Faulkner Foundation Award for best first novel of the year and was a National Book Award finalist.

"The Secret Integration," Pynchon's last-published short story, appeared in *The Saturday Evening Post* in 1964. Pynchon himself has said that story marked his progression from "apprentice" to "journeyman."[13] *The Crying of Lot 49* appeared in 1966, with prepublication excerpts in *Esquire* (1965) and *Cavalier* (1966), and received a Rosenthal Foundation Award. Curiously, Pynchon has disparaged *Lot 49* as a "story […] which was marketed as a 'novel,' and in which I seem to have forgotten most of what I thought I'd learned up till then."[14] *Gravity's Rainbow* (1973), widely considered Pynchon's masterpiece, shared a National Book Award with Isaac Bashevis Singer's *Crown of Feathers* and received runner-up honors for the annual Nebula Award from the Science Fiction Writers of America. It was also unanimously recommended by the fiction jury for a Pulitzer Prize, but the Pulitzer advisory board balked, members calling the novel "'unreadable,' 'turgid,' 'overwritten,' and in parts 'obscene.'"[15] Awarded the Howells Medal by the American Academy of Arts and Letters in 1975 for "the most distinguished work of American fiction of the previous five years," Pynchon politely refused it.[16] However, in 1988 he accepted a five-year, $310,000 MacArthur Foundation Fellowship. The American Academy of Arts and Sciences named Pynchon a Fellow in 2009.

Pynchon has published odds and ends of non-fiction too. These include at least one article on missile-handling safety (1960); essays on the Watts riots (1966), Luddism (1984) and sloth (1993); a review of Gabriel García Márquez's novel *Love in the Time of Cholera* (1988); introductions to books by Richard Fariña (1983), Donald Barthelme (1992), Jim Dodge (1997) and George Orwell (2003); liner notes for CDs by Spike Jones (1994) and the indie rock band Lotion (1995); an interview with Lotion (1996); a piece about the Halloween picnic for his son's school's newsletter (1999); a program note commemorating the tenth anniversary of *The Daily Show* (2006); and numerous promotional blurbs for books by other writers. In the seventeen-year interval between *Gravity's Rainbow* and *Vineland* (1990), he collected all his short stories except "Mortality and Mercy in Vienna" into *Slow Learner* (1984), adding a reflective introduction. Many reviewers celebrated this introduction for its supposed candor, but other readers have found it less revealing and more strategic. The novel *Mason & Dixon* appeared in 1997, *Against the Day* in 2006 and *Inherent Vice* in 2009.

Though publicity-averse, Pynchon has spoken out on some literary and political issues. In 1965, in *Holiday* magazine, he praised Oakley Hall's western novel *Warlock*. The next year, in a letter to the *New York Times Book Review*, he mocked French novelist Romain Gary for accusing him of stealing the name Genghis Cohen for a character in *The Crying of Lot 49*. Pynchon's name appears along with more than four hundred others on a 1968 open letter in the *New York Review of Books* protesting the Vietnam War. Signers pledged not to pay any increase in federal income taxes meant to help pay for the war. This signature landed Pynchon on an FBI index.[17] Pynchon joined in offering support and encouragement, published in the *New York Times Book Review* in 1989, to Salman Rushdie after the latter was put under a fatwa by Iran's Ayatollah Khomeini for writing *The Satanic Verses* (1988). Remarks attributed to Pynchon in a 2002 issue of *Playboy Japan* criticize the "affectless" reporting and the shallowness of network news, describe network and print journalism as "propaganda" and, sarcastically, recommend tobacco stock as a good investment given the anxieties aroused by the terrorist attacks of 9/11.[18] Pynchon's agent has disavowed these remarks on his behalf. In a 2006 letter released to the London *Daily Telegraph*, Pynchon defended Ian McEwan, as a fellow writer of historical fiction, against a charge of plagiarism for using details from a memoir of the Second World War in his novel *Atonement* (2001).

Hard information about Pynchon's private life is scarce. In its absence, gossip about girlfriends, drug use, favorite TV programs and pig fetishes, and trivia about eating habits and clothing preferences risk being given undue weight. Gaps and possible contradictions in the record are numerous, and what seems trustworthy may turn out to be untrue. For example, he is said to have considered "becoming a disk jockey," and to have been "considered as a film critic by *Esquire*" in 1959, and to have wanted the latter position perhaps in the mid 1960s.[19]

Apparently Pynchon lived mostly in Mexico from late 1962 until 1964, in Houston from 1964 to mid 1965, then mostly in California through the 1980s.[20] In letters to Faith and Kirkpatrick Sale in 1963 and 1964, Pynchon considered visiting them in Ghana; but he was prevented by a variety of personal "traumata," and by his making "[n]o real progress"[21] on "three, possibly four novels and assorted short stories I've been screwing around with."[22] (He confirmed the number of novels as four a year later.) Pynchon wanted to do research in Italy and Yugoslavia as well as Africa. Yet in late 1963 or early 1964, he applied to the University of California at Berkeley to pursue a second Bachelor's degree, in math, but was denied admission.

Another letter to the Sales reveals a surprising side to the literary taste and ambition of a writer early in his career who would soon become world renowned as a giant of postmodern fiction. Pynchon declared that "the traditional realistic" novel was "the only kind of novel that is worth a shit," and added, "[that] is what, someday, I would like to be able to write."[23]

In late 1965, Pynchon turned down an offer to teach at Bennington College. The number of novels he was working on at that time was back down to three.[24] The 1967 edition of the Cornell alumni directory lists Pynchon as married to Mary Tharaldsen and living in Oakland, California, around the time another source places him in Berkeley.[25] Several sources place him in Manhattan Beach, near Los Angeles, from roughly the mid sixties to at least the early seventies.[26] Manhattan Beach is taken to be the model for the fictional Gordita Beach in *Vineland* and *Inherent Vice*. A former landlady said Pynchon moved in 1975 from Manhattan Beach to Big Sur.[27] In the early to mid seventies he lived occasionally in the Sales' Greenwich Village apartment, below Donald Barthelme's, "when the Sales were away."[28] A 1974 letter Pynchon wrote from New York to novelists David Shetzline and M. F. Beal expresses disillusionment with national politics, disgust with cultural pretension and disenchantment with "a 'literary' life."[29]

Pynchon is said to have "walked the 233–mile length of the Mason–Dixon line" by the late seventies, and to have spent some weeks or months doing further research for *Mason & Dixon* in England at the end of the seventies.[30] Driver's license records give his address as Aptos, California, during the eighties, but whether he spent much time in Aptos or used it more as an address of convenience while living elsewhere is uncertain; Trinidad and Soquel, California, for example, are mentioned by various sources, as is Mexico. Since about 1989, he has lived in New York City with his wife, the literary agent Melanie Jackson, and their son. Melanie Jackson is a great-granddaughter of Theodore Roosevelt and a granddaughter of Supreme Court Justice and Nuremberg war-crimes prosecutor Robert H. Jackson.

Journalists' determination to out Pynchon peaked around the time *Mason & Dixon* was published. In 1996, *New York* magazine ran what Nancy Jo Sales claimed was a photograph of Pynchon taken from behind.[31] The next year, the London *Times*'s James Bone, an unapologetic stalker, published a head-on snapshot.[32] That same year, a CNN camera crew filmed Pynchon in his Manhattan neighborhood; but, in deference to Pynchon's telephoned objection, the network refrained from identifying him in the street scenes it broadcast. Pynchon is said to have told CNN that he believed "recluse" was journalistic "code" for "doesn't like to talk to reporters."[33]

The CNN footage is analyzed at some length in *Thomas Pynchon – A Journey into the Mind of <P>*, a documentary more about the Pynchon mystique than about Pynchon himself.[34] Richard Lane explains in inadvertently comic detail (He-has-a-pen-in-his-shirt-pocket-so-he-must-be-a-writer) who in the CNN clips he thinks is Pynchon. Some well-informed viewers believe Lane is mistaken. So Pynchon the man still largely eludes us, and perhaps that is just as well. As fascinating as his fiction may seem to make his life (including his defiance of the norms of celebrity culture), Pynchon the literary phenomenon is what makes us care in the first place. We hardly need to know about the life to appreciate the fiction.

NOTES

1 See Jules Siegel, "Who Is Thomas Pynchon … And Why Did He Take Off with My Wife?" *Playboy*, March 1977, pp. 97, 122, 168–74; and Andrew Gordon, "Smoking Dope with Thomas Pynchon: A Sixties Memoir," in Geoffrey Green, Donald J. Greiner and Larry McCaffery (eds.), *The Vineland Papers: Critical Takes on Pynchon's Novel* (Normal, IL: Dalkey Archive, 1994), pp. 167–78.

2 PenguinGroupUSA, "*Inherent Vice*, Thomas Pynchon – 9781594202247," www.youtube.com/watch?v=RjWKPdDko_U

3 Mathew Winston, "The Quest for Pynchon," *Twentieth-Century Literature*, 21.3 (1975), 279.

4 Deborah L. Madsen, "Colonial Legacies: The Pynchons of Springfield and the Hawthornes of Salem," in Klaus H. Schmidt and Fritz Fleischmann (eds.), *Early America Re-Explored: New Readings in Colonial, Early National, and Antebellum Culture* (New York: Peter Lang, 2000), p. 49.

5 Michael Hartnett, "Thomas Pynchon's Long Island Years," *Confrontation*, 30–31 (1985), 44–48; Charles Hollander, "Pynchon's *Juvenilia* and *Against the Day*," *GRAAT On-Line* 3 (2008), 38–55, www.graat.fr/5%20Hollander.pdf

6 Lance Schachterle, "Pynchon and Cornell Engineering Physics, 1953–54," *Pynchon Notes*, 26–27 (1990), 129–37.

7 Siegel, "Who Is Thomas Pynchon," p. 122.

8 Cf. Winston, "Quest," 284.

9 Quoted in Corlies M. Smith, interview with Luc Herman and John M. Krafft, December 29, 2002.

10 Lewis Nichols, "In and Out of Books," *New York Times Book Review*, April 28, 1963, p. 8; Pynchon quoted in David Hajdu, *Positively 4th Street: The Lives and Times of Joan Baez, Bob Dylan, Mimi Baez Fariña, and Richard Fariña* (New York: Farrar, 2001), p. 47.

11 Steven Weisenburger, "Thomas Pynchon at Twenty-Two: A Recovered Autobiographical Sketch," *American Literature*, 62.4 (1990), 696.

12 Adrian Wisnicki, "A Trove of New Works by Thomas Pynchon? *Bomarc Service News* Rediscovered," *Pynchon Notes*, 46–49 (2000–2001), 9–34.

13 Thomas Pynchon, *Slow Learner* (Boston: Little, Brown, 1984), p. 3.

14 *Ibid.*, p. 22.

15 Peter Kihss, "Pulitzer Jurors Dismayed on Pynchon," *New York Times*, May 8, 1974, p. 38.

16 William Styron, "Presentation to Thomas Pynchon of the Howells Medal for Fiction of the Academy," *Proceedings of the American Academy of Arts and Letters and the National Institute of Arts and Letters*, Second series, 26 (1976), 43–46.

17 Natalie Robins, *Alien Ink: The FBI's War on Freedom of Expression* (New York: Morrow, 1992), p. 411.

18 Thomas Pynchon, "Talk by Thomas Pynchon" [in Japanese], *Playboy Japan*, January 2002, p. 32.

19 Winston, "Quest," 284; Mel Gussow, "Pynchon's Letters Nudge His Mask," *New York Times*, March 4, 1998, p. E8.

20 Carolyn Kellogg, "When Thomas Pynchon Is Just Tom: A Remarkable Collection Debuts," *Los Angeles Times*, May 5, 2011, latimesblogs.latimes.com/jacketcopy/2011/05/thomas-pynchon-tom-a-remarkable-collection.html

21 Thomas Pynchon, letter to Faith and Kirkpatrick Sale, March 27, 1964 (Harry Ransom Humanities Research Center, The University of Texas at Austin).

22 Thomas Pynchon, letter to Faith and Kirkpatrick Sale, March 9, 1963 (Harry Ransom Humanities Research Center, The University of Texas at Austin).

23 Thomas Pynchon, letter to Faith and Kirkpatrick Sale, June 29, 1963 (Harry Ransom Humanities Research Center, The University of Texas at Austin).

24 Scott McLemee, "You Hide, They Seek," *Inside Higher Ed*, November 15, 2006, www.insidehighered.com/views/mclemee/mclemee158

25 *Directory of Living Alumni* (Ithaca: Cornell University Press, 1967), p. 580; Gordon, "Smoking," p. 171.

26 Garrison Frost, "Thomas Pynchon and the South Bay," *Aesthetic* (n.p., n.d. [2003]), www.theaesthetic.com/NewFiles/pynchon.html; Bill Pearlman, "Short Cuts," *London Review of Books*, December 17, 2009, p. 22; Siegel, "Who Is Thomas Pynchon," passim.

27 Garrison Frost, "Thomas and Evelyn," *Aesthetic* (n.p., September 5, 2007), www.theaesthetic.com/NewFiles/thomasandevelyn.html

28 Tracy Daugherty, *Hiding Man: A Biography of Donald Barthelme* (New York: St. Martin's, 2009), p. 373.

29 Thomas Pynchon, letter to David Shetzline and M. F. Beal, January 21, 1974.

30 Bill Roeder, "After the Rainbow," *Newsweek*, August 7, 1978, p. 7; Christopher Hitchens, "American Notes," *Times Literary Supplement*, July 12, 1985, p. 772; Tom Maschler, *Publisher* (London: Picador, 2005), pp. 95–97.

31 Nancy Jo Sales, "Meet Your Neighbor, Thomas Pynchon," *New York*, November 11, 1996, pp. 60–64.

32 James Bone, "Mystery Writer," *The Times Magazine* [London], June 14, 1997, pp. 26–29.

33 Joie Chen and Charles Feldman, "Who Has Seen Thomas Pynchon the Writer?" *The World Today* (CNN, June 5, 1997), 10:44 pm EDT; quoted in Phil Kloer, "Reclusive Novelist Breaks His Silence," *Atlanta Journal and Constitution*, June 5, 1997, p. 2C.

34 *Thomas Pynchon – A Journey into the Mind of <P>*, directed by Fosco and Donatello Dubini (Dubini Filmproduktion, 2001; DVD, 2006).

PART I

Canon

I

LUC HERMAN

Early Pynchon

Given the seventeen-year interval between the publication of *Gravity's Rainbow* and *Vineland*, critics may well have reason to find major differences between the two phases of Pynchon's literary career. Whatever the value of this periodization, the usual association of late style and absolute mastery does not quite apply, since it is for the climax of his first period that Pynchon has become part of the literary canon. If his first phase is indeed crowned by the two accepted masterpieces *The Crying of Lot 49* and *Gravity's Rainbow*, then Pynchon's first novel, *V.*, assumes a somewhat awkward position. Is it still part of the learning curve (with the author reaching his peak almost immediately afterwards), or is it the first full-bodied illustration of the postmodernism that would become associated with his name, mostly on the strength of the two books that follow? Maybe this question is too determined by these books' later importance, or even by the classical notion of authorial growth, which Pynchon himself reinforced in the introduction to the 1984 collection of his early stories, *Slow Learner*. The genesis of *V.* does seem to indicate that he was struggling in his first attempt at long fiction. In an August 1961 letter, Pynchon went as far as telling his editor that he didn't "know dick about writing novels yet and need[ed] all kinds of help."[1] However, judging from the speed, initiative and efficiency with which he would rewrite the version of the book he had first submitted, both the statement in the letter and his later self-presentation in *Slow Learner* can be construed as instances of modesty – false or authentic.

There is more to Pynchon before the two masterpieces than the short stories and *V.* The author's first publications on record go back to his senior year in high school. References in the Oyster Bay High School Yearbook of 1953 have allowed for the identification of six Pynchon juvenilia in the school newspaper, *Purple and Gold* – four columns entitled "Voice of the Hamster," a quick parody of *Sir Gawain and the Green Knight* ("Ye Legend of Sir Stupid and the Purple Knight") and a short report about a picture for the yearbook.[2] The columns take the form of letters written by a voluble student at "Hamster High" to a friend who attends Oyster Bay. Hamster High is Pynchon's first possible world in print, replete with exaggerated descriptions and fancy names (like that of the trigonometry teacher, Mr. Faggiaducci). Characters and events in the columns no doubt allowed fellow pupils to make connections with elements from their own school environment. In the short report, Pynchon himself gives the game away by suddenly describing "the Boys," a group of rowdy Hamster kids, as attending Oyster Bay. In two substantial attempts to link up the juvenilia with Pynchon's later work, suggestions range from early evidence of "puzzle-building skill"[3] to the clear foreshadowing of an "ability to alternate between intriguing ambiguity and sardonic desentimentalization."[4] While these interpretations inevitably give the *Purple and Gold* pieces too much weight, parts of the juvenilia do provide Pynchon aficionados with an uncanny reading experience, not least when the writer of the column letters brings up "a fascinating experiment in psychology entailing the instilling of paranoid hallucinations into the logical mind by psychoanalytic deletion of the super-ego. In other words, we are trying to see how much Faggiaducci can take before he flips his lid."[5]

Between 1959 and 1964, Pynchon published six short stories, five of which are collected in *Slow Learner*. Four of these were written at Cornell, after Pynchon had returned to college from his two-year stint in the navy and changed his major from Engineering Physics to English. Only one other piece from the Cornell period, a libretto, has come to light. In 1958, Pynchon and his friend Kirkpatrick Sale tried their hand at a musical.[6] Unfinished and still unpublished, "Minstrel Island" is a "lascivious Luddite satire" in which IBM dominates the world and aims to sanitize Minstrel Island, a colony for artists and dropouts.[7] Hero, their leader, tries to tease the executive woman, Broad, away from the company by making her fall in love with him. Extremely didactic and perhaps unwittingly grotesque in its attempt at contemporary allegory, the musical illustrates Pynchon's concerns about the impact of technology and also anticipates his use of songs in narrative. The name of its titular island points to an interest in the Middle Ages which Pynchon attributes in the *Slow Learner* introduction to one specific book, *The Wandering Scholars* (1927) by Helen Waddell.[8] Unlike the mobile intellectuals and artists of medieval times, however, Pynchon's minstrels have already retreated to a colony, where they may no longer be effective against their corporate enemy. The Luddite attitude (to which Pynchon would return much later in an important essay) is exposed for its failure to be genuinely subversive.[9]

It is not entirely clear why "Mortality and Mercy in Vienna" (1959) was not included in the 1984 collection.[10] The story combines elements that also show up elsewhere in the early work (such as party scenes, college learning, ethnic stereotypes and borrowings from the spy novel genre), but it manages to mix them in an intriguing way. Siegel, a junior diplomat, arrives early at a party in Washington and is put in charge by the host, whom he resembles. Guests confide in him as they used to in his double, and eventually an Ojibwa who has come along with a party regular succumbs to his Windigo psychosis and opens fire on the innocent bystanders. Siegel deliberately precipitates the attack before escaping for his own safety. Critics have speculated that the story was not republished because it can be perceived as validating violence.[11] The heavy-handed reference to Shakespeare's *Measure for Measure* in the story title and the simplistic contrast between a Jewish and a Jesuit voice within Siegel may also have made it look amateurish to Pynchon twenty-five years after its publication.

Pynchon's reclusiveness has turned his introduction to *Slow Learner*, by default, into a vital source of information for critics. The possibility that his self-presentation could be unreliable or at least influenced by the rhetoric of the genre has rarely been considered.[12] Although collecting his early stories could easily be seen as a lucrative way of ending a decade of almost complete silence, Pynchon takes the moral high road and offers his early efforts as a negative example to novice writers. Others "may be able to profit from [his] error" and so he has gladly undertaken this painful confrontation with the material he would prefer to forget.[13] Set up as a classic tale of the writer's apprenticeship, the introduction is indeed candid about beginners' mistakes. Like a conventional teacher, Pynchon even goes so far as to wag his finger at the "literary theft" he himself practiced.[14] His biggest fault was to prefer "fancy footwork" to the authenticity of fiction "found and taken up, always at a cost, from deeper, more shared levels of the life we all really live."[15] Tongue-in-cheek, disingenuous or sincere, the framework of education enables Pynchon to present interesting information about the conflict he allegedly faced between Beat innovation and the modernist tradition taught in college, about his relative lack of political awareness in the 1950s, and about the various elements that went into his stories.

If Ernest Hemingway was one of the writers held up for emulation at the beginning of Pynchon's literary career, then "The Small Rain" (1959), with its portentous juxtaposition of love and death, at least aims in Hemingway's direction. In the immediate aftermath of a hurricane which has hit the bayou country on the Gulf of Mexico, specialist Nathan "Lardass" Levine is assigned to the rescue operation and hooks up with Buttercup, a coed on the campus used as a staging area by the army. After they have made love, he feels the need to spell out the story's central connection: "In the midst of great death [...] the little death."[16] Filled to bursting with male posturing and insipid atmosphere ("The smell of decay hung in the air, like vermouth, it seemed to Levine, after you'd been drinking it all night"), the story is nevertheless endearing for its youthful attempt to tackle big themes.[17]

In "Low-lands" (1960), men again team up, and women appear as unpleasant and even dangerous outsiders.[18] Dennis Flange is said to have two consolations for his failed marriage to Cindy – his analyst and the sea. At the beginning of the story, he escapes from his wife with two drinking buddies. One of them is seaman Pig Bodine, a member of Flange's division in the Korean War, who will reappear in many Pynchon novels. They end up at a garbage dump, where more drinking leads to the telling of sea stories, and Flange is eventually lured away by the gypsy Nerissa, whose pet rat turns somersaults. "Low-lands" is successful in its development of a sea motif, but it also exposes what Pynchon would later describe as serious flaws. The story has some "racist" and "sexist" talk, for which he apologizes in the *Slow Learner* introduction with a reference to the spirit of the times.[19] The choice of the name Bolingbroke (from Shakespeare's *Richard II*) for the African American in charge of the dump betrays a misplaced reliance on cultural baggage to "make it literary."[20]

"Entropy" (1960), Pynchon's best-known short story, provides the first instance of the entropy theme central to much of his work. Meatball Mulligan plays host to a never-ending party in his apartment. Upstairs, Callisto and Aubade have created a sealed environment, "a tiny enclave of regularity in the city's chaos."[21] Life in this hothouse is still subject to entropy in the thermodynamic sense, a measure of the amount of heat that cannot be turned into energy. Defined in the story as "the measure of disorganization for a closed system," this kind of entropy increases unless work is done to create order.[22] Callisto tries to apply the related notion of heat-death to culture, and readers might be tempted to romanticize his world-weary pessimism. However, he is likely the object of satire for his pedantic yet under-informed and dangerous self-indulgence. Trying to save a bird by warming it, he kills it: since a bird's average body temperature is higher than a human being's, Callisto inadvertently takes heat away from the animal instead of furnishing it. The bird's death may thus signal that Callisto's desire for an isolated steady state is misguided and that his prediction of the heat-death of culture is premature. Self-enclosure and personal failure seem more pertinent to the end of his intellectual motion than does cosmic entropy. Downstairs at the party, Mulligan is told by his friend Saul about the end of the latter's relationship. His explanation thematizes the meaning of "entropy" in communication theory, where various forms of noise are said to make "for disorganization in the circuit."[23] While Pynchon dismisses "Entropy" because it was built around a notion he claims (somewhat unconvincingly) not to have understood well, the story does showcase the narrativization of science for which he has been known ever since.[24] Moreover, it also features the best party scenes in the whole of his early work.

In "Under the Rose" (1961), Pynchon tried his hand at the spy fiction he enjoyed so much in his youth. At the time of the Fashoda incident (1898), an important moment in the European "scramble for Africa," two English operatives in Egypt, Porpentine and Goodfellow, confront their opponents. The Baedeker tourist guide is the avowed source for the story's setting, and the action neatly incorporates parallels with the plot of Puccini's opera, *Manon Lescaut* (1893).[25] Pynchon stretches the genre code in other ways as well – one of the bad guys has an electric switch sewn into his arm, and Porpentine eventually suspects the opposition has acted under orders from a force that may not be quite human. Despite various explanatory passages that signal Pynchon's lack of experience with the imaginative evocation of the past, the reader nevertheless needs to be acquainted with the historical situation and the opera in order to create meaning from the text. If "Under the Rose" does not quite succeed in its own right as a spy story with a twist, its transformation into a chapter of *V.* has made it important for an understanding of Pynchon's early poetics.[26]

In the spring of 1962, nearly a year after he had first delivered a draft to the publisher, Pynchon rewrote the novel that would be called *V.* He was following up on three suggestions from his editor at J. B. Lippincott, Corlies Smith, but the correspondence between the two of them shows that Pynchon had merely been waiting for these suggestions in order to present his own ideas for an extensive revision. A typescript of the version first submitted to Lippincott can be consulted at the Harry Ransom Center in Austin.[27] In both versions, *V.* is a historical novel about love and death that pushes the boundaries of the genre. It combines chapters about the amorous tribulations of a group of young people in mid-fifties New York with an almost chronological sequence of chapters set in various locations in Europe and Africa between 1898 and 1943. The central characters of the New York plot are Benny Profane, a self-declared schlemiel who stumbles through life, surrenders to women and proves to be a true friend, and Herbert Stencil, whose obsessive search for the elusive, female V. mentioned in his father's journal leads him on the imaginative tour of the past that results in the novel's historical chapters. Neither character is successful in the conventional sense – Stencil does not find V., and Profane ends up not having "learned a goddam thing."[28]

Love is the main theme of the New York plot, and this part of the novel also includes magnificent set pieces, such as Profane's alligator hunt in the New York sewers and a minute description of a "nose job."[29] The various love interests in the New York chapters create a diverse picture of male attitudes towards the female Other – so diverse, indeed, that the survival of the Western worship of Woman thematized, however perversely, in Stencil's quest can by no means predominate.[30] Nor does this form of worship seem to solve what Pynchon may have seen as the sexual woes of his generation. On the contrary, perhaps: if V. does not quite induce the men who pursue her to become aggressive, her presence is repeatedly associated with episodes of violence and destruction, including the death by impalement of a young ballerina with whom she has fallen in love in 1913 Paris.

Although the love theme in the New York chapters might have been developed even more succinctly than it ultimately was, *V.* did benefit greatly from Pynchon's revision. Some chapters were dropped or severely cut, which, for instance, did away with a long description of a family sitcom episode that would have provided a view on society's recuperation of love. The sequence of chapters or parts of chapters was also substantially rearranged. Other changes, big and small, have had considerable effect on the novel's possible interpretations. The version of "Under the Rose" in the typescript at the Harry Ransom Center is already very different from the original short story. It has become a sequence of eight impersonations imagined by Stencil, which together still amount to a tale of spying and diplomacy in Egypt. In an effort to make sure the reader would not be confused by this first historical chapter, Pynchon wrote a brief introduction to it for the novel's final version, in which his narrator reflects on the operation of Stencil's historical imagination.[31] Far from succumbing to the frustration that will be the outcome of Stencil's quest, this passage seems to valorize his enticing historical evocations as testifying to an imaginative sense of history perhaps more valuable than the verification of every last fact. The introduction implies that historians such as James Frazer, Robert Graves and Henry Adams are antiquated because they only indulge in continuity and simple pattern. However, the poetic resilience of Stencil's historical imagination (also displayed by the narrator in the Epilogue) seems to compensate in part for the impossibility of coming to grips with the intimidating chaos of history in the first half of the twentieth century.

Henry Adams, who reduced the narrative of historical progress in his *Education* (1906) to just two notions, the Virgin and the Dynamo, is presumably named in the introduction to the Egypt chapter as an exemplar of old-fashioned historiography. Nevertheless, Adams seems to have been a crucial inspiration for *V.*, especially through his association of the life-affirming sublimity of Woman with the comparable but life-denying sublimity of Technology. Witness not only Pynchon's motif of the inanimate (which he overdoes, even after removing many instances of it for the final version), but also the development of his title character, who ends up as a kind of mechanical doll. What is more, Adams seems to have inspired important aspects of Stencil's historical method, at least one of which emerges in the course of the revision process. Adams realized that general concepts such as the Virgin and the Dynamo could no longer be imposed on the "multiple" world a "child born in 1900" would confront, but Stencil (who is born in 1901!) tries to overcome this difficulty by imaginatively projecting himself into the multiple characters whose perspectives mediate the events of the Egypt chapter.[32] This multiplication also affects his self-image. In the entire typescript of V., Stencil speaks about himself in the first person. In the final version, he has switched from first to third, which the introduction to the Egypt chapter comments on as follows: "Herbert Stencil, like small children at a certain stage and Henry Adams in the Education, as well as assorted autocrats since time out of mind, always referred to himself in the third person. This helped 'Stencil' appear as only one among a repertoire of identities."[33] In a letter to his editor, Pynchon explains that he made the change from first to third because he wanted to align Stencil's voice in the 1956 chapters with the narrative voice in the historical chapters.[34] In the light of the quotation from Adams, both self-multiplication and third-person self-reference appear as efforts to meet the demands of twentieth-century reality. Their ultimate success depends on the reader's willingness to accept the sophistication they bring to the struggle with chaos.

In his evocation of twentieth-century history, Pynchon deals with the Second World War through a chapter in the form of a letter, written from Malta, about the devastating siege of that island (1940–43). He displaces the Holocaust onto a chapter about events in Namibia in 1922 that conjure up the German genocide of the Herero people between 1904 and 1907, when the protectorate was still a German colony. The link is made quite explicit. Noting the 60,000 people that General von Trotha exterminated during his one year in South-West Africa, the narrator informally refers to the generally estimated total of Jewish casualties in World War II: "This is only 1 per cent of six million, but still pretty good."[35] To cap the whole process of rewriting, Pynchon redid the South-West Africa chapter "from the ground up."[36] The new version is considerably longer than the original and features a remarkable balance between historical accuracy and creative fictionalization, which turns the story of German engineer Kurt Mondaugen as retold by Stencil into arguably the novel's strongest testimony to the force of the historical imagination. Major changes include the expansion of Vera Meroving, the chapter's main version of the title figure; a much greater emphasis on the genocide; and the foregrounding of the historical imagination through the fact that Mondaugen dreams the genocide in a state of nightmarish fever. This dreaming connects the South-West Africa chapter with the new pages at the beginning of the Egypt chapter, where the conscious unconsciousness of a dream experience is offered as a model for the workings of the creative mind confronting the multiplicity diagnosed and dreaded by Adams.

The chapter in South-West Africa also provides a historical counterpart to the importance of race in the 1956 plot. Pynchon's pseudo-hipsters attend performances by the African American saxophone player, McClintic Sphere, who gets entangled in the New York events through his friendship with the record executive, Roony Winsome, and his affair with the Maltese girl, Paola Maijstral, in her part-time role as a prostitute. Since Pynchon's editor surmised the young author wasn't interested in writing a "protest novel," he suggested reducing Sphere's role.[37] Pynchon agreed that protest "was the furthest thing from [his] mind,"[38] and so made many cuts, one a long episode in which Sphere takes Winsome to Harlem for a militant speech by an African American patriarch.[39] The characterization of Sphere in the published novel represents another major improvement compared to the typescript, where the main black character amounts to little more than a mix of Beat-inspired clichés, liberal sentiment and limited personal experience. Nevertheless, just as Bolingbroke in "Low-lands" can be read as an instance of Pynchon's early romantic primitivism in the depiction of race, even the revised Sphere may demonstrate an early failure to move far beyond reliance on (liberal) stereotypes.[40] Pynchon was aware of the "doctrinaire liberal" nature of the friendship between Sphere and Winsome, but he did not altogether eliminate it in the published novel.[41] The jazzman's famous catchphrase, "Keep cool but care," can also be read as an indication of just how ethically responsible Pynchon wanted his main African American character to be.

In "The Secret Integration" (1964), the final story collected in *Slow Learner*, the "race issue" becomes the main focus.[42] Whites are harassing the new African American couple in a Berkshire neighborhood and, as a kind of climax to this aspect of the plot, dump a pickup truckload of garbage in their front yard. The rebellious young boys at the heart of the action not only play pranks on the grown-ups to show their contempt for adult society, but also have a "secret integration" with an imaginary friend, the son of the newcomers. Attitudes toward race are further thematized through another jazzman, the alcoholic Carl McAfee. Local AA members send one of the boys to the hotel where McAfee is staying as a gesture of racist indifference, contempt or hostility. Since the jazz musician cannot pay for his bottle, he gets into a fight with a Latino bellboy. Exposing racism as an element of acculturation, "The Secret Integration" is pessimistic about the liberal ideal of racial harmony and can thus be seen as a corrective to Pynchon's earlier work.

In the period under consideration in this chapter, Pynchon was clearly dedicated to improving as a writer. While continuing to struggle with themes such as love, violence and oppression, he was learning the craft much faster than he would make it seem when collecting his short stories in 1984. In two final self-deprecating moves which reinforce rather than undermine the framework of education, Pynchon concludes his introduction to *Slow Learner* by suggesting that learning goes on forever, and that, in *The Crying of Lot 49*, he seems "to have forgotten most of what [he] thought [he]'d learned up till then."[43] The short novel was so deservedly successful that this second point sounds surprisingly harsh. Despite its setting in early 1960s California, *Lot 49* confirmed Pynchon's *V.*-based reputation as an original historical novelist. In her role as executrix of her former lover's estate, Oedipa Maas keeps probing into the historical sources of contemporary reality, sometimes going as far back as the sixteenth century. An archaeologist of American society, she does not fail to encounter race in the process, which goes to show that Pynchon was not quite done with the issue.[44] A new development in Pynchon's depiction of race, *Lot 49* is still a far cry from the unfettered approach to blackness in *Gravity's Rainbow*.

NOTES

1 Thomas Pynchon, Letter to Corlies Smith, August 31, 1961.
2 These texts have been published in Clifford Mead, *Thomas Pynchon: A Bibliography of Primary and Secondary Materials* (Elmwood Park: Dalkey Archive Press, 1989), pp. 155–67.
3 Charles Hollander, "Pynchon's Juvenilia and *Against the Day*," GRAAT 3 (March 2008), 48, www.graat.fr/5%20Hollander.pdf
4 Michael Hartnett, "Thomas Pynchon's Long Island Years," *Confrontation*, 30–31 (November 1985), 45.
5 Mead, *Thomas Pynchon*, p. 161.
6 The libretto forms part of the Pynchon collection at the Harry Ransom Center (Austin, TX), which also contains a typescript of the first version of *V.* submitted to the publisher, a set of galleys for that novel, a photocopy of a complete, typed draft of *Vineland*, and eight letters Pynchon wrote to Kirkpatrick and Faith Sale at the beginning of the 1960s.
7 Rodney Gibbs, "A Portrait of the Luddite as a Young Man," *Denver Quarterly*, 39.1 (2004), 35.
8 Thomas Pynchon, *Slow Learner* (Boston: Little, Brown, 1984), p. 7.
9 Thomas Pynchon, "Is It O.K. to Be a Luddite?" *New York Times Book Review*, October 28, 1984, 1, 40–41.
10 Thomas Pynchon, "Mortality and Mercy in Vienna," *Epoch*, 9.4 (Spring 1959), 195–213.

11 Vincent King, "Giving Destruction a Name and a Face: Thomas Pynchon's 'Mortality and Mercy in Vienna,'" *Studies in Short Fiction*, 35 (1998), 14.
12 For an exception, see the section devoted to the introduction in Luc Herman and Bart Vervaeck, "'Didn't Know Any Better': Race and Unreliable Narration in 'Low-Lands' by Thomas Pynchon," in Elke D'hoker and Gunther Martens (eds.), *Narrative Unreliability in the Twentieth-Century First-Person Novel* (Berlin/New York: Walter de Gruyter, 2008), pp. 229–46.
13 Pynchon, *Slow Learner*, p. 15.
14 *Ibid.*, p. 16.
15 *Ibid.*, p. 21.
16 *Ibid.*, p. 50.
17 *Ibid.*, p. 44.
18 See Mark D. Hawthorne, "Homoerotic Bonding as Escape from Heterosexual Responsibility in Pynchon's *Slow Learner*," *Style*, 34.3 (Fall 2000), 512–29.
19 Pynchon, *Slow Learner*, p. 11.
20 *Ibid.*, p. 4.
21 *Ibid.*, p. 83.
22 *Ibid.*, p. 88.
23 *Ibid.*, p. 91.
24 *Ibid.*, pp. 12–14.
25 *Ibid.*, p. 17.
26 See e.g. Richard F. Patteson, "How True a Text? Chapter Three of *V.* and 'Under the Rose,'" *Southern Humanities Review*, 18.4 (Fall 1984), 299–308; Douglas Fowler, "Story Into Chapter: Thomas Pynchon's Transformation of 'Under the Rose,'" *Journal of Narrative Technique*, 14.1 (Winter 1984), 33–43; and M. Angeles Martinez, "From 'Under the Rose' to *V.*: A Linguistic Approach to Human Agency in Pynchon's Fiction," *Poetics Today*, 23.4 (Winter 2002), 633–56.
27 For an overview of the rewriting process, see Luc Herman and John M. Krafft, "Fast Learner: The Typescript of Pynchon's *V.* at the Harry Ransom Center in Austin," *Texas Studies in Literature and Language*, 49.1 (Spring 2007), 1–20.
28 Thomas Pynchon, *V.* (Philadelphia: Lippincott, 1963), p. 454.
29 *Ibid.*, pp. 95 ff.
30 In this respect, see Lila V. Graves, "Love and the Western World of Pynchon's *V.*," *Southern Humanities Review*, 47.1 (Spring 1982), 62–73, for a discussion of the importance for *V.* of Denis de Rougemont's *Love in the Western World* (1939; English translation 1956; final French version 1972).
31 Pynchon, *V.*, pp. 61–63. For an elaborate interpretation of this introduction, see Luc Herman, "Thomas Pynchon's Appeal to the Canon in the Final Version of *V.*," in Christophe Den Tandt (ed.), *Reading Without Maps? Cultural Landmarks in a Post-Canonical Age* (Brussels: Peter Lang, 2005), pp. 291–303.
32 Henry Adams, *The Education of Henry Adams* (New York: Vintage Books/The Library of America, 1990), p. 424.
33 Pynchon, *V.*, p. 62.
34 Thomas Pynchon, Letter to Corlies Smith, April 19, 1962.
35 Pynchon, *V.*, p. 245.
36 Pynchon, Letter, April 19, 1962. For a detailed comparison of the two versions, see Luc Herman and John M. Krafft, "'From the Ground Up': The Evolution of

the South-West Africa Chapter in Pynchon's *V.*," *Contemporary Literature*, 47.2 (2006), 261–88.

37 Corlies Smith, Letter to Thomas Pynchon, February 23, 1962.

38 Pynchon, Letter, April 19, 1962.

39 See Luc Herman and John M. Krafft, "Race in Early Pynchon: Rewriting Sphere in *V.*," *Critique*, 52.1 (2011), 1–13.

40 See Robert Holton, "'Closed Circuit': The White Male Predicament in Pynchon's Early Stories," in Niran Abbas (ed.), *Thomas Pynchon: Reading From the Margins* (Madison: Fairleigh Dickinson University Press, 2003), pp. 37–50.

41 Pynchon, Letter to Corlies Smith, March 13, 1962.

42 Pynchon, *Slow Learner*, p. 152.

43 *Ibid.*, p. 22.

44 See Steven Weisenburger, "Reading Race: *The Crying of Lot 49* and Early Pynchon," in Thomas H. Schaub (ed.), *Approaches to Teaching Pynchon's* The Crying of Lot 49 *and Other Works* (New York: Modern Language Association of America, 2008), pp. 52–58.

THOMAS HILL SCHAUB

The Crying of Lot 49 and other California novels

Though *The Crying of Lot 49* (1966), *Vineland* (1990) and *Inherent Vice* (2009) are all set in California, each is a parable of the American nation. Together they form a mini social and political history of the culture as it devolved from an era of myriad social changes and expanding opportunities to one of conservative reaction. Each book is set specifically in Southern California: Oedipa travels south to San Narciso, while the generative action in both *Vineland* and *Inherent Vice* takes place in (or near) Gordita Beach (a.k.a. Manhattan Beach in South Bay). Thus in Pynchon's imagination Southern California is the place where the nation impinges upon the characters of his novels, the place in which his characters begin to think about their lives within the framework of the nation, as Oedipa does near the end of *Lot 49* when she walks down a "stretch of railroad track" and realizes "she might have found The Tristero anywhere in her Republic," that America itself is "coded in Inverarity's testament."[1] A search drives the plot of all three novels: for Trystero in Oedipa's case, for Prairie's mother Frenesi in *Vineland*, and in *Inherent Vice*, Doc Sportello's pursuit of Mickey Wolfmann and Coy Harlingen, among others. In all three novels, the main characters find more than they bargained for, but Oedipa's search in *Lot 49* is forward-looking, as she seems to stumble across (or produce) alternative, possibly subversive energies on the threshold of making a difference in the consensus culture of the United States, while both *Vineland* and *Inherent Vice* are reflective novels, looking backward from within or under the impact of the reactionary politics of the Nixon and Reagan years.

Unlike his other fiction, the California novels return again and again to the same place and time: more or less from 1964 to 1971. *The Crying of Lot 49* takes place prior to both *Inherent Vice* and *Vineland*, in the years that would lead to violent dissent and state repression; *Vineland* begins on a morning in 1984 under the administration of Ronald Reagan, but soon returns via Prairie's research in the archives, and the memories of Zoyd and DL, to the late 1960s; while the action of *Inherent Vice* takes place entirely within the early years of Richard M. Nixon's presidency, the beginning of the war on drugs and the influx of federal funding for local police enforcement.

This return to the same period suggests that the mid to late 1960s represent a watershed moment not only in the nation's life but in Pynchon's own. Pynchon wrote *The Crying of Lot 49* just prior to the national upheaval that began in 1968, during what may be termed the psychedelic and Aquarian sixties, as a young man living in California and Mexico.[2] There was much that was encouraging: LSD use was still legal, the Free Speech Movement was under way at Berkeley, Betty Friedan's *The Feminine Mystique* (1963) inaugurated second-wave feminism, Michael Harrington's *The Other America* (1964) kick-started Lyndon Johnson's Great Society programs and the War on Poverty, the Civil Rights Act passed in 1964, followed by the Voting Rights Act in 1965. President Johnson had yet to order 500,000 troops into Vietnam. *The Crying of Lot 49* captures the mood then prevailing of a nation on the threshold of substantive transformations. Because the novel was composed during this period, the author's temporal distance from his work is virtually absent. *Lot 49* emerges from a different era, and is expressing a mood and perspective radically distinct from those we find in *Vineland* and *Inherent Vice*.

Unlike the California novels to come, *Lot 49* is a novel about the possibility of revolution, the proliferation of countercultures, and the secret withdrawal from the "cheered land" of middle-class life. The vehicle for these themes is Oedipa Maas, a California housewife charged with settling the estate of a former lover, Pierce Inverarity. In the process of doing so Oedipa discovers an alternative America, invisible to those celebrating the American Century. As a corollary of this discovery, Pynchon's novel at least leaves open the possibility that something unspoken but widely felt is afoot. If Pynchon's participation in this era's turbulence stayed within bounds of the aesthetic, we must nevertheless acknowledge his participation in the full-scale assault taking place in the 1960s on the realist-naturalist tradition that had been the vehicle of protest writing for sixty-five years or more. In this *The Crying of Lot 49* is like many fictions of the period, including Ken Kesey's *One Flew Over the Cuckoo's Nest* (1962), Kurt Vonnegut Jr.'s *Cat's Cradle* (1963), Leonard Cohen's *Beautiful Losers* (1966), Richard Fariña's *Been Down So Long It Looks Like Up to Me* (1966), Ishmael Reed's *Yellowback Radio Broke Down* (1969), Tom Robbins's *Another Roadside Attraction* (1971) and Mary Shetzline's *Amazon One* (1971), among dozens of novels that might be listed. This young generation of writers was determined to come out from under the authority of the "traditional" novel. Like the metafiction writers John Barth, Gilbert Sorrentino, Donald Barthelme, Robert Coover and William Gass, with whom they have little else in common, Pynchon and company viewed realism as a pernicious illusion. Pynchon leaves no doubt about his own allegiances in the blurb he supplied for Rudolph Wurlitzer's *Nog* (1969): "The novel of bullshit is dead."

The Crying of Lot 49 is unique even among these novels because of its insinuation that the text itself is a kind of plot perpetrated upon the reader, containing a secret meaning known only to the author. This is to speak of the novel's *effect* rather than to suggest there is such a secret yet to be discovered. Yet the importance of this effect cannot be overestimated, for quality of insinuation, of a textual paranoia induced within and energizing the reader, constitutes the affective politics of the novel. *Lot 49*'s coy ambiguities are the stylistic analogue of the restless expectancy of the sixties, captured in Stephen Stills's lyrics for the Buffalo Springfield song "For What It's Worth" (1967): "There's something happening here / What it is ain't exactly clear." Together with the sense of social change under way, the novel produces a degree of liberal sentimentality about the Republic through Oedipa's evident dismay at what she learns about the difference between the promise of the United States and what it had become. In Oedipa's lament for "a land where you could somehow walk, and not need the East San Narciso Freeway" there is an echo of the wavering radical in one of the "Camera Eye" sections of John Dos Passos's *The Big Money* (1936): "what leverage might pry the owners loose from power and bring back (I too Walt Whitman) our story-book democracy."[3] The novel leaves open the prospect of an "alternative" America – at the very least a way of remaining "alien" yet "relevant" to the nation.[4]

Efforts to plot Pynchon's cultural politics along some spectrum from left to right, however, encounter a degree of incoherence. *Lot 49* disparages the "symmetry of choices," of "zeroes and ones," of a "right and left," but the space between these extremes is occupied by the consensus culture of government and business that the novel represents as monopolistic and oppressive, a culture that has "conditioned" the citizenry to the "silence and paralysis" Oedipa encounters upon entering San Narciso.[5] Though Oedipa laments "excluded middles," the novel's utopian aspirations seem best characterized not by *included* middles but by the language of "surprise," "possibility," "chance" and "diversity." If left, right and center are unacceptable, diversity and possibility must be found in a different version of "consensus" that shares more with aspects of new age libertarianism than with liberal pluralism.

Pynchon wrote *The Crying of Lot 49* during the presidential contest of 1964 between Barry Goldwater and Lyndon Johnson, and it shows: Oedipa is a Young Republican, a member of the starter organization that became the Young Americans for Freedom, and the philatelist Genghis Cohen wears a Goldwater sweatshirt. When Goldwater announced his candidacy for the Republican Presidential nomination in January of 1964, he promised to "offer a choice, not an echo," and the anti-feminist Republican activist Phyllis Schlafly wrote *A Choice Not an Echo* (1964), a pamphlet distributed by the millions.[6] Goldwater's promise appealed not only to the conservative right, but to many in the country of all persuasions – like Stanley Koteks – who felt government and the military-industrial complex were squelching individual liberties, initiatives and rewards. This background provides a secondary reference to Oedipa's stay at the Echo Courts Motel. We needn't dislodge the myth of Narcissus and Echo from our understanding of the novel to see that the political question facing Oedipa and the reader is whether she discovers a choice (a "real alternative") or an echo of Pierce and the business-as-usual political economy he represents. After her night in San Francisco, Oedipa tells herself "here were God knew how many citizens, deliberately *choosing* not to communicate by US Mail."[7]

Pynchon makes the libertarian element of these choices explicit in one of the novel's magical moments in which diversity and possibility are temporarily realized. When Oedipa returns to her Berkeley hotel, she is swept onto the dance floor with a party of deaf mute delegates:

> Each couple on the floor danced whatever was in the fellow's head: tango, two-step, bossa nova, slop. But how long, Oedipa thought, could it go on before collisions became a serious hindrance? There would have to be collisions. The only alternative was some unthinkable order of music, many rhythms, all keys at once, a choreography in which each couple meshed easy, predestined. Something they all heard with an extra sense atrophied in herself. She followed her partner's lead, limp in the young mute's clasp, waiting for the collisions to begin. But none came. She was danced for half an hour before, by mysterious consensus, everybody took a break, without having felt any touch but the touch of her partner.[8]

This scene is one of a series in chapter 5, Oedipa's journey through the San Francisco night, in which she comes across a variety of isolated communities, such as the "circle of children" for whom the "night was empty of all terror" because "they had inside their circle an imaginary fire, and needed nothing but their own unpenetrated sense of community."[9] The dancers are without question an image of effortless community, the miracle of communication at work, however mysterious it is to Oedipa. Because of this communication, as hypothesized by Nefastis, collisions which must happen do not: the reader is treated to a miraculous scene in which individual will meshes seamlessly with social order. The dance of the deaf mutes is nothing less than utopian.

Oedipa herself interprets her experience as an anarchist miracle, recalling an encounter earlier in the chapter with Jesús Arrabal, who defined "miracle" as "another world's intrusion into this one [...] where revolutions break out spontaneously and leaderless, and the soul's talent for consensus allows the masses to work together without effort, automatic as the body itself."[10] Oedipa intuitively collapses Arrabal's idea of "intrusion" from the *outside* with the *immanence* figured in the dance. Oedipa's analogy thus intensifies the utopian dimension of the scene, suggesting an idea of transcendent community possible from within – by consensus. In this chapter Pynchon redefines the idea of "consensus" as a product of miracles and revolutions rather than of liberal politics and its traditions. Indeed, this "mysterious consensus" directly contradicts the "bland" consensus liberalism of the fifties that turned Oedipa into a Young Republican and New Critic. Cyrus Patell rightly makes a connection with Pynchon's Luddite essay: "to insist on the miraculous is to ... assert the limited wish that living things, earthly and otherwise, may on occasion become Big and Bad enough to take part in transcendent doings."[11]

Every use of the word "consensus" in *The Crying of Lot 49* occurs in chapter 5, which provides several fantasies of consensus: the Nefastis Machine, the anarchist miracle, the children in Golden Gate Park, the dance of the deaf mutes, and the coinciding spectra of the human voice in Mucho's "vision of consensus."[12] In each case, as Patell has argued, this consensus is associated with transcendence, as when Mucho concludes: "Then you'd have this big, God, maybe a couple hundred million chorus saying 'rich, chocolaty goodness' together, and it would all be the same voice."[13] Oedipa's encounters with Nefastis, Arrabal, the children, the deaf mutes and Mucho repeatedly undermine her liberal rationalism, just as the psychiatrist Hilarius does. When Oedipa tells Hilarius to "face up to your social responsibilities [... and a]ccept the reality principle," Hilarius rebuffs her commonsense Freudianism, advising Oedipa instead to cherish her fantasies. When you lose them, "you go over by that much to the others. You begin to cease to be."[14] Oedipa's biggest, most lushly blossoming fantasy, the metaphor combining her isolated encounters into the idea of an alternative society "congruent with the cheered land," is Trystero.[15]

In both *Vineland* and *Inherent Vice*, Pynchon is less interested in the possibilities for alternative communities than in the Althusserian focus upon mechanisms that maintain the status quo, strategies that hold things in place – and which kept social history in the United States from developing in more liberal, not to say radical, directions. Set in 1984, *Vineland* in particular attacks the new fascism exemplified by the war on drugs begun by Nixon and continued under Reagan; at the same time Pynchon also places responsibility for the conservative retrenchment upon the putative radicals of the sixties. The novel returns to this formative period via the archival research conducted by Prairie Wheeler, daughter of Zoyd Wheeler, who is searching for her mother Frenesi Gates, whom she learns was a guerilla filmmaker and member of 24fps, a radical film collective. Pynchon uses Prairie's search to focus upon the ways the revolutionaries of the sixties were themselves complicit in the betrayal of that era's possibilities.

In *Vineland*, primary among the mechanisms maintaining the status quo is the mediating power of television and film. *Vineland*'s critique of "tubal" culture would seem improbably belated were it not for the critique of representation that was theorized in the 1970s and 1980s and which informs Pynchon's novel. In the 1960s, many of those working for social change thought television and film were capable of radicalizing the society, but Prairie's viewing of the film archives of the 24fps collective – much of it her mother's footage – shows Frenesi's naive radical filmmaking at the College of the Surf co-opted by the government agent Brock Vond. Joseph Slade usefully describes the pitfalls of mediated information, and how easily the "electronic media [can] defuse outrage by distorting revolutionary messages that were none too well coded to begin with."[16] When Frenesi tells DL Chastain "we're really going to change the world this time," Pynchon renders a harsh judgment not only on his own generation but upon the first of his California novels. Talking to Zoyd, Isaiah Two Four drives both judgments home by invoking the very language of *Lot 49*: "'Whole problem 'th you folks's generation [...] is you believed in your Revolution [...] but you sure didn't understand much about the Tube. Minute the Tube got hold of you folks that was it, that whole *alternative America*, el deado meato."[17] Isaiah refers here to the power of television to distract, overpower, diffuse and subject, but the failure to understand the mediation of film and television applies directly to Frenesi herself, naively thinking of herself as a bystander "on her own," shooting coverage that would lead to Weed Atman's death yet "safe in a world-next-to-the-world."[18] As if he'd been reading Hayden White and Michel Foucault, Pynchon deconstructs the illusions of transparent representation, and the claims by historians to objective narrative. The novel seems to corroborate the message of the song that made Gil Scott-Heron famous: "The Revolution Will Not be Televised" (1970). Here as elsewhere in the novel, Pynchon's plot operates most persuasively on an allegorical level, for Vond's interventions are most compelling if understood as representative of the state's ability to control media. As Slade points out, "the real narcotic in *Vineland* is television. The principal addict is federal drug agent Hector Zuñiga, who commits himself to a Tubal detoxification facility" but cannot give up his ambition to shoot his own movie.[19] Throughout the novel, references to *The Brady Bunch*, *Jeopardy*, *The Flintstones*, *The Phil Donahue Show* and so on, make obvious the degree to which Hector's addiction is shared by everyone in the culture, to the extent that popular culture thinks the identities and lives of the novel's characters for them. Readers may be reminded of the moment of parodied transcendence in Don DeLillo's *White Noise*, when Jack Gladney overhears his daughter repeating "Toyota Celica" in her sleep.[20]

Vineland's satire goes beyond Adorno and Horkheimer's critique of the top-down culture industry to indict the citizenry itself. As numerous passages that might be adduced show, Pynchon places much of the onus for keeping things in place on the people themselves, by reason both of the ease with which they can be satisfied, and of the extent to which immediate sexual and material desires take precedence over long-term social change. Like the contempt for the Old Left registered in Norman Mailer's *Armies of the Night* (1968) and E. L. Doctorow's *The Book of Daniel* (1971), Pynchon's *Vineland* and *Inherent Vice* represent a subsequent generation's fault-finding with the formations that may be grouped beneath the "new left," from the psychedelic hippies and Haight Ashbury dropouts, to SDS and SNCC, to Abbie Hoffman and the Yippies, the Black Panthers and The Weather Underground. Pynchon's reprimand of the counterculture appears early in the novel when Hector Zuñiga upbraids Zoyd Wheeler: "*Caray*, you sixties people, it's amazing [...] All o' you are still children inside, livín your real life back then. Still waitín for that magic payoff."[21]

Indeed, this is a key insight of the novel: that the right didn't need to persecute the left because the counterculture children wanted the authority that was voted into office. "Brock saw the deep [...] need only to stay children forever, safe inside some extended national Family [...] Children longing for discipline."[22] Molly Hite convincingly argues that Pynchon makes Frenesi's betrayal central to the novel to show the complicity between sexuality and power, and the allure of co-optation by authority.[23] As in Vond's ability to co-opt the radical ambitions of Frenesi's film collective, Frenesi's otherwise implausible willingness to betray Weed Atman because of her sexual attraction to Brock Vond in uniform makes better sense if understood as an analogue for her generation's unacknowledged desire for authority, "as if some Cosmic Fascist had spliced in a DNA sequence requiring this form of seduction and initiation into the dark joys of social control."[24] Near the end of the novel Hector tells Zoyd, "they did a study, found out since about '81 kids were comin in all on their own askín about careers, no need for no separate facility anymore, so Brock's budget lines all went to the big Intimus shredder in the sky."[25]

To confirm the spirit that informs *The Crying of Lot 49* and the era in which it was written, there may be no more revealing (or hilarious) passage in the California novels than the one describing Cesare Lombroso's theory of "misoneism":

> Radicals, militants, revolutionaries, however they styled themselves, all sinned against this deep organic human principle, which Lombroso had named after the Greek for "hatred of anything new." It operated as a feedback device to keep societies coming along safely, coherently. Any sudden attempt to change things would be answered by an immediate misoneistic backlash, not only from the State but from the people themselves — Nixon's election in '68 seeming to Brock a perfect example of this.[26]

The passage explicitly opposes the meliorism of liberal politics to the radical break that is the requirement of revolution. For Pynchon, as for many generations of political theorists on the left, meliorism offers only the illusion of gradual change, providing in actuality for the continuation of the System. Whether Pynchon once imagined the United States – the Western world – to be on the verge of sudden change, *Vineland* perfectly captures that feeling after Nixon's election of the nation having stepped back from the cusp of radical transformation – "a people's miracle, an army of loving friends."[27]

Both *Vineland* and *Inherent Vice* show Lombroso's theory being realized through the complicities, infiltrations, and betrayals of individual characters. In *Lot 49* betrayal seems largely a matter of United States citizens being betrayed by government and business monopolies – "arid betrayals of spiritual poverty";[28] while in *Vineland* and *Inherent Vice*, "betrayal" is part of a discourse about snitches, informers, and run-of-the-mill compromise.[29] In both books, everyone is on the take: "betrayal became routine, government procedures for it so simple and greased that no one, Frenesi was finding out [...] could be considered safely above it, wherever 'above' was supposed to be, with money from the CIA, FBI, and others circulating everywhere."[30] Every transaction entangles one in a systemic complicity, from the use of credit cards by which shoppers voluntarily give information to the system, to changing one's outfit from T-shirt and bikini to "flatland gear."[31] Frenesi and her genetic line fall for uniforms, while Coy Harlingen confesses: "I wanted to do something for my country. Stupid as it sounds."[32] Like Tyrone Slothrop in northern Germany, Coy has fallen for that "nation-love" that helps hold things in place.[33]

Characteristically, there is an actual historical background to which Pynchon's text refers. Much of the nation may have read or seen television spots about the war on drugs, but the occupants of California's Mendocino and Humbolt Counties knew about it firsthand. The seemingly far-fetched depictions of re-education camps and helicopter raids depicted in *Vineland* masks the actual war on drugs, which created CAMP, or Campaign Against Marijuana Planting, in 1983 and which is still in operation. "With more than 110 agencies having participated, CAMP is the largest law enforcement task force in the United States" deploying "aggressive eradication techniques" including aerial surveillance, and transportation of officers. CAMP was preceded by a regional California agency, the Bureau of Narcotic Enforcement, that initiated a regional task force program in the mid 1970s. Each regional task force had a BNE Special Agent in charge, aka Hector Zuñiga.[34] Given the funding and material dedicated to this effort, Brock Vond saw "his future in the war against drugs" as a "great nation pursued its war on a botanical species."[35]

Any connection to Frenesi's "old sweet community" is considerably attenuated in Pynchon's most recent novel, *Inherent Vice*. Set in the Nixon years when many in the South Bay community are fleeing north to Vineland, Pynchon's satire on US fascism and the betrayal of possibility seems all but pre-empted and beside the point. In this novel, Pynchon returns to the private eye formula of *The Crying of Lot 49*, but adheres more closely to the plot resolution required of that genre. Like a Raymond Chandler novel, this one begins with a visit to private eye Larry "Doc" Sportello from his former girlfriend Shasta Hepworth, who asks Doc to rescue her current love interest from being committed to a mental hospital. The plot grows ever more complicated and interconnected from thereon, including the corrupt activities of the Los Angeles Police Department, the tracking down of Coy Harlingen, an informer and agent provocateur for the LAPD, the discovery of the mysterious Golden Fang Enterprises, and a conversation with Crocker Fenway, whose runaway daughter Japonica Doc had several times recovered for her parents.

This conversation with Fenway may be identified as the bottom line of Pynchon's current thinking about our "silver chances of song."[36] Once Coy Harlingen's "family and his freedom" have been negotiated, the dialogue turns to the subject of class conflict. Pynchon assigns Doc the role of the savvy member of the renter class talking tough with the big money: "For years now under everybody's nose there's been all this class hatred, slowly building. Where do you think that's headed?" Fenway remains unruffled: "It's about *being in place*," he tells Doc coolly.

> "We've been in place forever. Look around. Real estate, water rights, oil, cheap labor—all of that's ours, it's always been ours. And you, at the end of the day what are you? One more unit in this swarm of transients who come and go without pause in the sunny Southland, eager to be bought off with a car of a certain make, model, and year, a blonde in a bikini, thirty seconds on some

excuse for a wave—a chili dog, for Christ's sake." He shrugged. "We will never run out of you people. The supply is inexhaustible."[37]

Fenway's Brahminism personifies Lombroso's theory of misoneism. In his references to bikini blondes, waves and chili dogs, Fenway shows he has Doc's number. Fenway is one of the "Real Ones" whose quality of life Brock Vond covets, while Doc is one of "the destined losers whose only redemption would have to come through their usefulness to the State law-enforcement apparatus."[38]

Inherent Vice puts us much closer to the actual mechanisms of state control in play from the late 1960s to the mid 1970s: the agents of COINTELPRO infiltrating Black Nationalists and campus radicals, the LAPD, the P-DID ("Police Department Identification Number") that Pynchon parses as the "Public Disorder Intelligence Division"[39] and the ubiquitous Red Squads. In place since 1886, "Red Squads were police intelligence units that specialized in infiltrating, conducting counter-measures and gathering intelligence on political and social groups." During the era of *Inherent Vice*, mass actions against the war in Vietnam and public disorder led Red Squads to focus upon dissidents and protest movements across the spectrum. "The methods employed ranged from simple surveillance to isolated incidents of assassination," as the killing of Fred Hampton, deputy chairman of the Illinois Black Panthers, was understood to be.[40] Government repression such as this is the reference point for the activities of Adrian Prussia, who "found himself specializing in politicals—black and Chicano activists, antiwar protestors, campus bombers, and assorted other pinko fucks."[41]

In order to secure one advantage or another, the citizens of Gordita Beach cooperate where they can with the repressive state apparatus. Doc admits to Fenway, "If you and your friends and lunch companions don't all remain 'in place,' how will average PIs like me ever make a living?"[42] In a comic replay of Vond's realization that the flower children seek parental authority, Doc's lawyer imagines Charlie the Tuna in willing complicity with the system that kills him: "Yes! he, he *wants* to be caught, processed, put in a can, not just any can, you dig, it has to be Starkist! suicidal brand loyalty, man, deep parable of consumer capitalism"; and then draws the analogy: "the horrible thing is, is we *want* them to do it...."[43] One casualty of this focus on complicity is a diminished role for the underclass, the preterite, in these novels. As Pynchon's recognition has evolved of how thoroughly everything really is connected, the We-system has disappeared and along with it that sympathy for the "invisible yet congruent" citizenry that marks his fiction from *V.* and *The Crying of Lot 49* to *Gravity's Rainbow*.

The epigraph to *Inherent Vice* was one of many slogans popular during the general strike of May 1968 that for a time shut down the economy of France and came close to toppling the de Gaulle government: "Under the paving-stone, the beach!" David Stroban attributes the slogan to Guy Debord:

> In the 1960s Guy Debord had spoken of the yearning for the beach that lay hidden beneath the asphalt of the city streets, in a statement that seems to sum up the period well. Many people discovered new freedoms, new ways of living and, above all, their own energy and creativity.[44]

The beach emerges in *Inherent Vice* as the momentary alternative to the street and the hothouse, left, right and center – a "parenthesis of light" that Doc intuits "might close after all, and all be lost, taken back into darkness."[45] Like the cemetery ghosts beneath the San Narciso Freeway, and the Thanatoids of *Vineland*, the spirit of this time and place lies coded within the epigraph, introducing – in a sense, paved over by – the entertainment to come.

Many of those who have written about the works of Thomas Pynchon have asserted that his fictions provide an alternative vision originating outside the totalizing system of the nation and global capital. At the very least, readers of his fiction have seen in it a countercultural critique of mainstream middle-class life and values. The word "alternative" itself is a prominent term in *The Crying of Lot 49*. Even Pynchon's withdrawal from the public eye has been taken to be a self-protective, if not subversive, strategy to refuse the market's commodification of his personal life. Except for the way *Lot 49* engages the reader, the three novels set in California consistently portray the United States as a system from which there is no escape. If there are any "politics" left in Pynchon's imaginative energies today, they seem typified primarily by a wistful libertarianism – a comic and melancholy realization that the narrow self-interest of the nation's citizenry guarantees the enduring depredations of "late capitalism."[46]

By the time *Vineland* and *Inherent Vice* are published, Pynchon has lost all interest in "mysterious consensus," though an underlying resentment at the loss of what once seemed possible persists. When we last see Oedipa, she is "waiting for a symmetry of choices to break down, to go skew," but the middle class of *Inherent Vice* remains stuck in a "cycle of choices that are no choices."[47] His later novels still portray American life as something to be escaped, but with the caveat that all are complicit in the stubborn repetition of that life.[48] Consensus in these books is what it was before Oedipa stepped onto Sproul Plaza many years ago, that is, merely "suburban consensus."[49] Similarly, both *Vineland* and *Inherent Vice* contain abundant fantasy – but it is *just* fantasy, lacking the subversive implications it has for Oedipa and the reader in *Lot 49*: the family reunion of *Vineland* and Prairie's escape from Vond, Desmond "thinking he must be home," and the implausible resolutions of *Inherent Vice*, including Coy's release and reunion with his family, the return of Trillium to hers, and Shasta's reconnection with Doc.[50] Even though Pynchon situates Vineland's population within a history of dissent going back to the Wobblies, the forms and figures of community in *Vineland* and *Inherent Vice* are much less ambitious than in Pynchon's first California novel. In *Lot 49*, the "separate, silent world" Oedipa could have found "anywhere in her Republic" intimated a pervasive sense of change welling up in the disaffected citizenry, rising like a surfer's dream from the once becalmed ocean.[51] In the next two California novels there is no such imagined community. Frenesi's idea of "revolution" is "a mysterious people's oneness, drawing together toward the best chances of light," while Doc fondly remembers "outdoor rock concerts where thousands of people congregated to listen to music for free, and where it all got sort of blended together into a single public self."[52]

Though all three of the main characters in these novels – Oedipa, Frenesi and Doc – suffer varying degrees of the author's irony tinged with sympathy and nostalgia, for their stories of a three-decade long era of United States social history emerge from Pynchon's lived experience. As stories of Pynchon's youth and coming of age, the three novels identify southern California as analogous to Fitzgerald's Long Island and New York, once wondrous places receding into the past. In the last pages of *Inherent Vice* a temporary society forms in the ubiquitous fog, as drivers "set up a temporary commune to help each other home." Eventually, Doc imagines, he will peel off from this "caravan in a desert of perception" and wait for "the fog to burn away, and for something else this time, somehow, to be there instead."[53]

NOTES

1 Thomas Pynchon, *The Crying of Lot 49* (Philadelphia: Lippincott, 1966), pp. 177–80.
2 Garrison Frost, "Thomas Pynchon and the South Bay," www.theaesthetic.com/NewFiles/pynchon.html. On Pynchon during these years, see also Richard Fariña, *Long Time Coming and A Long Time Gone*, foreword by Joan Baez (New York: Dell, 1970).
3 Pynchon, *Lot 49*, p. 99; John Dos Passos, *The Big Money* (New York: Houghton Mifflin, 2000), pp. 118–19.
4 Pynchon, *Lot 49*, p. 182.
5 *Ibid.*, pp. 181, 26.
6 Barry Goldwater, "Announcement of candidacy for Republican nomination," www.4president.org/speeches/barrygoldwater1964

7 Pynchon, *Lot* 49, p. 124, italics mine.
8 *Ibid.*, p. 131.
9 *Ibid.*, p. 118.
10 *Ibid.*, p. 120.
11 Cyrus Patell, *Morrison, Pynchon, and the Problem of Liberal Ideology* (Durham: Duke University Press, 2001), p. 11. For Pynchon's essay itself, see "Is It O.K. to Be a Luddite?" *New York Times Book Review*, October 28, 1984, 1, 40–41.
12 Pynchon, *Lot* 49, p. 143.
13 *Ibid.*, p. 142.
14 *Ibid.*, pp. 136, 138.
15 *Ibid.*, p. 181. On *Lot* 49 as a novel about the power of metaphor to form community, see Edward Mendelson, "The Sacred, the Profane and *The Crying of Lot 49*," in Kenneth H. Baldwin and David K. Kirby (eds.), *Individual and Community: Variations on a Theme in American Fiction* (Durham: Duke University Press, 1975), pp. 182–222.
16 Joseph Slade, "Communication, Group Theory, and Perception in *Vineland*," in Geoffrey Green, Donald J. Greiner and Larry McCaffery (eds.), *The Vineland Papers: Critical Takes on Pynchon's Novel* (Normal, IL: Dalkey Archive Press, 1994), pp. 68–88 at p. 71.
17 Thomas Pynchon, *Vineland* (New York: Little, Brown, 1990), p. 373, italics mine.
18 *Ibid.*, 236, 237, 269.
19 *Ibid.*, p. 78.
20 Don DeLillo, *White Noise* (New York: Penguin, 1985), p. 155.
21 Pynchon, *Vineland*, p. 28.
22 *Ibid.*, p. 269.
23 Molly Hite, "Feminist Theory and the Politics of *Vineland*," in Green, Grenier and McCaffery (eds.), *Vineland Papers*, pp. 135–54.
24 Pynchon, *Vineland*, p. 83.
25 *Ibid.*, p. 347.
26 *Ibid.*, pp. 272–73.
27 *Ibid.*, p. 239.
28 *Ibid.*, p. 170.
29 See N. Katherine Hayles, "'Who Was Saved?': Families, Snitches, and Recuperation in Pynchon's *Vineland*," in Green, Grenier and McCaffery (eds.), *Vineland Papers*, p. 16.
30 Pynchon, *Vineland*, p. 239.
31 Thomas Pynchon, *Inherent Vice* (New York: Penguin Press, 2009), p. 1.
32 *Ibid.*, p. 161.
33 See Pynchon, *Vineland*, p. 255; Thomas Pynchon, *Gravity's Rainbow* (New York: Viking, 1973), p. 623.
34 See Office of the California Attorney General, "Campaign Against Marijuana Planting," www.ag.ca.gov/bne/camp.php; and Pynchon, *Vineland*, p. 220.
35 Pynchon, *Vineland*, pp. 130, 271.
36 Pynchon, *Gravity's Rainbow*, p. 63.
37 Pynchon, *Inherent Vice*, pp. 346–47.
38 Pynchon, *Vineland*, pp. 276, 354.
39 Pynchon, *Inherent Vice*, p. 122.

40 "Red Squad," en.wikipedia.org/wiki/Red_squad
41 Pynchon, *Inherent Vice*, p. 323.
42 *Ibid.*, p. 348.
43 Ibid., p. 119.
44 David Stroband, "Beneath the City Streets, the Beach: The Ideas and Work of Louis Le Roy," www.stichtingtijd.nl/2009_05_Beneath_the_City_Streets.doc
45 Pynchon, *Inherent Vice*, p. 254.
46 *Ibid.*, p 136.
47 Pynchon, *Lot 49*, p. 181; Pynchon, *Inherent Vice*, p. 38.
48 Pynchon, *Inherent Vice*, p. 192.
49 *Ibid.*, p. 349.
50 Pynchon, *Vineland*, p. 385.
51 Pynchon, *Lot 49*, p. 179.
52 Pynchon, *Vineland*, p. 117; Pynchon, *Inherent Vice*, p. 176.
53 Pynchon, *Inherent Vice*, pp. 368–69.

3

STEVEN WEISENBURGER

Gravity's Rainbow

Biographical and historical contexts

In November 1970, Thomas Pynchon took a sheet of quadrille paper and wrote Cornell English professor and F. Scott Fitzgerald biographer Arthur Mizener. Then living in Manhattan Beach, California, Pynchon was well into writing *Gravity's Rainbow* (1973). About that work he volunteered: "the further I get into this wretched profession the clearer it is I am doing very little consciously beyond some clerk routine – assembling, expediting – and that either (a) there is an Extrapersonal Source, or (b) readers are the ones who do most of the work, or all of the above. Which is not a bringdown to realize."[1] Option (b) describes what Roland Barthes had just named the "writerly text" – a fiction that invites readers to actively engage with and thus in a sense *to write* the text.[2] Option (a) playfully attributes his work to some paranormal process, though again there is nothing unusual about it. Historians commonly remark that following a broad and deep research effort one's narration of past events, things, places, people and their expressions will spill from one's notes onto pages. Thus the Archive seems to write itself into narration, hardly "a bringdown" because it frees the writer to concentrate on what lies beyond the "clerk routine" – the analytical and critical work of historiography.[3]

The glib tone signals that Pynchon had clearly assessed his powers as a historical novelist, which shone brightly in his first novel, *V.* (1963). *Gravity's Rainbow*, for a time entitled "Mindless Pleasures," would seal his greatness and define Pynchon alongside William Faulkner as a writer who uses history to represent core contradictions and dilemmas of the twin projects named "America" and "Modernity." Two decades after it was published literary critics and theorists had analyzed the historiographical innovations and narrative challenges of *Gravity's Rainbow*, recognizing it as *the* pathbreaking work of postwar US fiction.[4] During an epoch from 1960 to 2010 when the historical novel became fiction's pre-eminent form, *Gravity's*

Rainbow remained the *ne plus ultra*, ranked in poll after poll at or near the top with fictions such as Toni Morrison's *Beloved* (1987) and Don DeLillo's *Underworld* (1997). Like those books, *Gravity's Rainbow* brushes American history against the grain, and it is – despite contrary claims by John Gardner and others – a profoundly *moral fiction*.[5]

What were the sources and compass points of Pynchon's moral vision during the sixties? He opposed the Vietnam War, enrolling himself for example with other writers and editors "believing that American involvement in Vietnam is morally wrong" and therefore pledging not to pay federal income taxes that would go towards the war effort.[6] Otherwise, if Pynchon organized for or even just marched in support of the antiwar and/or the civil rights movement(s), such activities haven't yet made it into the public record. We do know that for two years after graduating from Cornell he labored in a bureaucratic warren of the US military-industrial complex. Only recently have details of his Boeing years come to light, including co-workers' recollections, and a portion (over a hundred pages) of his technical prose.[7] From this still-emerging archive we know that colleagues recalled a long-haired and mustachioed Pynchon distinguished for meticulous and tireless research, who wrote with more stylistic flair than anyone else while sprinkling folksy and humorous anecdotes through these dry pieces, and whose first in-print mention of the V-2 missile – soon to star as a kind of virtual protagonist in *Gravity's Rainbow* – appeared in a September 1962 article titled "Hydrazine Tank Cartridge Replacement." Pynchon wrote most extensively on the "Bomarc" winged surface-to-air missile, eerily similar to the A-9 that Nazi engineers built to bomb New York. He also wrote on the Minuteman inter-continental ballistic missile or ICBM, a solid-fuel multi-stage weapon built by émigré German rocket experts to fling a nuclear warhead six thousand miles inside a one-mile diameter target.[8] Touted as the "ultimate weapon" in 1961, it not only raised the nuclear ante against Soviet competitors but also eliminated the (mythical) US "missile gap."[9] Pynchon wrote for servicemen – mechanics, technicians, and missile-transport specialists – similar to those whom the German army had also tasked to transport, maintain, and operate V-2 missiles and launching equipment. As Pynchon eventually learned, those counterparts got their advice from the *A-4 Fibel*, a handbook for operating the *Aggregat-4*, the final configuration of what Allied forces dubbed the V-2.[10]

The ethical and critical implications of Pynchon's Boeing writings were, and are, significant. Fears of nuclear holocaust achieved their hysterical peak during his stint in Boeing missile support. Throughout the 1960 campaign, presidential candidate John F. Kennedy harped on claims that Republican leadership had allowed the US to lag behind the Soviets in the number and power of ICBMs. Told in early 1961 that the missile gap was "a fiction," Kennedy nonetheless ratcheted US missile production to unprecedented levels and built new launching sites nearer than ever to Soviet soil. Soviet leaders countered, striking a deal with Fidel Castro to put launch sites ninety miles from US shores, and so in October 1962 brought on the Cuban Missile Crisis that poised the world on the very brink of extinction.[11] At that moment, Pynchon had just left off writing for Boeing and was giving his whole attention to revising the manuscript of V. before moving to Mexico.[12] Still, during those twenty-two months at Boeing he had been a cog in the US war machine – closely involved in what was *the* most critical component of the military-industrial complex. He had as they would say "interfaced" with guided missile engineers and technicians in order to synthesize and translate their top-secret "work-product" for ordinary usage. He had done so at a moment when their humdrum labors linked each of them to a world-historical crisis skirting toward an unspeakable violence. Therefore like any other drone producing and servicing either side's "Pilotless Aircraft" during the Cold War, his work – his gift with writing itself – had left Pynchon inescapably complicit with the bureaucracy of mass destruction and terror.

He most certainly understood this. In an incisive early review George Levine remarked that in representing merciless modern warfare Pynchon's novel wisely refused "outrage" because he understood how the ordinariness of the bureaucratic work supporting any modern war effort turns "people into objects" just as certainly as infantry service does, and perhaps more insidiously than does infantry service. Military-industrial labor needs numbed moral sensibilities, and a corporate culture that will subtly "victimize people into victimizing" others with the weapons they build.[13] Other reviews, early essays and books also remarked on the significance in *Gravity's Rainbow* of ordinary bureaucrats – such as its apparent protagonist Tyrone Slothrop – laboring away in cubicles.[14] They illustrate what Georg Lukács, in *The Historical Novel*, identified as the form's essential "middling men." What these characters *do*, often in contrast with the desires and fantasies defining their inner lives, are keys to the conscience of *Gravity's Rainbow*.[15] Indeed each of this novel's six major characters fits the corporatized profile: US Army Lieutenant Tyrone Slothrop in his beaverboard carrel analyzing patterns of V-2 rocket strikes on London; Roger Mexico, his British army counterpart, using statistics in the same effort; Franz Pökler, a German technician seduced by the romance of space travel but finally just another technocratic worker-bee in behalf of Nazi weapons development; Lieutenant Weissmann, aka Dominus Blicero (Lord Death), officer of a Nazi V-2 unit who illustrates the truth of Herman Melville's remark that "the white civilized man" can be "the most ferocious animal on the face of the earth"; as well as Vaslav Tchitcherine, a Soviet weapons expert and secret agent assigned to snatch rocket parts, technologists and technologies for Stalin's use; and even Tchitcherine's half-black half-brother and mortal enemy Enzian, equally determined to snatch and in his own way to de-bureaucratize the Rockets powers, then to use them in reversing the deathward trajectory of his people, the South-West African Herero who had lived under the sign of erasure ever since the Germans' genocidal campaign against them in 1904–6.[16]

Their template was German rocket engineer Wernher von Braun (1912–77), who makes a cameo appearance in *Gravity's Rainbow*. His words also grace the novel's opening page, where Pynchon laid down a two-sentence epigraph taken from a brief von Braun text of 1962, proclaiming Nature's transformative powers and a technocrat's "belief in the continuity of our spiritual existence after death." When he wrote those words, von Braun – having surrendered in May 1945 to US forces and gone to work for the army's belated rocket effort (to close a real missile gap) – had transitioned into a leadership position at NASA. He had thus returned to his first desire, building manned space vehicles for landing men on the Moon, but this after three decades' work in weapons design and construction for two world powers. The NASA years made him famous, but von Braun's image was always shadowed by his work on Nazi rockets, his officer's rank in the SS, his meetings with Hitler. American politicians and Defense Department superiors preferred to avoid troubling aspects of von Braun's past. He willingly obliged, crafting an autobiography whose themes were always that in Germany he had been an apolitical scientist obsessed with peaceful space exploration; then, drafted into military service, he had been too distracted developing the A-4 rocket to notice that in its development phase at Peenemünde and during mass production at Nordhausen much of the labor was done by enslaved ethnics. At the Nordhausen facility thousands of them were living (barely) amidst hellish conditions at the Dora concentration camp.[17] Von Braun insisted that as a scientist he had no "right" to "moral viewpoints" on those facets of the German rocket program and that in any case as a soldier his "duty was to help win the war."[18] This narrative excuse held up for decades. Recent historical work has been very hard on it, particularly the elitism at its core: a blind faith in that romantic aura surrounding techno-scientific discovery, and in the related belief that "scientists and engineers … can be untainted by politics."[19] In fact, von Braun knew plenty about the uses of slave labor at the Peenemünde development facility, and directly witnessed conditions at Dora. Providing testimony in 1969 for a war crimes tribunal, he dissimulated what he knew and did – for example, about the punishment of a Dora inmate.[20] Building rockets in America, von Braun sought the grace of historical amnesia. US employers enabled that quest.

Pynchon had seen through such manipulations, and had done so way ahead of recent, revisionist von Braun biographers. Borrowing his novel's epigraph from that 1962 essay, he trimmed away the rocket scientist's remarks on how mankind's survival in an age of total war depends on "our adherence to ethical principles," high-minded words bathed in hypocrisy. He also trimmed away von Braun's *own* choice of an epigraph – words from Benjamin Franklin about the certainty of "justice" for one's "conduct" in this life.[21] Pynchon would have cut them because judging the ethical issue of von Braun's career – like the issue of his own experience "doing ... the clerk routine" at Boeing – is precisely what the pages of his narrative satire would work through aesthetically. His trimmed von Braun epigraph gives the reader who first opens *Gravity's Rainbow* an idea of the Romantic Scientist – which the story then upends and shatters. This is why Pynchon apportioned to so many of his characters – not just to the main six but to a wide array of others like Edward Pointsman and Carroll Eventyr – variants of the von Braun problem that remain *our problem*: the developed world's complicity in weapons of total destruction. In his distorting lens, the routinized terror of the late-modern security state finds its origin in the grotesquery and excess of that Rocket World whose locus he first knew at Boeing, then from sources on the V-2.

Pynchon could just as well have written his way toward that vision in a historical novel built around the development and deployment of the nuclear bomb which, when mated with the Rocket, synthesized the Cold War's main totem. In that case he would have researched America's makeshift wartime "atomic cities" like Los Alamos and Oak Ridge instead of makeshift German "rocket cities" like Peenemünde and Nordhausen, and he'd have read about figures like Robert Oppenheimer and General Leslie Groves instead of Wernher von Braun and Major Walter Dornberger. Indeed both efforts would be synthesized (as *Gravity's Rainbow* indicates) in the mating of Rocket and Hydrogen Bomb to produce, by 1961, "the ultimate weapon," the Minuteman missile.[22] But Thomas Pynchon had come to know Rocket-work. So *Gravity's Rainbow* represents the new, man-created but inhumane order that emerged in the V-2's aftermath and in Europe's post-War rubble. His novel's subject is the transnational order of capital, industries and markets, and especially those bureaucratized and militarized servants whom that new order dedicates to domination and death. In the most terrible of ironies, it always does so in the guises of peace and the total powers – some would say the *delusions* – of the National Security State.[23] So as the novel's refugees move across war-torn landscapes, readers realize how "a State begins to take form [...] a State that spans oceans and surface politics, sovereign [...] and the Rocket is its soul."[24]

Reckoning time and space

An elemental aspect of Rocket World's "signs and symptoms" is that a ballistic missile descends on its target at supersonic speed, and one therefore hears the sound of its arrival *after* it strikes.[25] If a "screaming comes across the sky" that any may hear, then they are saved – that time.[26] It's a paradoxical phenomenon that cuts several ways. Initially the reversal or shattering of ordinary cause-and-effect sequencing becomes a master trope in a novel that configures temporal sequences according to principles of reversal or, worse, of fracture, random dispersion, even mere fragments of order. Thus for anyone opening *Gravity's Rainbow* the first order of business is to deal with how extensively the storytelling has been decoupled from linear, deterministic and teleological assumptions about Time and History, assumptions that seduce one into a totalized understanding whereby "*everything is connected*, everything in the Creation."[27] Instead, from the novel's jumbled narrative sequencing we try to reconstruct an order of events, stretches of chronology enabling one to begin sensibly reckoning the force and form of Time, which is one of the ways that readers do writerly work. With this technique Pynchon's novel also marks an epistemological break whose counterpart is humanity's radically disrupted way of knowing the world of Nukes. Thankfully his narration does mark time by mentioning seasons and some dates, as well as moments on the Christian liturgical calendar. And the accrual of these indices does define a nine-month period in which the novel's main action occurs, from early December 1944 to early September 1945, a nearly closed circle or partial mandala to which Pynchon attached a myriad of leaps and loops backward, forward and around in historical time.[28] Even so, just what this emergent form signifies – perhaps a nine-month gestational period before the Cold War order is birthed? – remains in doubt because the text repeatedly either undercuts that kind of meaning-making or ascribes it to *paranoia*, which the novel understands as a deeply habituated, deterministic epistemology peculiar to modernity and especially to the deathward "Progress" of Germany and the United States.

Here too Pynchon implicates himself. For in morphing his own historical Puritan ancestors (chiefly William Pynchon, theologian and founder in 1636 of Springfield, Massachusetts) into fictional Slothrops, Pynchon both defines and satirizes twentieth-century political paranoia as a remnant or chronic abscess of Calvinist ways of thinking about divine power. Central to Puritanism was the belief in a stern and wrathful sovereign divinity, which may at any moment cast a sinner into Hell, with every such death sentence a synecdoche for a Judgment Day over all humanity. In a well known sermon of 1741, Jonathan Edwards represents this God instantly dropping sinners into the "fiery pit" as if each were an "abject" spider dangling over the flames on its own self-spun thread of evil.[29] In Pynchon's secular formulation, so does the Rocket spell instant death for Londoners as for all Mankind, unless something radically changes. Thus while the Rocket seems to operate in time with instant, total power over life, it does so in new – mechanical – modes. A system, or *Aggregat*, it emptily simulates pre-modern conceptions of a godlike sovereignty over life and death, randomizing and secularizing pre-modern conceptions of Man's access-points to sacred, eternal Time. And under the aegis of Technology it re-scripts collective beliefs in providential History, reckoned in *Gravity's Rainbow* as various individuated paranoid affects, anxieties and fantasies – Calvinism's diseased residues, again.[30]

The second of Rocket World's elemental signs and symptoms is that it reconfigures space, eliminating distance (for example, an ocean) as a national security advantage. So, just as this novel's readers reckon with a temporality decoupled from traditional teleological meaning, they also confront new modes of spatiality whose topological centers – capital cities as *foci* of meaning and value, of "civilization" – may be put under erasure. In this way the Rocket presages new forms of transnational sovereignty. For what indeed is London, to the Rocket? Like Antwerp, merely another target in a redrawn topology left decentered and boundaryless in the Rocket's aftermath. *Gravity's Rainbow* represents that new global power in how it narrates the Rocket's origins from superpower armies mated with international cartels like IG Farben and Standard Oil. And we see the power of its global reach from the novel's opening pages, depicting terrified Londoners' surreal evacuation of their city. Subsequent episodes increasingly leave behind metropoles like London or Berlin. Historical flashbacks and fantasy sequences swing reading into peripheries like England's Kent coast, or down a Boston toilet to the American southwest, and in later episodes to South-West Africa (now Namibia) and eventually into colonial outposts such as Mauritius, South America and the steppes of Kirghizstan. Partly these strange narrative jumps enable Pynchon to retrace histories of white colonialist conquest and domination of warmer territories and their non-white peoples. Every such leap or loop metaphorically recoups the novel's core image of missiles overmastering faraway map-points, throwing high-explosives and even a message over great spaces.[31] Indeed it isn't only paranoids like Slothrop who must reckon with the Rocket as a master signifier, with its powers physically and virtually to remap the geography of empire.

Everywhere in *Gravity's Rainbow* "Post-A4 humanity is moving."[32] Evacuees, refugees, displaced persons, stateless persons and surviving concentration camp internees stream through the novel's episodes. By any measure they are *the* dominant form of humanity under the sign of the Rocket. They bracket this novel from its first (London) episode to its seventy-third and last: there, in a final avatar, as "ghetto-suicidal" faces of 1970s Los Angelenos peering from automobiles rolling along the Santa Monica and Harbor freeways and recalling those in London Underground cars fleeing that city in 1944.[33] While Rocket-questing in post-War Europe, Slothrop encounters the same figures everywhere, as soon as he escapes – or is programmed to escape – the safe confines of Monte Carlo (itself a paradoxical and liminal space, its occupying forces imposing order; its gambling tables, randomness). All across the defeated Reich flows an abandoned humanity: in central Germany, around and through the Dora concentration camp that von Braun so wished to disremember; and in northern Germany, over a vast plain as a myriad of ethnic and national types such as "Czechs and Slovaks, Croats and Serbs, Tosks and Ghegs."[34] In this space only the War's surviving, ineffectual, "neutered" romantics go "Holy-Center-Approaching," nostalgically desiring order and total meaning at a point of supposed origin and sovereign power but instead stumbling over rubble into a space both literally and symbolically "stripped now, hollow and dark."[35] This is Rocket space, what Pynchon names "the Zone."

Here readers should tread cautiously. The irrepressibly nostalgic Tyrone Slothrop – he whose "Penis He Thought Was His Own" but who in any political sense is really "Just a neuter" – delights in fantasizing a Romantic Zone where, "maybe for a little while all the fences are down [...] the whole space of the Zone cleared, depolarized" and so a *tabula rasa* "without even nationality to fuck it up."[36] In the Romantic's view of it the Zone blooms with inchoate potentials – fences down, boundaries gone. There everything seems "a free, unhierarchical, anarchic space without cultural – symbolic and imaginary – inscriptions."[37] There the self-reliant man *seems* to stand tall and sovereign. To Greta Erdmann the Zone is a "native space" in which "I was free"; and there, too, Slothrop may appear "as properly constituted a state as any other in the Zone."[38] Dream on. For *Gravity's Rainbow* repeatedly undercuts any fantasies of popular sovereignty. When Greta imagines the Zone as a space of blithe liberation she is still "acting" under the slavish dominion of filmmaker Miklos Thanatz (whose patronymic signifies "Death"). And until he disappears from or is scattered into the text about four-fifths of the way through it, Slothrop has always acted as a both "partly willing and partly unwitting plaything of power."[39] The same holds true for most of the novel's key characters: Pointsman, Mexico, Pökler, Tchitcherine, Katje Borgesius, and certainly Lt. Weissmann, aka "Dominus Blicero" (Lord Death).

The Romantic Zone's counterpart is a dark *topos*, an Ironic Zone to which Pynchon gives a much more extended and realistic attention. Here the governing and very black humor is that death has no meaning; is merely the *summa totalis* of a mathematical equation (in rocketry), the function of an apparatus or the project of an agency. In the Ironic Zone we realize the blunt force of philosopher Thomas Hobbes's recognition (in *Leviathan*, 1651) that the masses of mankind live in "continual feare and danger of violent death" while their daily existence is "solitary, poore, nasty, brutish, and short" – conditions bureaucratized in Boston as "the State Street law firm of Salitieri, Poore, Nash, De Brutus, and Short."[40] In a striking passage near the novel's end, Pynchon figures non-human vitality, a raw Earthliness appearing to "human consciousness, that poor cripple" as so "violently pitched alive in constant flow" and such "an overpeaking of life clangorous and mad" that it seemed to demand Man's rational "dominion." The Ironic Zone is that time-space or chronotope which humanity imposes on this rawness and finally on itself. There Man's motto has become Extinction: "It is our mission to promote death."[41] Dodoes or Africans, it makes no difference; for the Zone has gone "past secular good and evil" and "we" individuals now have only to devote ourselves to the "impulse to empire, the mission to propagate death," a technical project "we had to work on, historically and personally."[42] This is the modern History that Pynchon writes with the capital H.

So the terminus of History's arc, and the Zone's archetypal space, is the death camp. In *V.* Pynchon had located one historical origin of it during the German campaign of extermination in South-West Africa. In *Gravity's Rainbow* he realizes the concentration camp as that uniquely modern space in which any sovereign power – or "They-system" – denationalizes and denaturalizes the subject, then turns it into a laboring machine until, its productivity exhausted, its life is snuffed. But the concentration camp is only the most blatantly violent exemplar of that Zonal ethos. Among its kinder, gentler versions are the aptly named "White Visitation," the Harvard lab where Dr. Jamf evidently conditioned Infant Tyrone, the engineering shops at Peenemünde, the entertainments at Zwölfkinder (a kind of Nazi Disneyland), or even the movie houses in which wartime viewers might, if they *really look*, recognize cinematic images of themselves "trapped inside Their frame" and "waiting for Their editorial blade."[43] A number of readers have remarked on Film as a means of social control and a deathwards lure.[44] Much more obviously, so is *every* colony a version of the Camp: in Kirghizstan where Russians "hunted Sarts, Kazakhs, Kirghiz, and Dungans [...] like wild game"; or in Mauritius where Dutch settlers hunted Dodoes to extinction. Slothrop himself has been colonized, his penis "like an instrument installed, wired by them into his body as a colonial outpost" and uncannily capable of keening to the "kingly voice of the Aggregat itself."[45] This is a plotline for which, our narrator remarks, "there ought to be a punch line [...] but there isn't" because its *telos* is extinction, signified as just a blank movie screen.[46]

Reading political subjects

From his earliest stories one of Pynchon's great themes has been the powers of state apparatuses to transform people into objects. A consistent motif in his work has been the automation of bodies in part or whole, processes of control and terror for which, in *Gravity's Rainbow*, the Rocket State has even ratified "Articles of Immachination."[47] The novel's ultimate symbol images Machine incorporating Man, as Blicero retrofits a V-2 rocket bearing the number 00000 so that it can take a youthful human payload named Gottfried ("God's Peace") into fiery death. Symbolically the arc of this rocket marks the historical transference of sovereign powers from Oven-state, whose principal *topoi* are the death-factories or *Konzentrationsläger*, to Rocket-state, whose principal *topoi* are the labs and cubicles of Cold War security states.[48] An inescapable meaning of this trope is that it equates the ontological status of the novel's named "middling" characters with those unnamed figures, the abject and abandoned DPs and Camp survivors streaming *en masse* across war-torn Europe. Yet most, like Pointsman or Tchitcherine, still have to reckon that equation. Interchangeable and expendable, they're all just as vulnerable to instant death on the decision of sovereign lords, members of the "power elite" who exist in the text only as mystified representations, as in the "giant photographs" of Stalin, Churchill and Truman put up in Berlin for the July 1945 Potsdam conference.[49] As for the masses, the technocrats on down to lowliest DPs who exist in subjection to those "human sultans [...] with no right at all to be where they are," only a few – the "Counterforce" – belatedly realize their enslavement.[50] And some of them – characters like Mexico, Pökler and Slothrop – come to an ethical realization of their own complicity in mass death.

How the novel scripts those ethically and politically charged moments is both challenging and crucial. From its opening episodes *Gravity's Rainbow* uses point of view to loop readers into characters' minds, using internal focalization to unfold their perceptions, thoughts and fantasies. In one of its most notable innovations in narrative technique, Pynchon often uses the focalized mind-space of one character as a passageway into that of another, perhaps even a character from the distant historical past (as a "fantasist-surrogate" working for the Allies, that is exactly Pirate Prentice's role).[51] At times this process of embedding focalizers inside one another creates some of the novel's most dizzying and extraordinary reading experiences – for example, the brilliant, circular sequence in episode 14, when a cameraman films Dutch double agent Katje Borgesius.[52] Here and through scores of similar episodes readers realize how the technologies of power operate. Take another, also from early in the novel, when behavioral psychologist Pointsman, mind filled with "Realpolitik Dreams," considers snatching one of London's wayward children, a girl, to use as subject in his operant conditioning experiments. Although the text focalizes through Pointsman here, its second person address identifies us with Pointsman scanning the Bus Station, noting gobs of "chewing-gum scuffed to charcoal black" on the cement floor, then the seated children: "You've never quite decided if they can see through to your vacuum. They won't yet look into your eyes, their slender legs are never still, knitted stockings droop (all elastic has gone to war), but charmingly: little heels kick against the canvas bags, the fraying valises under the wood bench."[53] This remarkable scene moves reading from the seeming objectivity of merely scoping details (gum), into imaginative identification with Pointsman, to the voyeur's desire (stockings), and finally (for readers) to horror, so seamlessly does the writing cross over from empathy to exploitation, desire to domination.[54] This movement reveals Pointsman as mere vacuum tube unwittingly wired into a system of domination. It tags him as one of the novel's "neuters."[55]

Take a contrasting moment from Slothrop's tour of Rocket assembly stations in the Nordhausen tunnels. Unlike Pointsman, he more than scopes: he critically interprets minutiae like the "fine splinters of steel" littering the floor around lathes that remind him how, "once upon a time," Camp inmates "bloodied" their knuckles "against grinding wheels" and those splinters "stabbed" the "pores, creases and quicks" of their fingers. Feeling those spirits haunting this place, Slothrop further recognizes that "History" leaves "you" no way out of even this tenuous identification with Dora's victims and also offers "no time-traveling capsule to find your way back" from the enveloping horror of that recognition, so beyond nostalgia. Next Slothrop thinks: "Ghosts used to be either likenesses of the dead or wraiths of the living," remnants of a past life or figures of its future; but now "the Zone" has "blurred badly" all such temporal sequencing so that under the "sovereign" Rocket every being is the sign of its own immanent erasure. This is "more than the bureaucracy of mass absence." Death collectively wills itself into a world-system, and anyone not outside of it has leagued with the living dead. In that sense the Camp inmate is indeed the "wraith" of our present, Nuclear Age existence.[56] Still, that awakening is one thing; what to do with it is another. Slothrop scatters, becoming at best an object of lore and a certain harebrained mythology. Roger Mexico stages a minor skirmish with "Them" while a member of the apparently short-lived "Counterforce." After an "act of courage" when he decided to "quit the game," Pökler visits Nordhausen seeking his interned family and experiences the ethical reckoning that von Braun avoided. Pökler realizes how all "his vacuums, his labyrinths, had been the other side of this. While he lived, and drew marks on paper, this invisible kingdom had kept on [...] Pökler vomited. He cried some."[57] Here his nausea and emotion index the ways that the Camp is a limit case on Pynchon's humor; also, that his sense of a "fugitive" politics is grounded in such embodied (gut-level) and empathetic responses.[58] Elsewhere in the camp Pökler finds "a random woman," barely alive, and sits with her, at last offering his "gold wedding ring" so that she might get "a few meals [...] or a ride home."[59] This is the novel's moral center, from which a politics might begin, scripted by one who also put "marks on paper."

Yet any further political results of this awakening are difficult if not impossible to gauge. Mostly *Gravity's Rainbow* concludes that "Their neglect is your freedom," so that one's only hope is to fly – humorously – beneath or beyond Their control.[60] Yet the novel cannot or will not show us Slothrop, for instance, doing so. Otherwise Dominus Blicero rules this novel's last pages, with his firing of the quintuple-zero Rocket and his dream of residing inside a hermetically sealed "great glass sphere" with just a "handful of men" where all are "frosty" white like the Moon.[61] On the one hand Blicero's dream metaphorizes von Braun's dream, realized in his direction of the 1969 lunar landing. On the other, it realizes late modernity's paradoxical, collective desire for a National Security State achieved with technologies of mass Death, of annihilation. Either way, the sign of the Rocket is that mere survival hinges on securing people's complicity with and subjection to a Power Elite's relentless sovereignty. Thus the novel ends, literally and figurally, with a suspended sentence.

NOTES

1 Thomas Pynchon to Arthur Mizener, November 25, 1970, Folder 8, Box 17 "Publishing Material," Steven Tomaske Memorial Papers, The Huntington, San Marino, California.
2 Roland Barthes, *S/Z: An Essay* (Paris: 1970; New York: Hill and Wang, 1974), pp. 200, 205–6, 215.

3 So Stephen Pyne advises throughout *Voice and Vision: A Guide to Writing History and Other Serious Nonfiction* (Cambridge, MA: Harvard University Press, 2009), for example pp. 261–62.

4 Linda Hutcheon, *A Poetics of Postmodernism: History, Theory, Fiction* (New York: Routledge, 1988).

5 John Gardner, *On Moral Fiction* (New York: Basic Books, 1979); see also James Wood, *The Broken Estate: Essays on Literature and Belief* (New York: Modern Library, 2000).

6 Two-page advertisement in *Ramparts*, 6.7 (February 1968), 60–61.

7 David Cowart, *Thomas Pynchon: The Art of Allusion* (Carbondale: Southern Illinois University Press, 1980), pp. 96–97; and Adrian Wisnicki, "A Trove of New Works by Thomas Pynchon? *Bomarc Service News* Rediscovered," *Pynchon Notes*, 46–49 (2000–2001), 9–34.

8 Neil Sheehan, *A Fiery Peace in a Cold War: Bernard Schriever and the Ultimate Weapon* (New York: Random House, 2009), p. 413.

9 *Bomarc Service News*, 38 (September 1962), 3–5; and Wisnicki, "A Trove," 19–20.

10 Steven Weisenburger, *A Gravity's Rainbow* Companion: *Sources and Contexts for Pynchon's Novel*, 2nd edn. (Athens: University of Georgia Press, 2006), p. 213.

11 Christopher A. Preble, *John F. Kennedy and the Missile Gap* (DeKalb: Northern Illinois University Press, 2004); and James C. Dick, "The Strategic Arms Race of 1957–61: Who Opened a Missile Gap?" *Journal of Politics*, 34, 4 (1972), 1062–1110.

12 Thomas Pynchon, Letter to Faith Sale, October 1, 1962, Harry Ransom Center, University of Texas, Austin.

13 George Levine, "V-2" (1973), repr. in Edward Mendelson (ed.), *Pynchon: A Collection of Critical Essays* (Englewood Cliffs: Prentice Hall, 1978), p. 187.

14 Richard Poirier, "Rocket Power," *Saturday Review of the Arts* (March 1973); repr. in Mendelson (ed.), *Pynchon*, pp. 167–78; Michael Wood, "Rocketing to Apocalypse," *New York Review of Books* (March 22, 1973), 22; and Edward Mendelson, "Gravity's Encyclopedia," in George Levine and David Leverenz (eds.), *Mindful Pleasures: Essays on Thomas Pynchon* (Boston: Little Brown, 1978), pp. 161–96; Dale Carter, *The Final Frontier: The Rise and Fall of the American Rocket State* (London: Verso, 1988).

15 Georg Lukács, *The Historical Novel* (1962; Lincoln: University of Nebraska Press, 1983), pp. 33–47.

16 Herman Melville, *Typee*, ed. Ruth Blair (New York: Oxford University Press, 1996), p. 152.

17 Luc Herman and Bruno Arich-Gerz, "Darstellungen von *Dora*," *Arcadia: Internationale Zeitschrift für Literaturwissenschaft*, 39, 2 (2004), 390–409.

18 Michael J. Neufeld, *Von Braun: Dreamer of Space, Engineer of War* (New York: Vintage, 2008), p. 162.

19 Wayne Biddle, *Dark Side of the Moon: Wernher von Braun, the Third Reich, and the Space Race* (New York: Norton, 2009), p. 85.

20 *Ibid.*, pp. 123–26.

21 For von Braun's text see Weisenburger, *Companion*, pp. 15–16.

22 Sheehan, *A Fiery Peace*, pp. 414–15.

23 Garry Wills, *Bomb Power: The Modern Presidency and the National Security State* (New York: Penguin, 2010); Douglas T. Stuart, *Creating the National Security State* (Princeton University Press, 2008).

24 Thomas Pynchon, *Gravity's Rainbow* (New York: Viking, 1973), p. 566.

25 *Ibid.*, p. 159.

26 *Ibid.*, p. 3.

27 *Ibid.*, p. 703. See Molly Hite, *Ideas of Order in the Novels of Thomas Pynchon* (Columbus: Ohio State University Press, 1983), pp. 95–100.

28 Weisenburger, *Companion*, pp. 9–12.

29 Jonathan Edwards, "Sinners in the Hands of an Angry God" (1741), in Nina Baym (ed.), *The Norton Anthology of American Literature*, 6th edn. (New York: Norton, 2003), vol. A, pp. 498–509.

30 See Thomas H. Schaub, *Pynchon: The Voice of Ambiguity* (Urbana: University of Illinois Press, 1981), pp. 76–101.

31 Pynchon, *Gravity's Rainbow*, p. 20.

32 *Ibid.*, p. 304.

33 *Ibid.*, p. 756.

34 *Ibid.*, p. 549.

35 *Ibid.*, pp. 523, 508, 510.

36 *Ibid.*, pp. 216–17, 556.

37 Hanjo Berressem, *Pynchon's Poetics: Interfacing Theory and Text* (Urbana: University of Illinois Press, 1993), p. 126.

38 Pynchon, *Gravity's Rainbow*, pp. 487, 291.

39 Carter, *Final Frontier*, p. 23.

40 Pynchon, *Gravity's Rainbow*, p. 591; Weisenburger, *Companion*, p. 309.

41 Pynchon, *Gravity's Rainbow*, p. 720.

42 *Ibid.*, pp. 590, 722, 720.

43 *Ibid.*, p. 694.

44 Cowart, *Thomas Pynchon*, p. 35; Alec McHoul and David Wills, *Writing Pynchon: Strategies in Fictional Analysis* (Urbana: University of Illinois Press, 1990), pp. 39–40.

45 Pynchon, *Gravity's Rainbow*, pp. 340, 285, 470.

46 *Ibid.*, p. 738.

47 *Ibid.*, p. 297.

48 *Ibid.*, pp. 102, 373; Carter, *Final Frontier*, 6 and passim.

49 C. Wright Mills, *The Power Elite* (New York: Oxford University Press, 1956).

50 Pynchon, *Gravity's Rainbow*, p. 521.

51 *Ibid.*, p. 12.

52 *Ibid.*, pp. 92–113; Steven Weisenburger, "Hyper-Embedded Narration in *Gravity's Rainbow*," *Pynchon Notes*, 34–35 (Spring–Fall 1994), 70–87.

53 Pynchon, *Gravity's Rainbow*, p. 50.

54 Hite, *Ideas of Order*, pp. 145–46.

55 Pynchon, *Gravity's Rainbow*, p. 677.

56 *Ibid.*, p. 303.

57 *Ibid.*, pp. 430, 432–33.

58 Respectively, Stefan Mattessich, *Lines of Flight: Discursive Time and Countercultural Desire in the Work of Thomas Pynchon* (Durham: Duke University Press, 2002), p. 159; and Samuel Thomas, *Pynchon and the Political* (New York: Routledge, 2006), p. 91.

59 Pynchon, *Gravity's Rainbow*, p. 433.

60 *Ibid.*, p. 694.

61 *Ibid.*, p. 723.

4

KATHRYN HUME

Mason & Dixon

In *Gravity's Rainbow*, Pynchon calls the colonial William Slothrop "the fork in the road America never took," a road that would have been kinder both to people who were powerless and to the land.[1] With *Mason & Dixon*, Pynchon explores that colonial period as the time in which the decisions were made that sent America down the wrong road. His symbol for these values, decisions and consequences is the surveying project carried out by Charles Mason and Jeremiah Dixon (1763–67). To settle the rival claims of the Penns and the Calverts over the boundary between Pennsylvania and Maryland, these surveyors cut a line eight or nine yards wide straight through the wilderness along latitude 39° 43′ 20″. This line created colony borders and ownership; damaged the plants, beasts and people whose territory it had been; and came to signify the divide between slave-holding colonies and those that banned slavery. Pynchon focuses on slavery more than the horrors of Indian-killing because Mason and Dixon's line defined the political oppositions of the new country and figured prominently in the Civil War a century later.

Mason & Dixon will seem highly fragmented, information-dense, and full of frustratingly incomplete lines in dialogues. A 773-page book that scorns coherence does make heavy demands on its audience, so in addition to wondering *how* to read it, one can ask *why* Pynchon should have constructed his storyworld in this fashion. This chapter will sketch one way to approach reading the novel – the *how* – by visualizing the text as layers of material and as networks of connected points. The *why* behind these images lies in Pynchon's sense that layering and connecting amplify power – for good or bad purposes – and his way of amplifying power here intensifies non-material, spiritual reality. In Dixon's words, layers accumulate force.

Aldous Huxley famously describes consciousness as a "reducing valve," and his three points – the reductive nature of consciousness, the existence of other worlds that we rarely see clearly because of our diminished sensitivity, and the limitations of local language to describe the otherworldly – are all pertinent to understanding Pynchon's enterprise.[2] Reading *Mason & Dixon* offers an experience analogous to suddenly finding our reducing valve open much wider than usual. In life, we exclude data we sense to be unthreatening, but when reading this book we must consciously absorb vastly more data than our valve lets through in everyday life. The many episodes concern archaic science, very detailed history, hundreds of characters, and apparently crazy fantasy. We struggle because we lack the tools to classify, interpret, and rank the importance of those data. Nor does Pynchon make that ranking easy, since he loves offering something seemingly fantastic that proves to be historical.[3] Pynchon's novels generally postulate other levels of reality – in *Gravity's Rainbow*, the phenomena associated with the Other Side, for instance. Pynchon suggests that such realities can be glimpsed if we let down our shields or open our valve. In *Mason & Dixon*, he frequently tries to indicate the presence of alternative realities, despite being hampered by a language that has no vocabulary for rendering their existence plausible.

Pynchon establishes this concern with wider consciousness early in the framing story, in which Wicks Cherrycoke, the parson who accompanied Mason and Dixon, tells his sister's children about that venture twenty years later. In the course of amusing his Philadelphia kin with fireside tales, Cherrycoke briefly alludes to a mystical experience he had when he was jailed for criticizing the authorities: "One of those moments Hindoos and Chinamen are ever said to be having, entire loss of Self, perfect union with All, sort of thing. Strange Lights, Fires, Voices indecipherable."[4] Mystics and explorers of hallucinogens often insist on the intense meaningfulness of such visions; such an experience, they claim, changes one's perception of reality and reveals realities beyond the trickle provided by consciousness. Few people achieve nirvana, but Pynchon seems to feel that our material and social worlds permit access to more transcendent elements than we realize. Making us cognizant of further realities as layers seems to be the principle upon which he constructs his eighteenth-century world.

Layers and networks

Pynchon develops two structural images that, taken together, tell us something of how he views the world in this novel, and may suggest a way of viewing the novel as well. The images are layers and networks, the latter being points connected by lines, and some of those points being nodes with many connections to other points. The layers correspond roughly to the space and time zones of the novel, chief of which are the early lives of Mason and Dixon in England, their observations in South Africa, their expedition in America and their post-America activities. Lesser sequences include scenes in India, Ireland, Canada and St Helena. His other zones are implied whenever an alternative reality intrudes. The networks of nodes and lines correspond, metaphorically at least, to themes and topics that are found in two or more of the layers, thus being visualizable as a three-dimensional network with extensions that also connect to themes in other Pynchon novels. Quite naturally, as readers struggle with the outpouring of information, they connect a past appearance of a theme to its current appearance.

Pynchon's showy discussion of layers suggests his reasons for creating so densely complex a book. A fop's Damascus blade evokes comments on the way those famously strong blades were made by twisting and working two sorts of steel together until they become many thin layers. A chef then expounds on lamination as the technique that creates mille-feuille pastries. Other characters invoke gold-beating and "the Leyden Pile, decks of Playing-Cards, Contrivances which, like the Lever or Pulley, quite multiply the apparent forces, often unto disproportionate results." To this list, Cherrycoke adds books (each page a layer) and a printer adds an "unbound Heap of Broadsides" that can be distributed, both phenomena making the accumulation of knowledge or political power possible.[5] Mason and Dixon witness Ben Franklin's famous scientific electrical experiments with Leyden jars; hence, when they see an ancient Indian mound that had been broken into, Dixon likens the layers they see to a Leyden jar.[6] Mason objects that whereas the jar's layers were "Gold-leaf, Silver foil, Glass— Philosophickal Materials," these are "dirt...ashes...crush'd seashells." Dixon argues, however, that "alternating Layers of different Substances are ever a Sign of the intention to Accumulate Force," in the case of the mounds, presumably magical or telluric power.[7]

The claim that layers accumulate power is what attracts Pynchon to this metaphor. Even the newly invented sandwich is identified as an example of lamination, and we see it concentrating power when a blood-rare beef sandwich is called the "Eucharist of this our Age."[8] The relationship between layers and accumulating power helps us visualize how and why Pynchon assembles this narrative as he does, why he values multiplicity over simplicity.[9] To give an obvious example, if we did not see Dixon learning how to survey and make maps in his youth, we would not understand how that skill, used to enclose commons and impoverish the poor farmers of England, would enable similarly oppressive social patterns in America.

The idea of layers also provides us one way of visualizing what Pynchon is doing with other worlds or alternative realities. Pynchon gives us a hollow earth with its own inhabitants, the hollow earth theory having been proposed as science (rather than mythology) in 1692 by Edmond Halley (of Halley's comet). That realm of reality is in a sense beneath our feet.

So are the telluric forces of ley lines. Pynchon gives us a few giant angels like those that appear in *Gravity's Rainbow*, suggesting a different reality above us.[10] Rebekah's ghost makes the land of the dead intrude upon our own, as also happened in *Vineland*. Animals that can perform human tasks, whether reading (*Against the Day*) or speaking (the Learnèd English Dog in *Mason & Dixon*, a dog in *Gravity's Rainbow*, a stag in *Against the Day*) suggest that we should explore non-human consciousness for new realities within our own level. Golems both small and large, were-animals, spectral beings such as the third Surveyor, the Black Dog and a Presence represent non-material realities that can break through to Mason and Dixon's material reality.[11] We hear of a world of giant vegetables so large that one could burrow into a beet and live in it. We find several examples of sentient or eternal machines: two clocks talk to one another; Vaucanson's mechanical duck acquires consciousness, life, and supernatural powers; R.C. swallows a watch that never needs winding, and it actively resists ejection.[12] The survey team finds a cabin magically much larger inside than out, and the activities inside resemble the partying found in elven or faerie worlds.[13] Yet further levels of reality include a lump of dough whose yeast talks and Mason's entrapment in a shadow world consisting of the eleven days lost to calendrical reform in 1752.[14]

Almost anything can give access to a layer of reality beyond our own. Mason looks too hard at the electrical spark produced by the electrical "eel," and he reports seeing "another Dispensation of Space, yea and Time."[15] Thinking he is just looking at a rare beast, he finds instead a disquieting alternative world. All of these can be seen as layers or worlds above ours, below it physically or in scale (yeast) or beyond but adjacent in some unspecified fashion. Pynchon does not pile them up hierarchically in true lamination, but we experience them as if each were a layer above or below us whose presence we can sometimes sense. If we accept Dixon's statement that layers always accumulate power, then Pynchon's frequent invocation of these layers seems meant to intensify something – our openness to non-material realities and sensitivity to their paranormal energies, at the very least.

Pynchon's other focal image, networks, emerges at the end of the novel. The dying Mason argues that the land is being tied together in a network of points and lines, which in Pynchon's value system is usually bad, since that involves ownership and control. However, astronomers' practice of tying the stars together and placing them in almanacs may be different, given that no ownership can attach to these mathematical lines. Mason claims that this stellar network produces an astral Gematria containing messages of great urgency for America.[16] The Gematria is the numeric coding applied to the Hebrew scriptures in Kabbalistic mysticism, and it supposedly produces messages for those who study it. If we connect the points, we will be able to read the messages, and what they concern is America. The overwhelming abundance of material with which Pynchon floods the reader challenges us to make such connections, and that is pretty much how we have to read this novel. What we get is an in-depth, interconnected vision of values and decisions taken around the world at different times that sent America in a particular direction culturally. This complex vision explains some of the dire drawbacks of America's culture and lifestyle.

Making sense of the information glut

To make reading easier, I would like to identify some of the chief thematic points that turn up on more than one of the chronological or ontological layers. This will give first-time readers something to which they can attach new material as it flows over them.

The chief layer that helps us organize our reading is the archetypal American plot: two men venturing into the wilderness together.[17] Mason is not quite the fugitive from civilization seen in Natty Bumppo, Ishmael, Huck Finn or Sal Paradise, but he shares their uneasiness with women and an unwillingness to settle down and fit in where his origins would have dictated. Dixon is not differentiated by race, as is often the case for the support character; his subordination stems from his being mechanic surveyor to Mason's mathematical astronomer, and he shares with many sidekicks the characteristic of being comfortable with himself and his body.[18] Mason's melancholia aligns him with the Puritan side of American culture; Dixon's outgoing enjoyment of liquor and women lets him embody the gusto and appetite for experience that is the hedonistic side of the same culture. The two-men-in-the-woods is essentially a cultural myth, the wilderness being one of the great foundational spaces of American fiction.[19]

One of the nodes within this layer that connects to many other layers consists of scientific observations and investigations. Readers can reconstruct much of mid-eighteenth-century science from Pynchon's references. Natural philosophers investigated electricity. They measured the transit of Venus across the face of the Sun in order to calculate the distance between Earth and Sun. Seagoing nations urgently sought ways to figure longitude while at sea. The discovery of Uranus – the first new planet in recorded history – upset long-held assumptions about the universe as a series of celestially perfect spheres. While observing his second Transit of Venus in Ireland, Mason suddenly sees the stars "no longer spread as upon a Dom'd Surface,— he now beholds them in the *Third Dimension* as well,— the Eye creating its own Zed-Axis, along which the star-chok'd depths near and far rush both inward and away, and soon, quite soon, billowing out of control."[20] Mason glimpses the universe as we understand it rather than as the nested spheres inherited from classical times, and we feel his wonder doubly because he couches modernity in the eighteenth-century prose style that is the medium of this novel from beginning to end. Pynchon can admit that science embodies great curiosity about the world, but its means and ends all have political implications, and he exposes ways in which science exerts political control and contributes even to such enterprises as slavery.[21]

Another node that connects most layers is power, and this connects not just to the phases of Mason and Dixon's lives, but to other Pynchon novels as well. *Gravity's Rainbow* features the Elect, the Preterite and Control. *Against the Day* gives us Capitalists and Labor. In *Mason & Dixon*, the terms reflect colonial empire, trade, slavery and mapping, but the underlying concern is the same: a small group that exercises power over a widely dispersed, much larger group of people who can find no effective way to fight back or gain freedom.[22] Many of the Royal Society's projects, such as figuring longitude, have implications for safeguarding ships for war, trade and empire. Pynchon makes much of the Astronomer Royal being married into the family of Clive of India, a connection that puts science in bed with trade and the military. To enforce ownership of land, whether commons or colonies, one needs maps, so map-making contributes to the power of the ruling few. Power is perhaps *the* core concept in all Pynchon's novels.

Whereas political power and control are present in Pynchon's story-worlds, *Mason & Dixon* also gives us non-human power in the form of telluric forces. Pynchon played with that possibility in *Gravity's Rainbow*, when Lyle Bland finds that "Earth is a living critter [... and] that Gravity, taken so for granted, is really something eerie, Messianic, extrasensory in Earth's mindbody."[23] In *Mason & Dixon*, Pynchon projects back on his eighteenth-century world the 1921 theory of ley lines or lines of power that run along the surface of the Earth. So strong are these telluric forces that Dixon and his teacher can supposedly fly above them. Equally anachronistically, Pynchon draws on Feng Shui to excoriate Mason and Dixon's visto, which is physically hacked straight across the wilderness, ignoring natural contours. According to this Asian philosophy, to "mark a right Line upon the Earth is to inflict upon the Dragon's very Flesh, a sword-slash, a long, perfect scar, impossible for any who live out here the year 'round to see as other than hateful Assault."[24] Telluric powers of a different sort are sensed by Dixon when he is carried off in the Arctic by inhabitants of Earth's interior. Pynchon is hostile to power exercised by humans, but he revels in telluric powers; they suggest that Earth has living and non-material dimensions, and also that alternative realities exist beneath our feet as well as above us.

Some of Pynchon's thematic nodes seem zany at first: beavers and the Black Hole of Calcutta, for instance, entice us to connect the references yet let him indulge in his characteristic humor.[25] Beavers exemplify chaos theory; they figure in New World cuisine possibilities; they appear as were-beavers; they play a role in Delaware Indian creation myths; and the tree-felling contest between a giant were-beaver and an ax wielder raises ecological uneasiness.[26] Science, mythology and pre-scientific beliefs all connect to this theme. The Black Hole of Calcutta yields erotic stimulation in a Cape Town brothel. It exposes the biased values of colonizers, who think nothing of a similar number of Indian lives lost every night in Calcutta. It serves as a model for Hell and as the plot for a musical. A chicken on the visto line provokes speculation on all the chickens from Ohio to the Chesapeake doing likewise, producing a "Chickens' Black Hole of Calcutta."[27] This infamous fragment of empire and its culturally biased attitude toward death thus connects to brothel sex, popular entertainment and the present-day overcrowded battery chickens of agribusiness. These all drive home Pynchon's point that many things are connected in ways we would not expect.

For temporal-political connections, we might look at what Christy L. Burns calls the parallactic method by which Pynchon melds the eighteenth century with the twentieth.[28] Pynchon wishes us to recognize our kinship to people in the earlier time. His eighteenth-century coffee houses ring with anachronistic orders for "Half and Half please, Mount Kenya Double-A, with Java High-land,— perhaps a slug o' boil'd Milk as well." George Washington smokes hemp with the surveyors, and Martha produces pastries to satisfy their munchies. A sailor called Pat O'Brian is expert in nautical knots. (The modern-day Patrick O'Brian of course wrote twenty immensely popular novels about England's navy during the Napoleonic wars.) Characters toss off lines such as "*Prandium gratis non est*" instead of the usual colloquialism, "There ain't no such thing as a free lunch." Mason dreams of the visto becoming a mall eighty miles long and of a discontinuous mall of anchored ships across the Atlantic marking longitude lines. The eighteenth century may seem very distant to Pynchon's audience, but he makes connections that help readers recognize similarity and therefore feel some responsibility for the evils done then and for their consequences in the present.[29]

Slavery is a node to which many themes connect. It is declared a necessary concomitant of capitalist trade.[30] It depresses Mason and Dixon in South Africa. We find it in the American colonies. Dixon attacks a slave merchant. Because science is always being carried out under the aegis not just of the Royal Society but also of the Dutch or British East India Company, Mason and Dixon cannot feel their mathematical work to be innocent in the commercial world so marked by slavery. Or, as Pynchon says in *Against the Day*, "all mathematics leads, doesn't it, sooner or later, to some kind of human suffering."[31]

More connective points could be identified, but let me mention just two: views from above and views from below. Pynchon's stories of people flying may reflect folklore, but Emerson's teaching his pupils to fly corresponds to the math he taught that will let them make maps, since those look down on the land from above. Pynchon frequently pairs the ideas of personal flying and map-making.[32] Paranoia represents the view from below, the uncertainty felt by the powerless over who is controlling them. Mason and Dixon often wonder who is really behind their mapping and measuring activities. What matters, is that views from above and views from below appear scattered throughout the novel. As we connect them, we gain a sense of Pynchon's worldview of those with power above and those who are helpless below. When you read Pynchon's other novels and see the same nodes there, you get a feel for all of Pynchon's work as forming a network.

Reading *Mason & Dixon*

Mason & Dixon is a novel not of action or character but of ideas, and those ideas may seem present in excess. With each appearing so vividly and with apparently equal emphasis, we cannot tell at first what can be relegated to background, if anything. Sorting materials into their zonal layer and looking for connections among those levels encourages readers to look at any new episode in terms of its links. Dixon's "numbing torrent of American Stimuli" forces us to hunt for connections rather than ignore them, as we are all too inclined to do when it comes to historical sins.[33] Those stimuli also batter down our defenses against the "other worlds" that mystics, students of consciousness, and Pynchon feel should be incorporated into materialist or scientific accounts of reality. Learning to open oneself to such possible worlds is one of the rewards of reading the book this way. What are those other worlds in this novel, though? Do these other worlds mean that Pynchon believes in the Hollow Earth or flying above ley lines?

Consider the Hollow Earth. Pynchon clearly enjoys that conceit; he uses it apparently frivolously in *Against the Day*, but in *Mason & Dixon* it generates a very vivid indictment of surface dwelling:

> wherever you may stand, given the Convexity, each of you is slightly *pointed away* from everybody else, all the time, out into that Void that most of you seldom notice. Here in the Earth Concave, everyone is pointed *at* everyone else,— ev'rybody's axes converge— forc'd at least thus to acknowledge one another,— an entirely different set of rules for how to behave.[34]

One need not take the Hollow Earth theory seriously to see the importance of the image Pynchon derives from it. This brilliant visualization of social values encourages us to think in terms of the whole world and all people. Then Pynchon elaborates further. One of the denizens pokes and examines Dixon. "Nothing too intrusive," he says, though Mason adds, "Nothing you remember, anyway" – thus reminding us of alien abduction stories.[35] After looking in Dixon's eyes and ears and mouth, this figure devastatingly asks him:

> Are you quite sure, now [...] that you wish to bet ev'rything upon the Body?— *this* Body?— moreover, to rely helplessly upon the Daily Harvest your Sensorium brings in,— keeping in mind that both will decline, the one in Health as the other in Variety, growing less and less trustworthy till at last they are no more?[36]

To rely only on the body and the material world is the premise of science and of modernity. In his other novels, Pynchon shows us many belief systems, including Buddhism, Kabbalism, Gnosticism, the Tibetan Book of the Dead, Zen, Shamanism, Native American myths, and Islam; *Mason & Dixon* adds Feng Shui to this list, but features the versions of Christianity most prominent at the time.[37] By pushing us to consider other worlds, Pynchon also suggests that a religious reality may be possible. He apparently wishes us to free ourselves from our dogmatic insistence on nothing but what our bodily senses can confirm. I suggest that he pictures the other realities as something like the layers that Mason and Dixon discuss, and imagines such multiplying of layers accumulates power. If we read attentively, make the connections, and come to see them as central to reality, then his layered structure pushes us beyond everyday materiality to higher and, to him, more satisfying non-material realms.

Pynchon is hard-put to come up with positives, given his basically negative image of our political world and his overwhelming sense that America made the wrong turn at the beginning: "America was the one place we should *not* have found [slaves]."[38] If one fights evils with power, then the power will spawn its own hierarchies of those who wield the power and those who are forced to carry out the will of others, a point made frequently in *Gravity's Rainbow*. In *Against the Day*, he seems to uphold the practice of anarchist dynamiting as an individual act of resistance to capitalism. For those who are not willing to risk their lives to improve society, he recommends investing one's effort in family and doing whatever minor acts one can to make the world better rather than worse. Even small acts to counter the system's evils may be helpful: a tree tells Slothrop in *Gravity's Rainbow* to steal the oil filter from an unguarded logging tractor.[39] Dixon's wrenching away a slave-driver's whip is a more courageous version of such a small intervention.[40]

Pynchon urges wider definitions of reality than those embodied in the physical and social world. He pushes us to open ourselves to visionary levels. Some of his non-material realities are unclassifiable, but some belong to recognized spiritual and religious systems, though he does not emphasize Christianity in *Mason & Dixon* quite as much as he does in *Against the Day*. Pynchon's point is that we need to acknowledge the possibilities. Striving to see connections is built into our process of reading *Mason & Dixon*. The other implied worlds or levels of reality are not problems to be solved, but rather possibilities to consider, new ways of conceiving our ontology. Pynchon promises us access to a richer world and new depths of meaning if we can open ourselves to these visionary moments in life as well as in reading.[41]

NOTES

1 Thomas Pynchon, *Gravity's Rainbow* (New York: Viking, 1973), p. 556.
2 Aldous Huxley, *The Doors of Perception/Heaven and Hell* (Harmondsworth: Penguin, 1972), pp. 21–22.
3 For such crazy but historical material, see e.g. www.thomaspynchon.com/mason-dixon/extra/swallow.html, which reports that someone named R.C. did swallow a team chronometer, and local legend says you can hear it at R.C.'s tombstone in White Clay Creek Preserve, Delaware.
4 Thomas Pynchon, *Mason & Dixon* (New York: Henry Holt, 1997), p. 10. Joseph Dewey analyzes Cherrycoke's spiritual quest in "The Sound of One Man Mapping: Wicks Cherrycoke and the Eastern (Re)solution," in Brooke Horvath and Irving Malin (eds.), *Pynchon and* Mason & Dixon (Newark: University of Delaware Press, 2000), pp. 112–31.
5 Pynchon, *Mason & Dixon*, p. 390.
6 *Ibid.*, p. 294.
7 *Ibid.*, p. 599. Pynchon's lamination images suggest he has in mind the many-layered voltaic pile (not invented until about 1800) rather than Leyden jars. The jars did have a foil-glass-foil layering, however, and Franklin makes a "battery" of twenty-four such jars, which multiplies the number of layers involved.
8 *Ibid.*, p. 367.
9 Charles Clerc calls attention to lamination in this novel; see his *Mason & Dixon & Pynchon* (Lanham: University Press of America, 2000), p. 139.
10 Pynchon, *Mason & Dixon*, p. 108.
11 *Ibid.*, pp. 685, passim, 605, 494, 635.
12 *Ibid.*, pp. 112, 372–81, 321–25.
13 *Ibid.*, p. 412.
14 *Ibid.*, p. 205.
15 *Ibid.*, pp. 433–34.
16 *Ibid.*, p. 772.

17 See Leslie A. Fiedler, *Love and Death in the American Novel* (New York: Scarborough Books, 1982), pp. 26–28.

18 For the men's failure to become real friends, see Celia M. Wallhead, "Mason and Dixon: Pynchon's Bickering Heroes," *Pynchon Notes*, 46–49 (2000–2001), 178–99.

19 See Richard Slotkin, *Regeneration Through Violence: The Mythology of the American Frontier, 1660–1860* (1973; New York: HarperPerennial, 1996), esp. p. 22.

20 Pynchon, *Mason & Dixon*, p. 725.

21 Pynchon basically undercuts the whole Enlightenment project because of what science does to the mindset of European cultures, as demonstrated by David Cowart, "The Luddite Vision: *Mason & Dixon*," *American Literature*, 71.2 (1999), 341–63.

22 See David Seed, "Mapping the Course of Empire in the New World," in Horvath and Malin (eds.), *Pynchon and* Mason & Dixon, pp. 84–99.

23 Pynchon, *Gravity's Rainbow*, p. 590.

24 Pynchon, *Mason & Dixon*, p. 542.

25 Samuel Cohen links Pynchon's use of the titular ampersand to making connections in "*Mason & Dixon* & the Ampersand," *Twentieth Century Literature*, 48.3 (2002), 264–91.

26 Pynchon, *Mason & Dixon*, pp. 364, 383, 619–22, 620, 618–22. For New World Cuisine, see Colin A. Clarke, "Consumption on the Frontier: Food and Sacrament in *Mason & Dixon*," in Elizabeth Jane Wall Hinds (eds.), *The Multiple Worlds of Pynchon's* Mason & Dixon (Rochester: Camden House, 2005), pp. 77–98.

27 Pynchon, *Mason & Dixon*, pp. 153, 153, 482–83, 562–63, 665.

28 Christy L. Burns, "Postmodern Historiography: Politics and the Parallactic Method in Thomas Pynchon's *Mason & Dixon*," *Postmodern Culture*, 14 (2003), n.p.

29 For the examples in this paragraph, see Pynchon, *Mason & Dixon*, pp. 298, 278–81, 54, 317, 701, 712–13.

30 *Ibid.*, p. 108.

31 Thomas Pynchon, *Against the Day* (New York: Penguin Press, 2006), p. 541.

32 Pynchon, *Mason & Dixon*, pp. 58, 222, 242, 504–5, 689. Brian McHale notes Pynchon's association of power with vertical perspective and of subjunctive possibilities with horizontality in "Mason & Dixon in the Zone, or, A Brief Poetics of Pynchon-Space," in Horvath and Malin (eds.), *Pynchon and* Mason & Dixon, pp. 43–62.

33 *Ibid.*, p. 496.

34 *Ibid.*, p. 741.

35 *Ibid.*, p. 742.

36 *Ibid.*

37 Pynchon's Christian concerns are analyzed by Dewey, "Sounds," and by Justin M. Scott Coe, "Haunting and Hunting: Bodily Resurrection and the Occupation of History in Thomas Pynchon's *Mason & Dixon*," in Hinds (ed.), *Multiple Worlds*, pp. 147–69. See also Kathryn Hume, "The Religious and Political Vision of Pynchon's *Against the Day*," *Philological Quarterly*, 86.1–2 (2007), 163–87, for Christian and specifically Catholic spirituality.

38 Pynchon, *Mason & Dixon*, p. 693.

39 Pynchon, *Gravity's Rainbow*, p. 553.
40 Pynchon, *Mason & Dixon*, pp. 698–700. What the individual can do in the face of evil is discussed in Jeff Baker, "Plucking the American Albatross: Pynchon's Irrealism in *Mason & Dixon*," in Horvath and Malin (eds.), *Pynchon and* Mason & Dixon, pp. 167–88, and Brian Thill, "The Sweetness of Immorality: *Mason & Dixon* and the American Sins of Consumption," in Hinds (ed.), *Multiple Worlds*, pp. 49–75.
41 My thanks to Katie Owens-Murphy, Jeffrey Gonzalez and Sean Moiles for their criticism and suggestions.

5

BERNARD DUYFHUIZEN

Against the Day

With *Against the Day* (2006), Thomas Pynchon sets his readers their largest challenge yet to process multiple plotlines, histories and genre traces. Throughout his novels Pynchon has experimented with mixing genres, writing parodies and pastiches, and creating multi-voiced texts, but with *Against the Day* he pushes the boundaries of his tendencies toward encyclopedic fiction. Summarizing fully and accurately the plot of *Against the Day* would be a daunting task, and even then the numerous intersections of plotlines are likely to end up a tangled mass. The novel spans some thirty years beginning in 1893, includes some 170 characters, and covers the globe from the west coast of America to inner Asia, locating many historical events in new juxtapositions – yet, the text repeats the mantra found in many Pynchon novels: "everything fits together, connects."[1] Many of the plotlines nod toward a specific genre that allows Pynchon to contextualize his narrative within an array of intertexts while simultaneously maintaining a reasonably consistent narrative voice. That consistent narrative voice is one familiar to Pynchon readers as it is based in the genre of Menippean satire, which he has used before to shape his various texts' political substructures. The Menippea's features are "stylistic multiplicity (and the philosophic pluralism it implies), fantasy and philosophy, intellection and encyclopedism, an 'anti-book' stance, a marginal cultural position, and carnivalization."[2] The "equations of history" that Pynchon scratches out on the blackboard of this text and the various genres he deploys represent an array of vectors that integrate and disintegrate both within the fiction and among the fictional intersections with actual historical events.[3]

Even though Pynchon litters his text with "maps" and occasional guidebooks, very few of them guide the characters, much less the reader, to an expected destination. Pynchon, writing about his early fiction in *Slow Learner*, cites the "trick" of using Baedeker guides to construct scenes in foreign locales, and though the reader may sense Baedeker behind *Against the Day*, no character ever brandishes one, nor does the narrator refer to the ubiquitous travel guide of the era.[4] Indeed, in *Against the Day*, citing an actual text, Pynchon pokes fun at our dilemma in pursuing the textually reflexive search for Shambhala:

> The bookseller nodded. "That is the *Rigpa Dzinpai Phonya*, or Knowledge-Bearing Messenger, by Rimpung [*sic*] Ngawang Jigdag, 1557. Directions for journeying to Shambhala are addressed by the author to a Yogi, who is a sort of fictional character, though at the same time real—a figure in a vision, and also Rinpungpa himself. I do know of a variant currently for sale, which contains lines that do not appear in other versions. Notably, 'Even if you forget everything else,' Rinpunga instructs the Yogi, 'remember one thing—when you come to a fork in the road, take it.' Easy for him to say, of course, being two people at once."[5]

The second Yogi here is Yogi Berra, legendary New York Yankee catcher and purveyor of oxymoronic wisdom. Although the text signals many other narrative genres, the overarching narrator increasingly asserts his satiric will over the text, inserting jokes, bad puns and anachronisms, blending the genre differences into what Mikhail Bakhtin would call a "heteroglossic" narrative containing multiple voices and multiple discourses.[6]

Against the Day opens in 1893 with the "celebrated aeronautics club known as the Chums of Chance" heading for the White City of the World's Columbian Exposition in Chicago.[7] But even before we are a page into the text "the exact degree of fictitiousness" or facticity of the Chums is made strange: "Darby, as my faithful readers will remember, was the 'baby' of the crew" – who is this narrator who has "faithful readers"?[8] Soon thereafter, the Chums' existence is pegged to a series of dime-novel boys' adventure tales: "see *The Chums of Chance and the Evil Halfwit*"; many more titles follow, culminating in *The Chums of Chance and the Wrath of the Yellow Fang*, which foreshadows Pynchon's next novel, *Inherent Vice* (2009).[9] The accessible style of the early Chums chapters, punctuated with colloquialisms and plenty of adverbs, marks the genre trace Pynchon invokes, but as the Chums chapters progress through the novel, they largely lose the boyishness and merge with the novel's satiric narrative voice. The reader would expect the boy Chums to grow up during the thirty-year span of the novel, but since they are "fictions," they suspend the laws of time just as their airship's constant expansion appears to suspend the laws of gravity. Thus Pynchon signals another genre echoed in the Chums chapters: science fiction, especially the early forms practiced by Jules Verne and H. G. Wells (whose novel *The Time Machine* (1895) is invoked as an intertext to a Chums adventure).[10] Like the "aphorism" from Yogi Berra, however, Pynchon routinely drops in anachronistic allusions to more recent science fictions such as *Star Trek* and *Star Wars*.

Pynchon has often included various sciences within his texts, and his readers often need to take crash courses in physics, chemistry, social theory or behaviorist psychology, to name a few, to keep up. In Pynchon's texts the genres of scientific discourse always intersect with the application of science to the lives of characters. In *Against the Day* this tradition continues from the real Nikola Tesla to the fictional Heino Vanderjuice, but the center stage here goes to various mathematical theories (Riemann surfaces, spaces and numbers, vectorism, quaternions, etc.). One can assume that many readers of *Against the Day* will appreciate the wiki site devoted to the novel for basic introductions to the mathematical concepts at play.[11] Significantly, Pynchon uses mathematics as another metaphor for how human beings attempt to grasp, understand and control everyday existence. In Pynchon's hands, however, the metaphor leads to playful notions like "bilocation" – the capacity of one person or thing to be seemingly in two locations at the same time. For instance, professors Renfrew and Werfner, whose names mirror one another and who appear to be one person existing in two places, work simultaneously for opposing English and German interests. As an instance of the "double agent," this example of bilocation leads to another genre Pynchon invokes: the espionage thriller.

In the latter half of the novel, the plotline surrounding Cyprian Latewood, an initially reluctant British agent, has Pynchon revisiting the "great game" of late-colonial, pre-World War I espionage. In the "Introduction" to *Slow Learner*, Pynchon points to the genre he is evoking: "I had grown up reading a lot of spy fiction, novels of intrigue, notably those of John Buchan."[12] However, Cyprian's overt homosexuality, which often turns masochistic, complicates his missions in the Balkans. Although one can also spot anachronistic allusions to the James Bond novels and films (another source Pynchon cites in *Slow Learner*), Cyprian is the antithesis of the Cold War macho misogynist.[13] Indeed, as his relationship develops with both Yashmeen Halfcourt, a former classmate at Cambridge, and Reef Traverse, an exiled American anarchist who becomes Yashmeen's lover, Cyprian's story echoes the genre of masochistic fiction launched by Leopold von Sacher Masoch in *Venus in Furs* (1870). Where that novel depicted the extremes of submission to masochistic desire, *Against the Day* displays a character who comes to a new understanding of his essential being. In his commitment to Yashmeen, Reef, and their child Ljubica, Cyprian finds a "love" that awakens a spirituality that allows him to quit the spy game. Pynchon has explored both homosexuality and masochism before, most notably in *Gravity's Rainbow*, but in *Against the Day* he displays the human dimensions within those behaviors – his presentation this time is a far cry from the melodramatic psycho-dramas of General Pudding and his Domina Nocturna or Slothrop and Greta Erdmann.

Kit Traverse, Reef's brother and Yashmeen's university friend, also becomes a quasi-agent when he accepts an assignment to find Yashmeen's father and to engage for British interests in the search for Shambhala. As another character tells Kit why he may need to abandon his mission quickly, "if we had to cover every contingency we might as well be writing espionage novels."[14] Of all the characters in *Against the Day*, Kit travels the farthest and by the greatest array of conveyances: horse, wagon, car, train, sailboat, ship, midget submarine, gondola, vaporetto and airplane. Moreover, in the novel's second half, when he is ostensibly on the run from his benefactor, the mogul Scarsdale Vibe, we see him engaging in many "local" occupations to make ends meet. Although Kit is not the only traveler, he may be the best evocation of the adventure travel writing genre that pervades the Menippean satire of *Against the Day*. Pynchon is building on the genre of the geographic novel he developed in *Mason & Dixon* with its map-making and surveying, but this time he deploys a wider array of characters to range farther across the globe, invoking the local color of each location through national foods, beverages, local establishments, and so on. At the same time, Pynchon makes over ninety references to maps or charts or to mapping or to unmapped regions, marking the arrogant project of Western colonialism to fill in what Joseph Conrad identified in *Heart of Darkness* (1899) as the blank spaces on the map.[15]

Both Kit and Reef, along with their brother Frank, are sons of Colorado miner and anarchist bomber Webb Traverse, who is brutally murdered by Scarsdale Vibe's hired gunslingers. Vibe is the archetype of the plutocratic class ("plutes"), and as such he is the focus of the political dimension in the novel's "American" chapters. Vibe is a rapacious businessman, seemingly involved in everything, who has no qualms about the workers he exploits or the enemies he eliminates. In Webb's story, Pynchon engages yet another genre, the anarchist novel, which had a certain vogue around the turn of the century with texts such as Henry James's *The Princess Casamassima* (1886), which the Chums' dog Pugnax is reading when the text opens; Conrad's *The Secret Agent* (1907); Robert Louis Stevenson's *The Dynamiter* (1885); G. K. Chesterton's *The Man Who Was Thursday* (1908); and Isabel Meredith's *A Girl Among the Anarchists* (1903). Lindsay Noseworth, one of the Chums of Chance, may wish that "the inexorably rising tide of World Anarchism ... [were] safely within the fictional leaves of some book," but within the storyworld of *Against the Day* and in some of the historical acts of anarchism cited in the novel, there appears to be no safe boundary.[16]

Although we aren't given many direct examples of Webb's bombings, the text implies that they are targeted primarily at the property of the owners who oppress the miners and try to squash the union. With much of the action set around Telluride, Colorado, Pynchon shows Vibe already planning for the post-mining exploitation of the land as the recreational destination it has become. Pynchon walks a fine line here since the localized and often legitimate anarchist concerns in 1900 have been superseded by the twenty-first century's global terrorist narrative, and he implicitly asks his reader to weigh the moral justifications that sometimes attend political violence. We can infer from the text that Pynchon sides with Webb rather than Vibe, but as the genre shifts to a revenge tale, we see that the cycle of violence once begun is hard to end.

Vibe hires Webb's killers, Deuce Kindred and Sloat Fresno; the Traverse brothers seek revenge as family members were expected to do in western dime-novel conventions. The revenge convention had plenty of real-life counterparts, including the story of Wyatt Earp, for instance. Only Frank, however, fulfills the vendetta when he accidentally encounters Sloat in Mexico. In depicting the scene, Pynchon deploys a prose equivalent of the slow-motion, stylized violence found in films such as those directed by Sam Peckinpah and Martin Scorsese:

> [Frank] found there right in front of him, sitting slouched and puffy-faced and as if waiting, the no-longer-elusive Sloat Fresno, quick as that, with his pistol already somehow in his hand, giving Frank time only to find his own and begin firing cold, no chance to rouse up any of those family emotions, none of that—old Sloat, who maybe never even recognized him, failing as it turned out even to get off his shot—blown over backwards, one of the chair legs breaking under his already dead weight so he was sent into half a spin, throwing a dark slash of blood that trailed in the air and feathered in a crescent slap, unheard in the noise of the shots, across the ancient soiling of the *pulquería* floor. *Fín.*[17]

Reef and Kit fail in their attempt to kill Vibe in Venice after witnessing Vibe's bodyguards murdering a would-be anarchist they had inadvertently recruited into their plan. Pynchon invokes the revenge plot, but reinvents it in the actions of Webb's fourth child, his daughter Lake.

The family revenge plot is older than Greek tragedy, and Pynchon at one point refers to the Traverse brothers as "Furies [...] no longer in pursuit,"[18] but it is Lake, who in marrying Deuce Kindred (a marriage worthy of Greek tragedy) embodies the Greek notion of the Fury pricking at whatever modicum of conscience Deuce has. At one point, he pleads with her: "'Lake... please forgive me....' Down on his knees again with another display of eyeball hydraulics, which was not as becoming in a man, she had discovered, as tales of romance in the ladies magazines would lead you to think."[19] Lake may have "dime novel [daydreams] full of lurid goings-on," but she is pragmatic, engaging only in scenarios she desires such as the pornographic *ménage à trois* with Deuce and Sloat – "she was always ready to oblige" – or *The Postman Always Rings Twice* encounter she has with Lew Basnight.[20] Here Pynchon anachronistically evokes the kitchen seduction/rape scene in the film version starring Jack Nicholson and Jessica Lange rather than the film starring John Garfield and Lana Turner (which Pynchon cites in *Inherent Vice*) or J. M. Cain's original novel. Yet Lake never exacts revenge herself – Deuce's comeuppance is at the hands of Basnight and Hollywood law enforcement who finger him as the serial killer of wannabe starlets. Thus "poetic justice" is meted out to all of Webb's killers but not within a conventional plot arc and a specific set of characters. Pynchon's writing in the Los Angeles chapters points toward the genre he engages directly in *Inherent Vice*: noir detective fiction of the 1930s and 1940s – the pulp fiction descendant of the dime novel.

The multi-generational Traverse story in *Against the Day* is also a pre-quel to the multi-generational Traverse story in Pynchon's earlier novel *Vineland* (1990). By employing the multi-generational convention, Pynchon works in a genre with a strong American precursor: William Faulkner. Faulkner's generations had to come to grips with the loss of the Civil War and the resulting upheavals in Southern culture; Pynchon's, on the other hand, struggle through the class war of American capitalism that pits owners against workers. Thus, Pynchon blends the struggles of the Traverse family with a muckraking style of historical re-visioning. Long before we meet Webb, the anarchist and class-war themes are introduced at the novel's outset in Chicago, home of Upton Sinclair's *The Jungle*; moreover, those themes carry through to some of the novel's European settings. Whereas the muckrakers of the American tradition kept a tight focus on a particular industry such as meatpacking, Pynchon extends the view to a wider swath of human and, maybe more specifically, American conditions. Jess Traverse, Reef's son, sums it up best in the school essay he writes "on What It Means to Be An American": "*It means do what they tell you and take what they give you and don't go on strike or their soldiers will shoot you down.*"[21] In *Vineland* the union issues have moved away from the mines to Hollywood's film industry, but Pynchon is saying that the struggle continues.

Although film has been a constant intertext in Pynchon's writing (with the logical exception of *Mason & Dixon*), with *Against the Day* we see the genre in its infancy when Merle Rideout, at the "DREAMTIME MOVY" theatre, fixes a faulty film projector that jammed at the

"Worst possible place it could've happened, she's hangin on to this log in the river—"

"—bein swept down to this waterfall off this big cliff—"

"—current's too strong for her to swim, he just found out, ridin hard to get there in time—"[22]

The scene is probably based on the famous parallel action shot sequence from D. W. Griffith's *Way Down East*, and in its suspense and illusion of danger this early snippet of film language demonstrates why film quickly replaced the dime novel to provide audiences with cliffhanging thrills. Griffith's film was released in 1920, so if it is the film playing when Merle fixes the jammed projector, then this is another anachronistic allusion. Merle, an itinerant inventor and photographer, ultimately migrates to California, home of moving pictures, to invent a fantastic device that allows one to see time within a static photograph, to see what happens in the life of the photograph's subject. With this particular example of science fiction, Pynchon comments on the temporal plane within static spatial arts. Whether it is Merle's photographs, Hunter Penhallow's paintings or Arturo Naunt's Angel of Death sculptures, Pynchon layers into his text additional genre conventions from the spatial arts, suggesting again the complex intersection of art and life. Interestingly, these examples of the spatial arts intersect with Dally Rideout, Merle's daughter.

Dally grows up within the text, and she becomes a consummate actor within various genres of stage performance. Fiercely independent, Dally leaves her father to go to New York to seek her mother, Erlys, who ran off with a traveling magician when Dally was young. In 1900s New York, Dally finds work as the ingénue/victim of "chop suey stories" – street "comediettas" based on the "white-slave simulation industry" out to "catch the fancy of the Occidental rubberneck[ing]" tourist visiting Chinatown.[23] These street melodramas enact the dominant culture's fears of orientalism and the "yellow terror" of turn-of-the-century anti-immigration politics. Naturally for a Pynchon novel:

> At this point a curious thing happened. As if all the expensive make-believe had somehow slopped over into "real life," the actual tong war in the neighborhood now heated up in earnest [...] Mock Duck himself appeared in the street down in his well-known spinning squat, firing two revolvers at a time in all directions as pushcart vegetables were destroyed and pedestrians went diving for cover.[24]

The "chop suey story" morphs not only into "real life" but into "reel life" genre conventions of late twentieth-century Hong Kong action movies. Dally's experience additionally "slop[s] over into real life" when considered alongside Mary Ting Yi Lui's social history *The Chinatown Trunk Mystery*, which details miscegenation between Chinese men and immigrant Irish women. When Dally asks about auditioning for her part she is told, "Red hair! Freckles! Audition enough O.K.!"[25] Lui's study also includes a discussion of Chinatown "tourist guidebooks," designed to allow safe visits to this "foreign and inscrutable" neighborhood.[26]

Fortunately for Dally, her street performances attract the attention of impresario R. Wilshire Vibe (Scarsdale's brother), who specializes in the genre of musical theatre with clearly racist/colonialist overtones if the titles are anything to go by: *African Antics* ("basically a coon revue," he tells Dally), *Shanghai Scampers* and *Dagoes with Knives* (the last a "Bowery version of William Shakespeare's *Julius Caesar*").[27] Although Dally never appears in any of these questionable shows, she eventually appears on the London stage after again running into Wilshire, whose West End productions (*Wogs Begin at Wigan* and *Roguish Redheads*) prove that racist stereotyping is transatlantic. One of the last times Dally appears in *Against the Day* she is humming and whistling Paris show tunes ("there was a lively musical-comedy scene [...] in postwar Paris"), hanging out with her friend Jarri (who has been "resurrected" from her untimely "stage" death in *V*.), and playing a small part in the operetta *Fossettes l'Enflammeuse*.[28]

Throughout his writing, Pynchon often inserts song lyrics amid the prose to suggest that the text can't help but break into song. Sometimes the songs come from the characters, but other times they appear to be inserted simply to provide an opportunity for playful genre slippage. Of the twenty-one song lyrics in *Against the Day*, a couple come from *Waltzing in Whitechapel, or, A Ripping Romance*, "including one intended to be sung Gilbert and Sullivan style by a chorus of constables to a matching number of streetwalkers."[29] Of course the irony of a musical inspired by the murder spree of Jack the Ripper (replicated by Deuce's spree in Hollywood) is not that strange when one considers the long, successful run of the Broadway musical based on the fictional murdering barber Sweeney Todd, made famous in the Victorian penny dreadful serial *The String of Pearls*.[30]

Every thread in *Against the Day* is woven into a tapestry of genre traces, voices, allusions and parodies, and Pynchon has knotted his text with cultural artifacts that define a time of momentous cultural and social change. He captures the time surrounding the mass destruction of World War I, and as with *Gravity's Rainbow* he does not directly represent the war. Yet by enclosing this "war to end all wars" within his text, Pynchon poignantly comments on that cataclysmic event and its ongoing aftermath – as Miles Blundell, of the Chums of Chance, observes:

Back at the beginning of this . . . they must have been boys, so much like us. . . . They knew they were standing before a great chasm none could see the bottom of. But they launched themselves into it anyway. Cheering and laughing. It was their own grand 'Adventure.' They were juvenile heroes of a World-Narrative—unreflective and free, they went on hurling themselves into those depths by tens of thousands until one day they awoke, those who were still alive, and instead of finding themselves posed nobly against some dramatic moral geography, they were down cringing in a mud trench swarming with rats and smelling of shit and death.[31]

In a text constantly shuttling between the playful and the poignant, *Against the Day* is ultimately a "World-Narrative" that for Pynchon, writing in post-9/11 New York and letting his satiric guard down, is still being written, as yet another generation of "juvenile heroes" launch themselves into yet another great chasm. In *Against the Day* Pynchon takes the reader on a global journey of pratfalls and pathos, relentlessly asking us to reexamine our world – its modern economic and political origins and its enduring human drive to resist abusive structures of control.

NOTES

1   Thomas Pynchon, *Against the Day* (New York: Penguin Press, 2006), p. 24.
2   Eliot Braha, quoted in Theodore D. Kharpertian, *A Hand to Turn the Time: The Menippean Satires of Thomas Pynchon* (Rutherford: Fairleigh Dickinson University Press, 1990), p. 15. See also Charles Hollander, "Pynchon's Inferno," *Cornell Alumni News*, November 1978, 24–30.
3   Pynchon, *Against the Day*, p. 797.
4   Thomas Pynchon, *Slow Learner* (Boston: Little, Brown, 1984), p. 21.
5   Pynchon, *Against the Day*, p. 766.
6   Mikhail Bakhtin, *The Dialogic Imagination*, ed. Michael Holquist (Austin: University of Texas Press, 1981).
7   Pynchon, *Against the Day*, p. 3.
8   *Ibid.*, pp. 36, 3.
9   *Ibid.*, pp. 5, 1019.
10 *Ibid.*, p. 398.
11 "Pynchon Wiki: *Against the Day*," against-the-day.pynchonwiki.com
12 Pynchon, *Slow Learner*, p. 18.
13 *Ibid.*, p. 11. See for instance Pynchon, *Against the Day*, p. 1025.
14 Pynchon, *Against the Day*, p. 632.
15 In *Inherent Vice* (New York: Penguin Press, 2009), p. 194, Pynchon reminds us of the "useful notion" that "the map is not the territory," and he has been reminding us since his first novel *V.* that readers need to look behind the surfaces of Baedekerland to see the real life of every locale.
16 Pynchon, *Against the Day*, p. 6.
17 *Ibid.*, p. 395.
18 *Ibid.*, p. 485.

19 *Ibid.*, p. 484.
20 *Ibid.*, pp. 483, 268, 1051–52.
21 *Ibid.*, p. 1076.
22 *Ibid.*, p. 450.
23 *Ibid.*, p. 339.
24 *Ibid.*, p. 341.
25 *Ibid.*, p. 339.
26 Mary Ting Yi Lui, *The Chinatown Trunk Mystery: Murder, Miscegenation, and other Dangerous Encounters in Turn-of-the-Century New York City* (Princeton University Press, 2004), p. 21.
27 Pynchon, *Against the Day*, p. 344.
28 *Ibid.*, pp. 1065, 1066.
29 *Ibid.*, p. 679.
30 *Ibid.*, pp. 679–80.
31 *Ibid.*, pp. 1023–24.

PART II

Poetics

6

DAVID COWART

Pynchon in literary history

Even relatively early in his career critics compared Pynchon to writers like Rabelais, Swift and Melville. Like Cervantes or Sterne or Joyce (who died only four years after Pynchon's birth), Pynchon takes naturally to grand, comedic visions of the culture that has shaped his imagination and sensibility. He has affinities with the great epic poets as well. His catalogues – of disasters, of trash in a used car, of stamp anomalies, of pre-war British candies – link him to Homer, to Spenser, to his countryman Walt Whitman. Like Milton, he can recount a creation story fraught with sexual politics (Eve, Lilith and Adam become, in *Vineland* [1990], Frenesi, DL and Brock Vond) or imagine history's omega (the descending Rocket in the closing pages of *Gravity's Rainbow* [1973]). In *Mason & Dixon* (1997), like Virgil chronicling the mythic genesis of the fatherland, Pynchon imagines the moment at which the disparate ingredients of the American nation first came together. Like Swift, Pynchon can imagine a flying island (the tumescent airship of the Chums of Chance in *Against the Day* [2006]). Like Dante, he can evoke hellish abjection (Brigadier Pudding) and even conduct readers on a tour of the infernal regions, as announced by an epigraph purporting to come from the doubly apocryphal *Gospel of Thomas* ("Oxyrhynchus papyrus number classified"): "Dear Mom, I put a couple of people in hell today."[1]

Any artist of great ambition or great gifts invites a crucial question: does she or he effect change or merely consolidate some inherited aesthetic? Properly to gauge the achievement of Thomas Pynchon, one must go back to the earliest phase of his career, back to the moment at which this "individual talent," as Eliot would say, contemplated the "tradition" of which he would become a part. For Pynchon, a proximate part of that heritage would have been the work of the modernists, whose pervasive influence and authority he and his contemporaries could hardly have avoided. But for serious writers of fiction coming of age at mid-century, modernism was no longer a complete ecosystem of letters, self-sustaining and inviolable. Many in that generation had begun the work of reframing its premises, setting the stage for a displacement less tentative than what either the belated naturalism of Richard Wright (*Native Son* [1940]) and Norman Mailer (*The Naked and the Dead* [1948]) or the briefly robust Beat movement had accomplished. With the aging of Faulkner, Hemingway, Ellison and Eliot, Pynchon and company – the generation born in the nineteen twenties and thirties – sought a theme answerable to late-fifties sensibilities.

Pynchon himself seems early on to have viewed the modernist aesthetic as overdue for some creative subversion. Long before he would reflect (in the *Slow Learner* introduction of 1984) that T. S. Eliot had not been a particularly benign presence in his apprentice prose, Fausto Maijstral, in *V.*, can be heard waxing wry about the dubious influence of that poet on his literary confrères (he quotes a deft parody of "Ash Wednesday"). In the introduction (1983) to a reissue of *Been Down So Long It Looks Like Up to Me* (1966), by the same token, Pynchon recalls his and Richard Fariña's attending a party at Cornell dressed up as Fitzgerald and Hemingway respectively. Indeed, such icons may have supplied only postures to imitate with varying degrees of irony.

Shortly after graduating from Cornell, Pynchon applied (unsuccessfully) for a Ford Foundation Fellowship. The application, as summarized by Steven Weisenburger, provides glimpses of the literature Pynchon himself saw, early on, as formative. He tips his hat to the occasional parental or grandparental presence (Voltaire, Byron, Henry James), but most of the authors he names figure as older literary brothers or uncles (writers still active during Pynchon's formative years). In addition to T. S. Eliot and a couple of science-fiction authors (Ray Bradbury and Alfred Bester), he mentions Faulkner, Thomas Wolfe, F. Scott Fitzgerald, Nelson Algren and the Beats (from whom he claims, at this early stage, to have distanced himself).[2] These names provide a first census of the company he has since joined.

Twenty-five years later, in the *Slow Learner* introduction, he waxes somewhat more nostalgic about the Beats. He mentions Kerouac and Burroughs, emphasizing the impact their fictions had in a decade as buttoned-down as the 1950s. He calls Kerouac's *On the Road* (1957) "one of the great American novels." Such work, he notes, provides one context for his own early efforts, notably "Entropy" (1960) – "as close to a Beat story as anything I was writing then") – which strikes the mature writer as an attempt at "sophisticating the Beat spirit with second-hand science."[3]

He also lists Henry Adams, certain nineteenth-century scientists, Norbert Wiener, Edmund Wilson, Machiavelli, Helen Waddell, John le Carré, Shakespeare, Graham Greene and Spike Jones (for whose posthumous CD *Spiked* Pynchon would, years later, write liner notes). Briefly mentioning Philip Roth and Herbert Gold, he salutes Saul Bellow for *The Adventures of*

Augie March (1953) and Norman Mailer for "The White Negro" (1957). He notes, too, the impact of *Howl* (1956), *Lolita* (1955) and *Tropic of Cancer* (1934; not published in the United States until 1961), along with such periodicals as the *Chicago Review*, the short-lived *Big Table* (only five issues), *Evergreen Review* and *Playboy*. He invokes, finally, a number of popular writers (John Buchan, E. Phillips Oppenheim, Helen MacInnes, Geoffrey Household), and one would err to think of his having, as it were, outgrown them. Much of his originality – and much of what makes him postmodern – reveals itself in his ironic appropriation of tropes endemic to formula fiction. His pastiche style embraces such "low" material as much as it does high art. Thus he makes of pastiche something wonderfully original, something his followers and imitators would in many forms make the formal and stylistic touchstones of postmodern narrative art.

For the most part, the statements in the *Slow Learner* introduction correlate with the evidence of Pynchon's allusions, which extend across all of American letters, not to mention great tracts of British and world literature. Ranging from Machiavelli to Mary Shelley, from Jacobean tragedy to Emerson, from Rilke to the Argentine poet José Hernández (author of *Martín Fierro*, [1872, 1879]), and from Charles Dodgson to Federico García Lorca, Pynchon's allusions reveal a remarkably wide breadth of reading, as well as a global sensibility and literary ambition. Of course it is one thing to mention a writer, another really to embrace that writer's aesthetic or moral vision. Thus one discerns only a casual connection to, say, the Emily Dickinson quoted in *Gravity's Rainbow*, but real affinities with the Transcendentalists (especially Emerson, whom he quotes in *Vineland*), with Melville and, later in his career, with the American realists and naturalists who described the great octopus of American capital (Pynchon recapitulates their anatomy in *Against the Day*). Another kind of literary relationship exists with the Puritans, among them the author's own seventeenth-century ancestor William Pynchon, author of a heterodox 1650 treatise, *The Meritorious Price of Our Redemption*. Thus a "sect of most pure Puritans" figures in *The Crying of Lot 49* (1966), and Roger Mexico, in *Gravity's Rainbow*, deplores "the damned Calvinist insanity."[4] Here, too, Pynchon adapts and subverts certain Puritan doctrines: election, preterition and what he calls "orders behind the visible."[5]

Pynchon refers, too, to a number of works that do not actually exist: the journals of Father Fairing in *V.*, *The Courier's Tragedy* and *Cashiered* in *Lot 49*, *Alpdrücken* in *Gravity's Rainbow*, *The Ghastly Fop* in *Mason & Dixon*, the various adventures of the Chums of Chance in *Against the Day*. Insofar as these faux-texts, however outrageous or bizarre, commend themselves to at least momentary plausibility, they resemble the imaginary works that figure so often in the fictions of the Argentine master Jorge Luis Borges. They reveal, too, the erudition that Pynchon brings to pastiche. Each of these imaginary works distills some textual essence – often with a discernible model. Thus *Alpdrücken* contains, as it were, the whole of German expressionist film, and Diocletian Blobb's *Peregrinations* (in *Lot 49*) condenses the seventeenth-century travel writings of Thomas Coryat, Fynes Moryson and Peter Mundy. The Chums of Chance parody Tom Swift, identified at one point as their "colleague," and his predecessors, The Rover Boys.[6] *The Courier's Tragedy* compiles plot elements and stylistic features favored by Webster, Heywood, Marston, Ford and Massinger – the Jacobean playwrights of whose names 'Wharfinger' is an acrostic.

Not that Pynchon invokes only literary texts. He peppers his fictions with references to film, TV, cartoons and music of every stripe – from all those "German symphonies" sporting "both a number and a nickname" to Dion, Frank Zappa and the many others who convince him, as he declares in the *Slow Learner* introduction, that "rock 'n' roll will never die."[7] One of the running jokes in *Vineland* involves imagined biopics in which a film or television personality takes the role of some famous personage to whom she or he bears an uncanny resemblance: like the twinned image in a piece of Iceland spar ("the doubly-refracting calcite" frequently invoked in *Against the Day*), Pat Sajak stars in *The Frank Gorshin Story*, Woody Allen in *Young Kissinger* and so on.[8]

Culture wars redux

The quarrel between the ancients and the moderns survives today as a nagging doubt, on the part of some critics, regarding the legitimacy of a politicized standard of literary achievement. That is, some judge writers by their sensitivity to issues of race, gender and class, while others persist in preferring Oscar Wilde's simple criterion for excellence: "Books are well written, or badly written. That is all."[9] To determine a writer's place in literary history, in any event, one must consider the validity of current criteria for literary achievement and compare them to an older and perhaps more durable aesthetic chastened – where not elbowed aside altogether – by perspectivist thinking about canonicity. One can, as it happens, make the case for Pynchon either way.

Certainly he can lay claim to the traditional prerequisites of permanence: he writes beautifully and creates humane, insightful fictions that grapple resourcefully with history and the passions that make it. Shapely, sublime and verbally rich, his imagined worlds vie for legitimacy with what Tyrone Slothrop, in *Gravity's Rainbow*, calls "the authentic item."[10] Dispensing, early on, with traditional handling of character and plot, Pynchon eventually came to engage what in the introduction to *Slow Learner* he calls the "deeper, more shared levels of the life we all really live."[11] Early and late, however, his fictions merit the praise famously uttered by the Jane Austen heroine who defends the novel as a "work in which the greatest powers of the mind are displayed, in which the most thorough knowledge of human nature, the happiest delineation of its varieties, the liveliest effusions of wit and humour are conveyed to the world in the best-chosen language."[12] Happily, current criticism – for example, Elaine Scarry's *On Beauty and Being Just* (1999) – has begun to feel its way back into aesthetic categories that Austen's Catherine Morland would have recognized. Indeed, as a connoisseur of the Gothic, Catherine Morland would share Pynchon's appreciation of "beauty as Rilke defined it, the onset of terror just able to be borne."[13] The beautiful becomes intrinsic again to evaluation and judgment and merit.

At the same time, Pynchon's readers discern as much sensitivity to questions of race, gender, class and the colonial or postcolonial fate of "pigmented populations" as the politicized criticism of the age could wish.[14] Always sympathetic to the struggle of the colonized (as the reader sees in the Egypt and South-West Africa chapters of *V.*), Pynchon can take credit for insisting that the world remember what the Herero suffered in German South-West Africa in 1904. With great subtlety, Pynchon allows the Herero and Bastard communities in *V.* to remain virtually faceless amid the horrors perpetrated by their colonial masters – only to make his account of the hapless "Sarah" the more harrowing. In *Gravity's Rainbow*, Pynchon's sympathy for the oppressed or marginalized (he calls them the preterite, those passed over) leads him to an elaborate counter-Freudian play on the blackness of Enzian and his fellow *Schwarzkommando*. Erecting the great 00001 rocket just after VE Day, the black rocket troops reassert, among other things, the manhood compromised by their colonial history.

Pynchon represents ethnicity with great compassion, wit, subtlety – and a saving irreverence. In *Vineland* particularly Pynchon charms readers with clever experiments in the representation of ethnic accents in English – not to mention what the reader grasps as an English rendering of foreign speech. The explosive, exclamatory statements of the Japanese characters capture the quality of their language as experienced by Western patrons of art cinema. More common is the effect of foreign typography, spelling, diacritical marks and punctuation imported into English. Deft and aurally precise, this technique never becomes tendentious or patronizing. That is, even as Pynchon captures the locutions of Chicanos by writing "i" as "í" (or with Spanish-style bracketing question marks and exclamation points), he never descends to the Speedy Gonzalez/José Jiménez stereotype. That said, Hector or Vato is, in his way, every bit as comic as that travesty of Gallic naughtiness, the Marquis de Sod (the lawn entrepreneur of local TV commercials).

Depicting African Americans, on the other hand, Pynchon blends irreverence with warmth and sensitivity. Readers encounter Cleveland "Blood" Bonnefoy (another *Vineland* character); McClintic Sphere in *V.*; Carl Barrington, the imaginary friend, and McAfee, the musician, in "The Secret Integration"; and Gershom, George Washington's resourcefully impertinent slave in *Mason & Dixon* (at one point in that novel Jeremiah Dixon relieves a slave-driver of both whip and human property). Elsewhere, the author exposes stereotype and the subconscious dread behind it. Under the influence of sodium amythal, Tyrone Slothrop, in *Gravity's Rainbow*, becomes a self-disclosing *tabula* of bizarre racial fears: "'Good golly he sure is *all* asshole ain't he?' [...] 'Grab him 'fo' he gits away!' 'Yowzah!'"[15]

In all of his fictions, Pynchon scrutinizes history's omissions and misrepresentations. Nor does he neglect the history of letters. In his immense ambition and in the encyclopedic or Menippean energies he deploys, Pynchon performs the very idea of literature – from its primitive beginnings through the capillary branchings of postmodern and post-postmodern practice. By turns comic, satiric, ironic and romantic, he effortlessly shifts, too, between lyric and epic expression. *The Courier's Tragedy*, in *Lot 49*, reveals his grasp, even, of dramaturgy. A burlesque of Jacobean revenge drama, it is an especially assured performance, its language, its double couplets, its archaic diction, its assemblage of plot elements across a wide spectrum all conspiring to reveal an iceberg's worth of highly specialized literary knowledge. It also prompts consideration of whether Pynchon engages the possibilities of tragedy in a less antic vein. He seems in fact to defy the pundits who think the conditions of modern life inimical to real tragic elevation. To be sure, in *Gravity's Rainbow* one discerns nothing so splendid as tragedy in the unheroic fate of a Leni Pökler, who probably does not survive the Dora slave labor camp's liberation, or a Brigadier Pudding, who dies not with a bang – not at some grand moment of ambition frustrated or fated reversal – but literally with a whimper: "Me little Mary hurts."[16] From Victoria Wren to Webb Traverse and from Enzian to his half-brother Tchitcherine, however, Pynchon also presents figures who, in mythic stature and fate, rise to a tragic level. In their stories, readers may trace most of the features Aristotle laid out in the *Poetics*: the pity and fear, the elevated language, the moral stature of the protagonist, the flaw, the reversal and recognition. Like Sophocles, whose greatest tragic protagonist he feminizes as *Lot 49*'s Oedipa Maas, Pynchon shows the source of a nation's anguish in one oblivious heart.

Oedipa, like Oedipus, wanders an "infected city," herself the bacillus carried "to its far blood's branchings." [17]

The encyclopedic vision

Over thirty years ago, Edward Mendelson identified Pynchon as a writer of "encyclopedic" novels – fictions in which an author undertakes to treat her or his culture comprehensively.[18] Readers encounter Pynchon's encyclopedism in the guise of what Oedipa Maas, in *Lot 49*, calls "part of a plot, an elaborate, seduction, *plot*."[19] Pynchon seduces the reader with the promise of something like the big picture: read this book and you'll understand the age and its enormities. If in fact one does achieve considerable understanding, the insight takes an unexpected form. A Pynchon novel commonly stages for us the recognition of our hunger to know and understand. One learns, first, that the desire to know can be warped by the desire that the known take a certain congenial or at least comprehensible form. Beyond that painful recognition, however, lies something even more worth the knowing, which is the actual working of systems logic, whether the system be language or cosmos.

In the first part of his career, Pynchon develops wonderfully elaborate quest plots, predicated on recursivity. But none of Pynchon's novels ends with the grail possessed. Reified as V., the Trystero, the Rocket, the goal of each quest is knowledge that metastasizes and flees before the seeker. Thus the quest never ends, and in fact its goal becomes something like Jacques Derrida's "transcendental signified," whose "absence [...] extends the domain and the interplay of signification infinitely."[20] In *Lot 49*, Oedipa Maas rightly "wondered whether, at the end of this (if it were supposed to end) she too might not be left with only compiled memories of clues, announcements, intimations, but never the central truth itself, which must somehow each time be too bright for her memory to hold; which must always blaze out, destroying its own message irreversibly, leaving an overexposed blank when the ordinary world came back."[21] Like the knight of the grail quest romance, Oedipa (along with Herbert Stencil of *V.* and Tyrone Slothrop of *Gravity's Rainbow*), must ask the essential questions in the right way.

The quest becomes less perfectly self-sustaining in *Vineland*, which marks a turning point, a graduation, as it were, from the old mythopoesis. *Vineland*'s Prairie Wheeler is a transitional figure – in her relatively unproblematic mother search (a regendered Telemachiad) readers see the attenuation of the quest-plot that serves Pynchon so well in *V.*, *Lot 49* and *Gravity's Rainbow*. In his later works, Pynchon sets himself the task of engaging the world's complexities and the confusions of history without the safety net provided by the quest narrative. This is at once an explanation of the increasing difficulty of Pynchon (some reviewers found *Against the Day* unnecessarily taxing) and a measure of his integrity. Even in *Inherent Vice* (2009), which seems to embrace the conventions of detective novels, Pynchon foregoes the easy gratifications of linear narrative.

Yet one can still quite profitably read Pynchon against the critical economies of mid century – those contemporaneous with his formative years and early career. Names and movements would include M. H. Abrams (with whom Pynchon studied at Cornell), Joseph Campbell, the Chicago School (mentioned in the *Slow Learner* introduction), and such New Critics as Cleanth Brooks, who shares his first name with the protagonist of Pynchon's early story "Mortality and Mercy in Vienna" (1959), and R. W. B. Lewis, who recognized the importance of the American Adam archetype in the nation's literature (versions of this figure abound in Pynchon: Oedipa Maas, Tyrone Slothrop, Brock Vond, Mason and Dixon, the Traverses and perhaps even Benny Profane).

Northrop Frye (1912–91) remains an especially good thinker to match with Pynchon. Both are brilliant humanists with an immense range of erudition. In *The Anatomy of Criticism* (1957), which established itself as a critical juggernaut just as Pynchon, discharged from the navy, resumed his college education, Frye reintroduced the critical community to the strange genre known as Menippean satire – work characterized, from antiquity into modern times, by its ungainliness, its voluminous, encyclopedic ambitions, its scatology, its digressiveness and its descents into the fantastic. Frye named *The Golden Ass, Satyricon, Gargantua et Pantagruel, Candide, Gulliver's Travels* and *Tristram Shandy* as typical examples. The importance of such historicizing for contemporary letters was considerable. Like the Molière character who delights to learn that he has been speaking "prose" all his life, a number of novelists – John Barth, Robert Coover, William Gaddis and Joseph Heller, in addition to Pynchon – could congratulate themselves on being natural Menippean masters.

As complement to the Menippean, Frye also sketched the attributes of the encyclopedic. Everything he says about "encyclopaedic form," moreover, finds its mirror in Pynchon's work: "In the mythical mode the encyclopaedic form is the sacred scripture, and in the other modes we should expect to find encyclopaedic forms which constitute a series of increasingly human *analogies* of mythical or scriptural revelation."[22] Thus the narrator of *Gravity's Rainbow* invokes the "scholasticism" of "Rocket state-cosmology" and imagines "a rush of wind and fire" that will take believers "to the chambers of the Rocket throne," believers "who study the Rocket as Torah, letter by letter."[23] In the post-romantic imagination, says Frye, "the central episodic theme is the theme of the pure but transient vision, the aesthetic or time-less moment ... The comparison of such instants with the vast panorama unrolled by history ... is the main theme of the encyclopaedic tendency."[24] This visionary moment – commonly occulted by sobriety – takes various forms in Pynchon. In *Lot 49*, it is the epileptic's untranslatable epiphany – or simply that of an aged alcoholic: "She knew that the sailor had seen worlds no other men had seen if only because there was that high magic to low puns, because DT's must give access to dt's of spectra beyond the known sun, music made purely of Antarctic loneliness and fright."[25] This language and these tropes (he invokes the Antarctic with some frequency) figure repeatedly in Pynchon's novels. In *Gravity's Rainbow*, Pynchon evokes "the charismatic flash no Sunday-afternoon Agfa plate could ever bear, the print through the rippling solution each time flaring up to the same annihilating white."[26] On a much larger scale, the Soviet operative Vaslav Tchitcherine experiences the mysterious and never explained Kirghiz Light. From a "single great episode of light" to the "heavenwide blast" of the 1908 Tunguska Event in Siberia, Pynchon invokes more such episodes of radiant brightness in his vast 2006 novel *Against the Day*.[27] These mysterious phenomena anchor an epic meditation on the power of light itself – whether to obliterate or to illuminate.

Melville wrote only one truly encyclopedic novel (Maurice Blanchot speaks of *Moby-Dick*'s "offering itself as the written equivalent of the universe"), but Pynchon writes one after another. Replicating the cultural universe in words, he realizes a Borgesian fantasy.[28] He actually writes a succession of novels that are, as it were, volumes of a great and strange reference work – rather like the encyclopedia in Borges's story "Tlön, Uqbar, Orbis Tertius," which calls an imaginary world into existence. Thus Pynchon regales readers of *Mason & Dixon* with everything – or what seems like everything – about British North America in the mid eighteenth century. Readers of *Gravity's Rainbow* learn everything about the Faustian seductions of knowledge and power. In *Vineland* they contemplate everything about the 1960s from the dispiriting vantage of America's 1984. In *Lot 49* they explore centuries of postal history. In *Against the Day* they survey the arrival, all across the world, of the twentieth century. All of this began with what might be called the elliptical inclusivity of *V.*, in which Pynchon assembles that century in a fragmented, faux-modernist guise. The technique novelizes what Frye describes as the specifically modernist "practice of cutting out predication, of simply juxtaposing images without making any assertions about their relationship."[29] Of course, the reader who reassembles the fragments discovers a principle that gives the lie to many a modernist illusion: the need for coherence creates an illusion of coherence. The need for myth creates a myth that is factitious. No malign female entity actually "explains" a chaotic and bloody age; neither Trystero nor Rocket anchors or legitimizes our burgeoning paranoia. Nor do the myths of the real world have anything like the universal validity they seemed to present to the moderns, fresh from their readings of Sir James George Frazer, Jane Harrison and other mythographers. As the narrator of Oakley Hall's 1958 novel *Warlock* observes, "The human animal is set apart from other beasts by his infinite capacity for creating fictions."[30] A long-time admirer of *Warlock*, Pynchon observes and ironically participates in this mythopoesis.

One considers Pynchon's place in literary history, then, at almost exactly half a century since publication of his first novel, *V.*, in 1963. Pynchon made his presence felt roughly six months ahead of Lee Harvey Oswald and his violent self-insertion into history (through what Don DeLillo, twenty-five years later, would call "the seven seconds that broke the back of the American century").[31] Although heads of state had been assassinated before (as Pynchon repeatedly shows in *Against the Day*), Oswald augured things to come, and some would say he ushered in postmodernity itself. If artists have a prophetic function, one credits a remarkable prescience to the author of *V.*, who put his finger, early in 1963, on a pulse that had scarcely begun to throb. Successive fictions seemed also to reflect the spirit of the times. In 1966, publication of *The Crying of Lot 49* coincided with Derrida's presentation of "Structure, Sign and Play in the Discourse of the Human Sciences" at the "Languages of Criticism and the Sciences" conference at Johns Hopkins. The year that saw the World Trade Center dedicated, 1973, also saw publication of *Gravity's Rainbow*. Its opening pages, an elaborate fantasy of escaping a great building that has been bombed, take on fresh meaning after 9/11; the same goes for the closing pages, in which an imagined missile drops toward another building full of people. Pynchon's great novel came out, in fact, in a year characterized by Andreas Killen as "a cultural watershed, a moment of major realignments and shifts in American politics, culture, and society."[32] *Vineland*, which looks back at the 1960s from the vantage of a Reagan-ridden 1984, bears the publication date 1990 but appeared in bookstores at the end of 1989, the year that saw the breaching of the Berlin Wall and the end, many would say, of the Cold War. *Mason & Dixon* appeared in 1997, half way through the Clinton presidency. *Against the Day* appeared in 2006, three years into the second Iraq war. *Inherent Vice* came out in 2009, the year the first black president took office in the United States.

Logging each succeeding Pynchon novel against its historical moment, one discerns intimations of synchronicity. But do Pynchon's successive fictions in fact coincide with, comment on, or even anticipate events charged with millennial significance – or does the literary historian merely wish it so? This question – random vs. patterned – lies at the heart of the Pynchon aesthetic, as it happens. The author devotes a long passage in his first novel to a simple but compelling catalogue of the disasters that took place in a single year (as gleaned, the narrator observes, from an almanac). His point: that the random discloses no patterns. By the same token, just as postmodernism itself evolves from gauge of sixties paranoia to more subtle engagement with a critical moment in history, the matching of books and public events reveals significance only to those predisposed to entrail-reading. But the symptomatic temptation – or desire – to see a pattern finds its mirror in hermeneutics itself. Just as humanity manufactures shapely narratives and other fictions of coherence about history and the human condition, so may readers find more to Pynchon's prescience than is perhaps there. Even the most subtle readers stand ever ready to discover in texts the messages they consider most enlightened or congenial – or timely. This tendency has given us various avatars: atheistic Pynchon, religious Pynchon, Marxist Pynchon, Pynchon the Amerian visionary, Pynchon the iconoclast, modern Pynchon, postmodern Pynchon, post-postmodern Pynchon and so on. The irony is that, in good postmodern fashion, all of these are true.

Now everybody –

This discussion began with reflections on Pynchon's antecedents, the American and world writers the author read and admired and matched himself against – it would be fitting to conclude with those whom, however indirectly and at whatever distance, he mentors. At times he must figure as a daunting presence. But younger writers seem grateful for the path forged through a culture's tangled historical thicket – and for the inspiring example of a wonderfully flexible style in which to register their age and its confusion. They seek not to smash this literary rock but to come in under its shadow.

Twenty years or so younger than the master, Richard Powers (b. 1957), William Vollmann (b. 1959) and David Foster Wallace (1962–2008) have seemed most obviously to be consolidating the Pynchon manner, extending the "encyclopedic" range of his subject matter. Admittedly Wallace, best known for his vast and magisterial *Infinite Jest* (1996), on occasion expressed discomfort at the inevitable comparisons of his work and that of Pynchon. The prolific Vollmann, on the other hand, seems completely undaunted by this terrible father. A National Book Award winner for *Europe Central* (2005), he has authored an immense number of books, both fiction and non-fiction. Of special note is his series of novels on encounters between native Americans and Europeans, *Seven Dreams*, of which four out of a projected seven volumes have appeared (they begin with *The Ice Shirt* [1990] and run, thus far, to 2,600 pages). Part of an emergent apostolic succession, these writers affect the catalogue, the anatomy, the grand Homeric list. Occasionally – notably in Powers – readers encounter the homage direct: the narrator of *Galatea 2.2* (1995), for example, mentions having read *Gravity's Rainbow* in high school. The sensitive but feckless Franklin Todd, in *The Gold Bug Variations* (1991), salutes Pynchon as his favorite living novelist. The protagonist of *Generosity: An Enhancement* (2009) falls asleep and "dreams himself into a Pynchon novel, with an international cartel trading in the arcane incunabula hidden in people's cells. His own sperm carries a sequence on the *Index Librorum Prohibitorum* ..."[33] Possibly more polymath than Pynchon himself, Powers bridges C. P. Snow's Two Cultures in virtually every paragraph.[34]

The Summer 2005 issue of *Bookforum* provides space for a number of Pynchon's successors (and a handful of contemporaries, including DeLillo, Tom Robbins, Gerald Howard) to express their admiration and, to varying degrees, indebtedness. As represented here, the Tribe of Pyn includes not only Robert Polito (b. 1951), Kathryn Kramer (b. 1953), Carter Scholz (b. 1953), Erik Davis (b. 1967), Jim Shepard (b. 1956) and Andrew Hultkrans (b. 1966), but also Lydia Davis (b. 1947), much praised for her *Collected Stories* (2009); Jay Cantor (b. 1948), author of *Krazy Kat* (1988); Percival Everett (b. 1956), author of *Wounded* (2005); Lorrie Moore (b. 1957), author of *A Gate at the Stairs* (2009); George Saunders (b. 1958), author of *Pastoralia* (2001); Joanna Scott (b. 1960), author of *Tourmaline* (2002); Jeffrey Eugenides (b. 1960), author of *Middlesex* (2002); and Rick Moody (b. 1961), author of *The Ice Storm* (1994). Other testimonials include those of Steve Erickson ("[f]or American literature in the last half of the twentieth century, Pynchon is the line in the sand that Faulkner was in the first half"), Trey Ellis ("Pynchon ... describes the modern condition so accurately that all other novelists ... owe him our creative lives") and Emily Barton, who "in college ... sang in a band named ... Imipolex G" for a very special fabric in *Gravity's Rainbow* ("I couldn't write as I do without reckoning with his optimistic cynicism or his perverse understanding of history").[35]

Pynchon's place in literary history will depend, to some degree, on the achievement of those he inspires. It will also depend on the long-term viability of the postmodern aesthetic he helped to found in 1963. The genius of postmodernism may lie in its ability to alternate – for some decades now – between the marginal and the mainstream. Frequently pronounced moribund or superannuated by something clumsily interpellated as "post-postmodern," it seems, rather, to shapeshift in step with an age still confused about authority, referentiality in the sign, and the distinction between story and history. In film, in television, in politics and public discourse, in literature high and low, and even in children's entertainments, postmodernism seems increasingly a default mode, something woven into the very fabric of the cultural moment. Now and in the future, in any event, anyone wishing to ride the millennial interface will need to engage the thinking of Thomas Pynchon.

NOTES

1 Thomas Pynchon, *Gravity's Rainbow* (New York: Viking, 1973), p. 537.
2 Steven Weisenburger, "Thomas Pynchon: A Recovered Autobiographical Sketch," *American Literature*, 62.4 (1990), 692–97. This document is no longer publically available.
3 Thomas Pynchon, "Introduction," *Slow Learner* (Boston: Little, Brown, 1984), pp. 7, 14.
4 Thomas Pynchon, *The Crying of Lot 49* (Philadelphia: Lippincott, 1966), p. 155; Pynchon, *Gravity's Rainbow*, p. 57.
5 Pynchon, *Gravity's Rainbow*, p. 188.
6 Thomas Pynchon, *Against the Day* (New York: Penguin, 2006), p. 794.
7 Pynchon, *Lot 49*, p. 18; Pynchon, *Slow Learner*, p. 23.
8 Pynchon, *Against the Day*, p. 114.
9 Oscar Wilde, *The Artist As Critic: Critical Writings of Oscar Wilde* (New York: Random House, 1969), p. 235.
10 Pynchon, *Gravity's Rainbow*, p. 184.
11 Pynchon, *Slow Learner*, p. 21.
12 Jane Austen, *Northanger Abbey*, in R. W. Chapman (ed.), *The Novels of Jane Austen*, v: *Northanger Abbey and Persuasion* (New York: Oxford, 1933), p. 38.
13 Thomas Pynchon, "Foreword," in George Orwell, *Nineteen Eighty-Four* (New York: Plume, 2003), p. xx.
14 Thomas Pynchon, *V.* (Philadelphia: Lippincott, 1963), p. 245.
15 Pynchon, *Gravity's Rainbow*, p. 64.
16 *Ibid.*, p. 533.
17 Pynchon, *Lot 49*, p. 117.
18 See Edward Mendelson, "Gravity's Encyclopedia," in George Levine and David Leverenz (eds.), *Essays on Thomas Pynchon* (Boston: Little, Brown, 1976), pp. 161–95.
19 Pynchon, *Lot 49*, p. 31.
20 Jacques Derrida, *Writing and Difference* (University of Chicago Press, 1978), p. 280.
21 Pynchon, *Lot 49*, p. 95.
22 Northrop Frye, *Anatomy of Criticism: Four Essays* (Princeton University Press, 1957), pp. 322, 56. Note the similar account on p. 315.
23 Pynchon, *Gravity's Rainbow*, pp. 726, 727.
24 Frye, *Anatomy*, p. 61.
25 Pynchon, *Lot 49*, p. 129.

26 Pynchon, *Gravity's Rainbow*, p. 579.
27 Pynchon, *Against the Day*, pp. 165, 779.
28 Maurice Blanchot, *Faux Pas* (Stanford University Press, 2001), p. 239.
29 Frye, *Anatomy*, p. 61.
30 Oakley Hall, *Warlock* (New York: Viking, 1958), p. 388. Pynchon wrote a brief appreciation of this novel a few years after it came out. See "A Gift of Books," *Holiday*, 38.6 (1965), 164–65.
31 Don DeLillo, *Libra* (New York: Viking, 1988), p. 181.
32 Andreas Killen, *1973 Nervous Breakdown: Watergate, Warhol, and the Birth of Post-Sixties America* (New York: Bloomsbury, 2006), p. 51.
33 Richard Powers, *Generosity: An Enhancement* (New York: Farrar, Straus and Giroux, 2009), p. 169.
34 See C. P. Snow, *The Two Cultures: And a Second Look: An Expanded Version of The Two Cultures and the Scientific Revolution* (Cambridge University Press, 1964).
35 These remarks appear as boxed text in a special section, "Pynchon from A to V," *Bookforum* (Summer 2005), pp. 36, 38, 40.

7

BRIAN MCHALE

Pynchon's postmodernism

Period concepts are moving targets, elusive and malleable, none more so than "postmodernism." When did postmodernism begin (if it ever did), and has it ended yet? Is there a postmodern period style, and if so, what are its features? Is it a specifically aesthetic category, or does it apply to culture and society generally? These and other questions remain literally debatable and unresolved, perhaps unresolvable. Postmodernism has been characterized a multitude of ways, some compatible with each other, others not.[1] No matter how it is characterized, however, the fiction of Thomas Pynchon appears to be universally regarded as central to its canon. For instance, on the first page of his landmark essay on postmodernism, Fredric Jameson includes Pynchon – inevitably, it would seem – on his shortlist of exemplary postmodernists, alongside Andy Warhol, John Cage, Phillip Glass, William Burroughs, Ishmael Reed, the French *nouveaux romanciers* and others.[2] Indeed, so ubiquitous is Pynchon in the discourses about postmodernism that we might go so far as to say, not that postmodern theory depends on Pynchon's fiction for exemplification, but that, without Pynchon's fiction, there might never have been such a pressing need to develop a theory of literary postmodernism in the first place.

Among the many theories of postmodernism, a few have come to seem indispensable, not because they are incontestable or uncontroversial, but because they empower us to frame useful working hypotheses about specific texts, genres and aesthetic or cultural practices. Adapting a distinction developed in modernist studies, we might differentiate between theories of postmodern*ism* – the aesthetic forms and practices of the postmodern period – and theories of postmodern*ity* – the historical and cultural conditions that presumably gave rise to those forms and practices. For instance, Jean-François Lyotard's account of the postmodern condition is a theory of postmodern*ity*, with important consequences for aesthetic forms and practices; so, too, is Jean Baudrillard's theory of simulation. Accounts of double-coding by Charles Jencks and others, or of postmodern irony and pastiche, or Linda Hutcheon's account of historiographic metafiction, are all in the first place theories of postmodern*ism*, though they perhaps imply a general condition of culture and society; so, too, is my own account of an ontological poetics of postmodern fiction. Most comprehensive of all is Jameson's theory, which straddles the distinction between postmodernity and postmodernism, offering an account of specific forms and practices that is also a general theory of the postmodern condition. Whether we consider theories of postmodernity or theories of postmodernism, however, Pynchon remains central, as even the briefest sampling of theoretical approaches will confirm.

Some postmodern*ities*

Incredulity. In an early (1979) and enormously influential account, Lyotard identified the postmodern condition with a general incredulity toward the master narratives that up until now had underwritten and sustained modern culture and society in the West.[3] We no longer place our faith, he claimed, in the narratives of progress, enlightenment and human liberation that served to legitimate modernity. Skeptical of such "grand narratives," we postmoderns instead value the self-legitimating language-games, or little narratives (*petits récits*), of local groups, particular institutions and sub-cultural enclaves. Although Lyotard himself has little to say directly about the consequences of postmodern incredulity for aesthetic practices, his theory animates Hutcheon's account of historiographic metafiction, the genre of skeptical, self-reflective historical fiction that she associates with literary postmodernism.[4] If incredulity toward master narratives constitutes the postmodern condition, then historiographic metafiction is something like its ideal vehicle of literary expression.

All of Pynchon's novels qualify as historiographic metafictions, including his novels of contemporary reality, *The Crying of Lot 49* (1966), *Vineland* (1990).[5] Pynchon's fiction relentlessly questions and undermines all of the West's master narratives: the narrative of Enlightenment in *Mason & Dixon* (1997) and elsewhere; of technological and scientific progress in *Gravity's Rainbow* (1973); of liberal optimism and the Hegelian dialectic of history in *V.* (1963) and *Against the Day* (2006); of empire and American manifest destiny in *V.*, *Mason & Dixon* and *Against the Day*; and so on. Pynchon's postmoderns, like Lyotard's, place their faith in the little narratives that sustain small-scale separatist cultural enclaves, such as the diverse undergrounds that come to light in the course of *The Crying of Lot 49*, the anarchic Counterforce of *Gravity's Rainbow*, the convents and the anarchist or drop-out enclaves of *Vineland* and *Against the Day*, even the ephemeral workers' utopia of the Becker-Traverse picnic at the end of *Vineland*. If one sought a model of what Lyotard's postmodern condition, fully realized, would look like, one could start with the Zone of *Gravity's Rainbow* – the space of anarchic freedom, multiplicity and social improvisation that opens up in Germany between the fall of the Third Reich and the consolidation of the Occupation – or the patchwork of micro-worlds making up subjunctive America in *Mason & Dixon* (see below).

Simulation. Equally influential, though differently oriented, originating in media studies, is Baudrillard's theory of simulation and the precession of simulacra, which has come to be identified with postmodernity.[6] By "precession of simulacra," Baudrillard means that images of reality, especially mass-media images – what we used to think of as *re*-presentations of reality – have come increasingly to precede and pre-empt reality itself, so that we experience the image – the simulacrum – before and even instead of the reality. A classic case (appropriately fictional) is the "most photographed barn in America" in Don DeLillo's *White Noise* (1985), a site worth photographing only because others have already photographed it; the simulacrum pre-empts the thing itself.[7] Everything in a mass-mediated social order is simulacral, including terrorism and war – which is not to say that either of these is any less lethal in postmodernity, but only that they are inscribed in advance, pre-emptively, in the mass-media that supposedly "cover" them. Presciently, Baudrillard, seems to anticipate, decades before the fact, our own era of reality television and celebrities famous for being famous.

Simulacra precede and pre-empt reality already in Pynchon's *The Crying of Lot 49*, where real lawyers and televised simulations of lawyers exchange roles, and the reality of San Narciso is doubled and pre-empted by television advertising. This tendency in Pynchon's fiction peaks two and a half decades later, in *Vineland*, where the precession of simulacra has fatally compromised reality. Here characters conform their own behavior, and their expectations about others and about the world at large, to television models; they allow the genre conventions of cop shows, sitcoms, soap operas, movies-of-the-week, and so on, to shape their lived realities. Similarly, in *Inherent Vice* (2009), a companion-novel to *Vineland*, Doc Sportello models himself on the private detectives of genre fiction. Most consequentially, however, Hollywood-movie simulacra literally pre-empt the reality of *Gravity's Rainbow*, not just locally, in scenes modeled on war movies, musical comedy song-and-dance numbers, Hollywood romances, and so on, but also globally when the entire narrative world is revealed retrospectively to have been the world of a movie.

Decentering. Another powerful theory of postmodernity reflects the impact of the postmodern condition on individual subjectivity. Where modernists explored the alienation of the individual subject, postmodernists, registering the implications of poststructuralist theory (contemporary with postmodernism, but not necessarily identical to it), sought to capture the experience of fragmentation or decentering of the subject. Jameson, for instance, sees the peculiar disjointedness of many characteristic postmodern artworks, their tendency to disintegrate into "a rubble of distinct and unrelated signifiers," as a consequence and correlative of the decentering of the postmodern subject.[8] He goes so far as to compare postmodernism, perhaps ill-advisedly, to schizophrenia.[9]

Even more so than with other varieties of postmodernity, here Pynchon is the inevitable reference. The elusive Lady V., object of Stencil's quest in Pynchon's first novel, is physically disassembled, literalizing the theoretical motif of the fragmented, decentered subject. V., however, offers little more than a rough draft for the spectacular disintegration of *Gravity's Rainbow*'s Tyrone Slothrop, who is "sent into the Zone to be present at his own assembly – perhaps, heavily paranoid voices have whispered, *his time's assembly*," but ends up "being broken down instead, and scattered."[10] Notoriously, by the time we reach the novel's final, radically disjointed and centrifugal episodes, "it's doubtful if [Slothrop] can ever be 'found' again, in the conventional sense of 'positively identified and detained.'"[11] If decentered subjectivity is the postmodern condition, then Slothrop is its poster child.

In Jameson's account, decentered subjectivity is generally negative in its consequences, associated with schizophrenic breaks, but this is not inevitably the case. One might also imagine oppositional and liberatory possibilities for decentered subjectivity, as in Donna Haraway's model of the cyborg subject – a hybrid subject, neither all-natural nor all-artificial, neither all-self nor all-other, and (crucially for Haraway's feminist politics) neither all-female nor all-male, but a composite, pieced together, and therefore capable of offering resistance to forms of domination that require individuals to be self-identical, one thing or another. "The cyborg," Haraway writes, "is a kind of disassembled and reassembled postmodern collective and personal self."[12] Cyborg figures in Pynchon's fiction are mainly negative; think of Bongo-Shaftsbury, the sinister assassin in *V.*, with the electric throw-switch sewn into the flesh of his arm, or Gottfried integrated into the apparatus of the rocket's warhead in *Gravity's Rainbow*, or Hector Zuñiga in *Vineland*, literally wedded to his television. But there are also a few sympathetic cyborgs, mainly machines aspiring to (partial) humanity, ranging from SHOCK and SHROUD, the animate crash-test dummies of *V.*, to Vaucanson's mechanical duck in *Mason & Dixon*, which not only attains intelligence and autonomy, but flies away to freedom.

Some postmodern*isms*

Double-coding. Of all the theories of postmodernism as an aesthetic practice, surely the best-known and most influential is the thesis that, in the postmodern era, the distinction between high culture and mass or popular culture that the modernists had striven so hard to maintain and police has finally, definitively broken down. This thesis, articulated with considerable intellectual rigor by Andreas Huyssen, attained broad public recognition through the efforts of the architecture critic Charles Jencks, a consummate salesman of the idea of postmodernism.[13] It is Jencks who is responsible for the notion of double-coding. Postmodern buildings, he argues, communicate on two different levels, to two different constituencies at once: on one level, through their modernist structural techniques and in-group ironies, they communicate with a minority constituency of architects and connoisseurs; on another level, they reach a broader public of consumers through their playful and pleasurable allusions to familiar historical styles of architecture.[14] Jencks saw analogies to his notion of architectural double-coding in postmodern literary manifestoes by John Barth and Umberto Eco, and in artistic practices across a range of postmodern art forms including, for instance, Eco's own novel *The Name of the Rose* (1980), which is simultaneously an exemplary historiographic metafiction (in Hutcheon's sense) and a popular bestseller.[15] Larry McCaffery, another able propagandist, coined the term "avant-pop" to label the kind of double-coded works that straddle or collapse the distinction between avant-garde experimentalism and popular culture.[16]

The notion of double-coding helps explain the paradox of Pynchon's status as simultaneously the object of academic research, widely taught in university courses, and a countercultural writer with a popular "cult" following.[17] Pynchon's fiction displays avant-garde difficulty and high-cultural allusiveness, and calls upon readers to bring to bear more or less esoteric knowledge from a range of demanding specialist fields. But its high-cultural demands are counterbalanced by low-cultural entertainment value. Pynchon's novels offer all kinds of "mindless pleasures" (the original title of the book that became *Gravity's Rainbow*): silly names and tasteless puns ("there was that high magic to low puns," Oedipa muses in *The Crying of Lot 49*), flagrant anachronism, cartoonish characters, abundant slapstick comedy, chase scenes, pornography (especially in *Gravity's Rainbow* and *Against the Day*, but also in the "V. in Love" episode of *V.*), pop-song lyrics and musical comedy song-and-dance numbers, and so on.[18] Especially characteristic of Pynchon is the unstable, disorienting interaction of his complex style with models derived from popular genre fiction, movies and television (see below): the very definition of avant-pop.

Irony and pastiche. The postmodern attitude, according to the fiction writer Max Apple, is "a mixture of world weariness and cleverness, an attempt to make you think that I'm half kidding, though you're not quite sure about what"[19] – an ironic attitude, in short, but involving irony of a peculiarly unfocused or unmoored kind. The postmodern period style, it is generally acknowledged, is ironic; but then, so was the modernist period style before it. How does postmodernist irony differ from the modernist kind? Alan Wilde argues that modernist irony was disjunctive; striving to recover an ideal integration and coherence, it acknowledged the disconnectedness of things, and sought at least to control disconnection even if it could not ultimately resolve it. Postmodern irony, by contrast, is suspensive: it "simply (or not so simply)" accepts "the world in all its disorder," abandoning the quest for integration altogether.[20] Akin to this understanding of postmodern irony is Jameson's highly influential concept of postmodern pastiche, the imitation of a style or genre without any of the satirical pointedness that characterizes parody. Pastiche is neutral mimicry, lacking parody's ulterior motives – "blank parody," as Jameson famously puts it.[21] Postmodern suspensive irony is to irony as pastiche is to parody, one might say.

The ironies in Pynchon's novels are varied and complex, but many of them are suspensive in Wilde's sense. When we encounter the sorts of cues that in any other novel would trigger ironic reading – silly naming, for instance, or flagrant anachronism – we are often compelled to wonder what exactly the point of Pynchon's irony might be. Sometimes, when there appears to be little at stake, we simply enjoy the gag and let it go at that, but at other moments the stakes are higher. When, for instance, in *Mason & Dixon*, Pynchon anachronistically attributes the clothing style and speech patterns of a 1990s Goth chick to a Brooklyn milkmaid of the 1760s, we laugh and move on; but when, at one of the novel's moments of high seriousness, involving Dixon's confrontation with American slavery, Pynchon gives a Baltimore slave driver children anachronistically named Tiffany and Jason, we have to wonder what exactly is at stake.[22] Pynchon appears to be half kidding here, but about what?

Pastiches of genre styles – blank parodies, in Jameson's sense – abound in Pynchon's fiction. Various high-modernist styles are pastiched in the course of *V.* Spy novels are pastiched in "Under the Rose" (a story recycled as a chapter of *V.*), and again later on in *Gravity's Rainbow*, and later still in *Against the Day*. Hollywood war movies and Jacobean revenge tragedy are pastiched in *The Crying of Lot 49*. The whole gamut of forties movie genres is pastiched in *Gravity's Rainbow* – war movies, musical comedies, romance, horror movies and animated cartoons, as well as superhero comics and radio shows. A similar range of eighties television genres is pastiched in

Vineland. Mason & Dixon is a wall-to-wall pastiche of eighteenth-century comic-picaresque fiction, with excursions into other genres of the same era (captivity narrative, Gothic novel, etc.). Hardboiled detective fiction and film noir are pastiched in *Inherent Vice*. *Against the Day*, in particular, amounts to an anthology of early twentieth-century entertainment fiction, including genres such as dime-novel westerns, juvenile adventure of the "Tom Swift" type, spy "shockers," detective stories of both the Edwardian and hardboiled types, scientific romance, African and Polar adventure fiction, college novels – a virtual library of pastiche.

Another poetics of postmodernism, or, Pynchon's worlds

Accounts of literary postmodernism almost invariably contrast postmodernist practice with modernism – unsurprisingly, perhaps, since some sort of relationship with modernism is inscribed in the very term "postmodernism" itself. Thus, modernism polices the boundary between high and popular culture, while postmodernism collapses that distinction; modernism practices disjunctive irony and pointed parody, while postmodern irony is suspensive and postmodern pastiche is "blank"; and so on. In every case, Pynchon's practice can be aligned with the postmodernist side of the opposition; or, the other way around, Pynchon is one of the writers whose practice compels us to recognize that there *is* a postmodernist poetics distinct from modernism. Another version of postmodernism, my own, focuses on a different aspect of modernism and its transformation by postmodernists.[23] In this case, too, Pynchon's practice is exemplary.

My thesis is that postmodernism is subject to a different dominant than modernism.[24] Modernist narrative fiction is dominated by issues that could be grouped under the heading of epistemology (theory of knowledge). Its techniques and devices are generally geared toward investigating human perception and cognition, differences in perspective, the subjective experience of time, the circulation and (un)reliability of knowledge, and so on. Postmodernist fiction, by contrast, is dominated by ontology (theory of being). Its characteristic techniques and devices are designed to explore issues of fictionality, modes of being and the differences among them, the nature and plurality of worlds, how such worlds are made and unmade, and so on. In shorthand: where modernism was a poetics of epistemology, postmodernism is a poetics of ontology.

Literary-historical change rarely involves the wholesale replacement of outmoded features and values by new ones, but more typically involves a reshuffling of existing features in the light of a new dominant function. Responding to changes in the world at large (such as the onset of late capitalism, in Jameson's terms) as well as the internal dynamics of literary history, dominants shift; what had formerly been foregrounded recedes to the background, while background elements advance to the foreground. Modernist features persist in postmodern narratives, but subject to a different dominant.

Modernist epistemological quests – quests for knowledge and certainty – still structure *V.* and *The Crying of Lot 49*; however, these quests remain unresolved, and the questing detective is left in limbo. By the time of *Gravity's Rainbow*, modernist problems of epistemology are subject to a new dominant. Slothrop's double epistemological quest – to discover the fate of Rocket 00000 and to uncover the truth of his own upbringing – is undertaken in a world that proves to be so volatile and indeterminate, so plural, that the quest is rendered moot; indeed, as we have seen, the questing detective himself disintegrates. Henceforth, the dominant of all subsequent Pynchon novels will be ontological (though detective-story epistemological questing does return in *Inherent Vice*). Many of Pynchon's characteristic techniques and devices serve to foreground issues of ontology – of worlds and being in those worlds – including strategies for pluralizing worlds; strategies for proliferating levels of reality internal to the storyworld; strategies for suspending reality between literal and figurative status; and strategies for exposing to view, and troubling, the very process of bringing worlds into being.

Plurality of worlds. All narratives produce multiple possible worlds – potential states of affairs, subjective realities, plans, expectations, speculations, dreams, fantasies; but these are normally subordinated to a single actual world, which they orbit like satellites. Pynchon's novels proliferate such potential and subjective alternative realities. His characters are exceptionally prone to fantasize and hallucinate (e.g., Prentice, Slothrop, Enzian and Tchitcherine, among others, in *Gravity's Rainbow*; Doc Sportello in *Inherent Vice*) and to dream (e.g., Mason in *Mason & Dixon*); moreover, it is often difficult to determine where fantasy, hallucination or dream leaves off and reality begins. Beyond proliferating subjective realities, Pynchon's novels also multiply objective (or apparently objective) alternative worlds – "lost" worlds, parallel worlds, passages between worlds, visitations from other worlds, and so on – juxtaposing them and exploring the tensions between them.

Pynchon's "lost" worlds – some of them sought but never found, others actually visited – include Vheissu in *V.*, the Hollow Earth in *Mason & Dixon* and *Against the Day*, Shambala in *Against the Day*, and Lemuria in *Inherent Vice*. Among his parallel, alternative or lateral worlds are the heterotopian multi-world space of the Zone in *Gravity's Rainbow*; the Thanatoid village and Tsorrek, the world of the dead, in *Vineland*; the "Delaware Triangle" (also called "The Wedge") and the eleven days lost to calendrical reform in *Mason & Dixon*; and, in *Against the Day*, the "lateral solutions" into which the Chums of Chance drift at Candlebrow University, and the Counter-Earth to which they voyage near the novel's end.

The Golden Gate Bridge serves as a kind of passage between worlds in *Vineland*; crossing it, we are told, "represents a transition in the metaphysics of the region."[25] In *Against the Day*, the Straits of Gibraltar and the Prophet's Gate near Kashgar in Inner Asia are both portals between worlds; so, too, evidently, is a water-logged construction site in *Inherent Vice*. Lew Basnight is apparently blown from one world into another in *Against the Day*.

Miraculous visitations from other worlds recur throughout Pynchon's fiction – "miraculous" in the sense of "anarchist miracle" which, as we learn in *The Crying of Lot 49*, is "another world's intrusion into this one," "a kiss of cosmic pool balls."[26] Examples include the angels and the other forms of otherworldly visitation that abound in *Gravity's Rainbow*; Mason's ghostly hauntings and the various wilderness apparitions of *Mason & Dixon*; the time-traveling Trespassers of *Against the Day*; and many others.[27] Akin to these visitations from other worlds are cameo appearances by historical figures who have, as it were, strayed from history into fiction – e.g., Walter Rathenau and Mickey Rooney in *Gravity's Rainbow*, Benjamin Franklin, George Washington, Thomas Jefferson in *Mason & Dixon*, Nikola Tesla and Bela Lugosi in *Against the Day* – as well as the migration of characters from one novel to another across the Pynchon canon – Clayton "Bloody" Chiclitz from *The Crying of Lot 49* to *Gravity's Rainbow*, Takeshi Fumimota from *Gravity's Rainbow* to *Vineland*, Melanie L'Heuremaudit from *V.* to *Against the Day*, and so on.

Strange loops. The narrative world can be pluralized, and ontology foregrounded, not only by juxtaposing worlds but also by layering or stacking them, for instance by nesting one plane of narrative reality inside another – a narrator at one level tells a story in which a second-order narrator in turn tells a story, and so on, potentially ad infinitum; or by describing an artwork (real or invented) belonging to a different medium – a painting, play, movie, etc. – thereby *re*mediating it. The most complex case of stacking or layering of narrative levels in Pynchon's fiction occurs in *Mason & Dixon*, where the Reverend Wicks Cherrycoke narrates the adventures of Mason and Dixon, while secondary narrators who occupy the same level as Mason and Dixon narrate further, doubly inset stories. Remediation (also called, with reference to paintings, ekphrasis) occurs conspicuously in *The Crying of Lot 49*, which remediates a (real) painting by Remedios Varo, a war movie broadcast on television, and the performance of a Jacobean revenge tragedy. Internal proliferation through stacking and remediation creates opportunities for a variety of paradoxes that further foreground the storyworld's ontology: metalepses, when the boundary between ontological levels is violated or overrun; strange loops, when an inset or nested world proves to be continuous with the primary world that frames it; *trompe l'oeil*, when an inset level is mistaken for the primary level; and *mise en abyme*, when an inset text or artwork mirrors the primary narrative.

Metaleptic violations of narrative levels occur (or threaten to occur) throughout *Gravity's Rainbow*, whenever the narrator (who is heterodiegetic, i.e., he does not exist at the level of the novel's world) appears to address the characters, at a lower level than his, or the reader, at a higher level.[28] For example, "Caught *you* with your hand in your pants! Go on, show us all what you were doing or leave the area, we don't need your kind around," and "Check out Ishmael Reed. He knows more about it than you'll ever find here."[29] As for Pynchon's strange loops, the strangest of them, arguably, involves "The Captive's Tale" in *Mason & Dixon*. The events of the "Captive's Tale" seem to be pitched at the same narrative level as Mason and Dixon's adventures, and indeed the tale's heroine and her protector eventually join Mason and Dixon's party. But "The Captive's Tale" also forms an episode of the Gothic novel *The Ghastly Fop*, which characters throughout *Mason & Dixon*, at all levels, are reading. So the Captive and her tale exist both at a primary level and at an inset level: a strange loop. "The chances for any paradox here, really, are less than you think," the narrator of *Gravity's Rainbow* assures us in an analogous situation, when the Floundering Four are revealed to be spectators of their own onstage adventures.[30] He is bluffing: in both cases, the chances for paradox are very good indeed.

Similarly paradoxical, though in a slightly different way, are the opening events of *Gravity's Rainbow* – which we initially assume to be occurring in the real world, but which prove to be Pirate Prentice's nightmare – and the end of the same novel, when the entire world of *Gravity's Rainbow* is revealed retrospectively to be a movie which we – "old fans who've always been at the movies" – have been watching.[31] In other words, these are instances of *trompe l'oeil*, a trick by which we are induced to mistake events at one level of reality for events at another. Finally, instances of *mise en abyme* – inset texts or remediated artworks that duplicate, in whole or in part, the primary narrative itself – include *Bordando el manto terrestre*, the Remedios Varo painting from *The Crying of Lot 49*, and *The Courier's Tragedy*, the remediated Jacobean play from the same novel; and, from *Against the Day*, the *Chums of Chance* novels that are mentioned throughout (including *The Chums of Chance at the Ends of the Earth*, read at one point by Reef Traverse), Professor Renfrew's "Map of the World," and

The Book of the Masked, all of which mirror aspects of *Against the Day* itself.

Figurative worlds. Metaphors and related figures of speech normally involve one element that belongs to the text's real world (the tenor of the metaphor) and another that does not (its vehicle); but works of postmodern fiction, including Pynchon's novels, often trouble the hierarchy of presence and absence in figurative language, making it difficult to distinguish what is literally there from what is merely figurative. This difficulty arises for Oedipa Maas in *The Crying of Lot 49* when she encounters John Nefastis's thermodynamically impossible machine, which literalizes Maxwell's Demon, a thought experiment (a species of metaphor): "The Demon makes the metaphor not only verbally graceful," Nefastis explains, "but also objectively true."[32] In this case, the literalizing of the metaphor is attributed to a character, Nefastis, and can be dismissed as aberrant. Harder to dismiss are the many instances of figurative language attributable to the novel's narrator which similarly threaten to burst their metaphorical frames and join the real world. Such metaphors-becoming-literal abound in *Gravity's Rainbow*, where they expand in size and complexity until they approach the condition of free-standing micro-worlds, second-order realities that compete with the novel's first-order world. A particularly flagrant example is the figure that begins, "Living inside the System is like riding in a bus driven by a maniac bent on suicide," and then continues for a further twenty-five lines to specify, in fine-grained detail, the bus-driver's manic monologue, the stops on the trip, the reboarding process, the advertisements above the seats – an entire miniature world, concrete enough to make the reader forget temporarily that it is all just a figure of speech.[33]

A different strategy is that of *Against the Day* where, instead of *Gravity's Rainbow*'s massively over-extended figures, we find threaded throughout the novel assertions that would normally be taken metaphorically but might just as plausibly be literal here, given the peculiar norms of this novel's world. When one says that someone "disappeared" or "vanished" one is normally using a dead metaphor, meaning simply that they left quickly or unobtrusively: "Amid a great creak and scrape of beer-house furniture, Kit's companions had swiftly vanished."[34] But in this novel, in which some characters literally do vanish – Dally Rideout from a magician's CABINET OF MYSTERY, Yashmeen Halfcourt by passing through a wall, and so on – it is sometimes hard to determine whether disappearances are literal or figurative. "Dr. Rao abruptly vanished"; "[Mushtaq] had simply vanished": literally or figuratively?[35] Cumulatively, such moments of ontological hesitation induce a kind of shimmer of indeterminacy, throwing the novel's entire world into doubt – placing it under erasure.

Worlds under erasure. Inducing hesitation between literal and figurative status is not the only means of de-realizing worlds. The same effect can be achieved, for instance, by positing an event or sequence of events and then contradicting it, multiplying competing sequences to create a "garden of forking paths," or by projecting a state of affairs in the fictional world and then *de*constructing, *un*narrating or rescinding it, thereby placing it *sous rature*, under erasure.[36] Such strategies foreground ontology by exposing to view the operations by which narrative worlds are made and, more to the point, unmade. These are among the most radically destabilizing devices in the postmodernist repertoire and, unsurprisingly, they are well-represented in the Pynchon canon.

The forking-paths strategy of multiplying contradictory sequences underlies the motif of bilocation that is so conspicuous in *Against the Day*. For instance, the ocean-liner *Stupendica* bilocates, literally pursuing two different courses at once, one version of it continuing on its way to Europe while its military double, the dreadnaught *Emperor Maximilian*, with Kit Traverse on board, proceeds to the coast of Morocco. Of the many episodes placed under erasure throughout Pynchon's fiction, none is more memorable, or more disturbing, than the passage from *Gravity's Rainbow* in which the rocket engineer Franz Pökler commits incest with his putative daughter Ilse, and then flees with her to Denmark, defecting from the V-2 program. Our readerly investment in the narrated event is considerable and complicated, no doubt a mix of revulsion (at the incest) and relief (at the defection), so we are pulled up short when it is abruptly rescinded: "No. What Pökler did was" comfort Ilse, not have sex or run away with her.[37]

Most consequential, perhaps, of all the erased episodes in Pynchon's fiction is the account of the America that Mason and Dixon find beyond the terminus of their Line, where they encounter a displaced French court, Spanish, Chinese and Russian enclaves, an underworld city, a sect of sky-worshippers, and much else, and from which they return to claim the prize for discovering a new planet, Uranus, and to extend their Line eastward across the Atlantic on buoys, around which develop a kind of floating city and theme park. Or rather, this is what *would have happened if* they had continued beyond the terminus – which they did not, either in history or in this novel. The entire episode, in other words, with all of its rich circumstances and quirky detail, unfolds in the subjunctive mode, under erasure: "Suppose that Mason and Dixon and their Line cross Ohio after all, and continue West."[38] As the narrator of *Gravity's Rainbow* puts it, in a similar situation: "Of course it happened. Of course it didn't happen."[39]

Coda: cognitive mapping

In Jameson's view, the postmodern condition above all presents a challenge to cognitive mapping: to the postmodern subject's capacity to know where, literally and figuratively, she or he is located in the space of late capitalism.[40] Some instances of postmodernist cultural expression, it appears, only aggravate the problem of cognitive mapping, while others may provide opportunities for solving it. Thus, for instance, a building like Portman's Bonaventure Hotel in Los Angeles, by immersing the subject "up to your eyes and your body" in hyperspace, demonstrates the near impossibility of cognitive mapping, while a building like Frank Gehry's private home in Santa Monica might actually provide conceptual and imaginative tools for mapping one's place in the world system.[41]

On which side does Pynchon's fiction fall, that of the problem or that of the solution? Jameson suggests that conspiracy theory and the paranoid sensibility, which abound in postmodern entertainment fiction (e.g. high-tech thrillers, cyberpunk science fiction), reflect "degraded attempts" at cognitive mapping, distracting and deflecting us from recognizing our true situation.[42] Insofar as Pynchon's novels, early and later, belong to this category of paranoid-conspiracy fiction – indeed, epitomize it – they must be regarded as hindrances more than help, Bonaventure Hotels of contemporary fiction.

However, I want to argue that the complex spatialities of Pynchon's texts – their proliferation of worlds, lateral and alternative, their paradoxes and short-circuits, their doubtful, shimmering, on-again off-again realities – imply different, more constructive possibilities of cognitive mapping. Granted, the spaces of Pynchon's texts are only virtual, not built – text-based illusions, not enclosures of glass and steel. But what if we could learn how to navigate these paradoxical spaces, even if only virtually; what if we could become familiar, even comfortable, with their strangeness, perhaps to the point of experiencing them as a kind of second nature? Could this conceivably help us come to terms with the all-but-intractable problems of cognitive mapping in the world at large? If we could come to feel "at home" in Pynchon's texts as one might (Jameson imagines) learn to inhabit Gehry's house, is it possible that this might empower us cognitively to begin finding our place and our way in postmodernity itself?

NOTES

1 See Hans Bertens, *The Idea of the Postmodern: A History* (London: Routledge, 1995).

2 Fredric Jameson, *Postmodernism, or, The Cultural Logic of Late Capitalism* (Durham: Duke University Press, 1991), p. 1.

3 Jean-François Lyotard, *The Postmodern Condition: A Report on Knowledge* (1979; Minneapolis: University of Minnesota Press, 1984).

4 Linda Hutcheon, *A Poetics of Postmodernism: History, Theory, Fiction* (New York: Routledge, 1988).

5 For details, see Amy Elias's chapter in the present volume.

6 Jean Baudrillard, "Simulacra and Simulations" (1981) in Mark Postman (ed.), *Selected Writings* (Stanford University Press, 1988), pp. 166–84. See also Daniel J. Boorstin, *The Image: A Guide to Pseudo-Events in America* (1961; New York: Atheneum, 1985).

7 Don DeLillo, *White Noise* (New York: Viking, 1985), pp. 12–13.

8 Jameson, *Postmodernism*, p. 26.

9 *Ibid.*, pp. 14–16, 25–31.

10 Thomas Pynchon, *Gravity's Rainbow* (New York: Viking, 1973), p. 738.

11 *Ibid.*, p. 712. For many more details, see Deborah Madsen's chapter in the present volume.

12 Donna Haraway, "A Cyborg Manifesto: Science, Technology, and Socialist-Feminism in the Late Twentieth Century," in Haraway, *Simians, Cyborgs and Women: The Reinvention of Nature* (New York; Routledge, 1991), p. 163.

13 Andreas Huyssen, *After the Great Divide: Modernism, Mass Culture, Postmodernism* (Bloomington: Indiana University Press, 1986).

14 Charles Jencks, *What is Post-Modernism?* (London: Academy Editions/New York: St. Martin's Press, 1986).

15 John Barth, "The Literature of Replenishment" (1979) in Barth, *The Friday Book: Essays and Other Nonfiction* (New York: Putnam's, 1984), pp. 193–206; Umberto Eco, *Postscript to The Name of the Rose* (San Diego: Harcourt Brace Jovanovich, 1984).

16 Larry McCaffery (ed.), *After Yesterday's Crash: The Avant-Pop Anthology* (New York: Penguin, 1995).

17 See Michael Bérubé, *Marginal Forces/Cultural Centers: Tolson, Pynchon, and the Politics of the Canon* (Ithaca: Cornell University Press, 1992).

18 Thomas Pynchon, *The Crying of Lot 49* (Philadelphia: Lippincott, 1966), p. 129.

19 Max Apple, "Post-Modernism," in Apple, *Free Agents* (New York: Harper & Row, 1984), p. 137.

20 Alan Wilde, *Horizons of Assent: Modernism, Postmodernism, and the Ironic Imagination* (Baltimore: Johns Hopkins University Press, 1981), p. 10.

21 Jameson, *Postmodernism*, p. 17.

22 Thomas Pynchon, *Mason & Dixon* (New York: Henry Holt & Co, 1997), pp. 400, 699.

23 Brian McHale, *Postmodernist Fiction* (New York: Methuen, 1987) and *Constructing Postmodernism* (London: Routledge, 1992).

24 See Roman Jakobson, "The Dominant" (1935), in Ladislav Matejka and Krystyna Pomorska (eds.), *Readings in Russian Poetics: Formalist and Structuralist Views* (Cambridge, MA: MIT Press, 1971), pp. 105–10.

25 Thomas Pynchon, *Vineland* (New York: Little, Brown, 1990), p. 314.

26 Pynchon, *Lot 49*, pp. 120, 124

27 Brian McHale, "Gravity's Angels in America, or, Pynchon's Angelology Revisited," *Pynchon Notes*, 42–43 (1998), 303–16.
28 McHale, *Constructing*, pp. 87–114.
29 Pynchon, *Gravity's Rainbow*, pp. 695–96, 588.
30 *Ibid.*, p. 680.
31 *Ibid.*, p. 760.
32 Pynchon, *Lot 49*, p. 106.
33 Pynchon, *Gravity's Rainbow*, p. 412.
34 Thomas Pynchon, *Against the Day* (New York: Penguin Press, 2006), p. 589.
35 *Ibid.*, pp. 539, 760.
36 The allusion is to Jorge Luis Borges's story "The Garden of Forking Paths" (1941).
37 Pynchon, *Gravity's Rainbow*, p. 421.
38 Pynchon, *Mason & Dixon*, p. 706.
39 Pynchon, *Gravity's Rainbow*, p. 667.
40 See Amy Elias's chapter in the present volume.
41 Jameson, *Postmodernism*, pp. 38–54, 97–129.
42 *Ibid.*, p. 38.

8

DAVID SEED

Pynchon's intertexts

In 2006 when Ian McEwan was accused of plagiarism in his novel *Atonement*, Thomas Pynchon unusually broke his silence to publish a letter of support, where he declared:

> Oddly enough, most of us who write historical fiction do feel some obligation to accuracy [...] Unless we were actually there, we must turn to people who were, or to letters, contemporary reporting, the encyclopedia, the Internet, until, with luck, at some point, we can begin to make a few things of our own up. To discover in the course of research some engaging detail we know can be put into a story where it will do some good can hardly be classed as a felonious act– it is simply what we do.[1]

Giving us a rare glimpse of his working methods, Pynchon points out in effect that his fiction consists to an important extent of a montage of historical material garnered from diverse sources. This does not mean that the only thorough reading of Pynchon must be a study of his sources, but rather that we should approach his texts as fields where different representational systems and verbal registers are constantly encountering one another. Julia Kristeva's explanation of intertextuality is particularly helpful here since she describes a process of transposition, revealing "the signifying process' ability to pass from one sign system to another, to exchange and permutate them."[2] Pynchon's works juxtapose sections from different sign systems in order to evoke not history itself but rather the texts that collectively go towards our formation of history. In that respect they could be seen as examples of what Linda Hutcheon has described as the "historiographic metafiction" practiced by E. L. Doctorow, Robert Coover and others, where intertextuality reconfigures the reader's relation with the past.[3] For all his skill at depicting historical characters, Pynchon's narratives present discursive fields where the reader encounters the texts that have gone before. One consequence of this is that textual assembly always becomes an important topic in his work.

In Thomas Pynchon's first novel, *V.* (1963), the historical sections open in 1898 and Pynchon uses the Baedeker guidebooks, which had become required reading for any tourist, to situate his characters. Pynchon himself had entered the Baedeker world in 1961 with the publication of his story "Under the Rose." Set in Egypt in 1898, the story links travel with empire through its spy protagonist. The action opens in Alexandria, then moves to Cairo and concludes at the Kheops (now spelt Cheops) pyramid complex, following the well-trodden route that Western tourists would have taken. Pynchon draws verbatim on the 1898 Baedeker handbook to Egypt for the details of the journey between the two cities and more generally in his use of "itineraries" and in his location of buildings by "blocks." The protagonist is a tourist in masquerade, habituating the most widely used hotels and public means of transport. Mapping has remained a constant preoccupation throughout Pynchon's fiction right up to the construction of the Balkan railway lines in *Against the Day* and in this early story he uses Baedeker to impose a stylized grid on the action. The landscape of the story contains landmarks like the railway stations and key hotels, and limits the role of any Egyptian characters to anonymous minor functionaries; in that sense Pynchon mimics Baedeker's colonial ethos.[4] In *V.* Pynchon heavily revises this story to give perspectives to non-European characters and also draws out the ideology of Baedeker land: "This is a curious country, populated only by a breed called 'tourists.' Its landscape is one of inanimate monuments and buildings; near-inanimate barmen, taxi-drivers, bellhops, guides: there to do any bidding, to various degrees of efficiency, on receipt of the recommended baksheesh, pourboire, mancia, tip."[5] Pynchon summarizes the world of tourism as a supranational "coordinate system" which reassures the traveler by reducing every location to its standard pattern. Chapter 7 of *V.* can thus be read as a travesty of tourism in its account of a farcical attempt to steal Botticelli's *The Birth of Venus* from the Uffizi Gallery in Florence. Baedeker asterisked this work as demanding particular attention whereas Pynchon displaces this convention on to the would-be thief himself, as if he were an unconscious product of the system he is supposedly attacking.

Baedeker land in *V.* functions as an estranging system within which characters enact their different imperial allegiances. *The Crying of Lot 49* (1966) multiplies the number of such systems, which it evokes by foregrounding the media throughout. Embedded within the narrative is a work which Pynchon has applied in his depiction of Oedipa's California environment: Marshall McLuhan's *Understanding Media: The Extensions of Man* (1964). McLuhan presents a view of contemporary society as containing a complex field of overlapping media systems which interconnect with the individual at every turn. Connectedness is thus one of McLuhan's main emphases and also one of the determinants of Oedipa's predicament since she is constantly bombarded with more information than she can process. The action of the novel begins with a message (a letter); Oedipa drives in a rented car to a motel, whose manager is a pop singer; there she is visited by a lawyer who resembles a TV actor. And so the process continues. Every new experience introduces yet another permutation of the media so disconcerting that by the middle of the novel Oedipa has developed a paranoid sense of everything being interconnected. In that respect she is developing an awareness summarized by McLuhan as follows: "Concern with *effect* rather than *meaning* is a basic change of our electric time, for effect involves the whole situation, and not a single level of information movement."[6] One of Oedipa's problems is precisely that, as her discursive field extends outwards to more and more alien areas of information such as nineteenth-century philately and cybernetics, she begins to experience an information overload.

McLuhan describes the cumulative impact of the modern media as inducing a state of narcosis (compare Pynchon's repeated allusions to drugtaking) which he relates to the myth of Narcissus, yet another connection with the novel. At his most enthusiastic moment he declares that a computer promises a "Pentecostal condition of universal understanding and unity," a view which Pynchon turns to comedy by suggesting the possibility of revelations which never quite materialize.[7] Oedipa is constantly struggling to map out emerging cultural connections, and here Pynchon deploys a complex rhetoric of resemblances. At one point as she gazes across a California cityscape, its layout reminds her of the printed circuit of a transistor radio, and this moment is symptomatic of the whole novel. The content of one medium is another medium for McLuhan. Oedipa's constant search for truth, for a final piece of information which will make everything clear, is doomed to failure because, as McLuhan showed, the media impact through their processes and not through any detachable "content." One of the results is that the distinction between her subjective and social experience becomes hopelessly blurred.

As many commentators have pointed out, *The Crying of Lot 49* contains an unusual number of references to its own status as a text, especially through the summary and discussion of Pynchon's Jacobean pastiche drama, *The Courier's Tragedy*. Metafiction regularly makes the reception or processing of a narrative part of its subject and Pynchon's novel is no exception. This text-within-a-text tantalizes the reader and Oedipa alike because, except for brief quotations, the text of the play itself is never given directly, only summarized and discussed. Pynchon's account of the performance which Oedipa attends comically highlights the sheer variety of violent acts in the play and uses contemporary slang ("the Duke, of course, is in his apartment busy knocking off a piece") to encourage the reader to approach the work as constructed spectacle.[8] The stability of the text is disturbed by the suggestion that it is a script dependent on a director for its embodiment and disturbed again by Oedipa's discovery that different versions exist. Her futile attempts to verify verbal details act like a comic warning to the reader not to expect informational closure.

Gravity's Rainbow (1973) also foregrounds interpretation, but demonstrates a consistent hostility towards deterministic explanations of human behavior and draws on two starkly contrasting theories to establish its narrative. Volume 2 of Pavlov's *Lectures on Conditioned Reflexes*, published in translation in 1941, is quoted and debated within the text. Pavlov's volume becomes known in the novel, like Goldstein's subversive tract in *Nineteen Eighty-Four*, simply as "The Book," for reasons which will become apparent shortly. One of Pavlov's guiding principles was that "the true mechanical explanation always remains the ideal of the natural sciences ... The whole of the exact sciences of today make only a long chain of progressive approximations of mechanical interpretation, approximations all the steps of which are united by the supreme principle of determinism: no effect without cause."[9] This passage, part-quoted in the novel, reduces living subjects to abstract response mechanisms. Pavlov's lectures and related writings on behaviorism gave Pynchon a lexical set of terms like "mosaic," "conditioning" and above all "reflex," which always occur with absurd or negative connotations in *Gravity's Rainbow*; and gave him also a model of experimentation which is ridiculed throughout the novel and criticized for being unethical. The would-be practitioner of Pavlov's theories is Edward Pointsman, whose very name (a manual operator of railway lines) suggests mechanism, and who is trying to investigate the etiology of Tyrone Slothrop's sexual responses to the falling of the Nazi V-2 rockets. Pointsman is attempting to interpret this link in a linear cause-and-effect way that is even contradicted by the V-2s themselves, which can only be heard coming after they have exploded. The issue here is one not simply one of psychological theory but also of narrative continuity, since the complex shifts in *Gravity's Rainbow* absolutely prevent the reader from forming the sort of simplistic explanations which Pointsman is seeking. The general importance of Pavlov in the novel is to focus the many references to measuring and controlling human behavior, an importance which Pynchon stresses again in his introduction to a 2003 edition of *Nineteen Eighty-Four* (1948) where he draws a clear continuity between Pavlovian conditioning and political manipulation.[10] In *Gravity's Rainbow* the mismatch between Pointsman's behavior and his claims of scientific objectivity make an important ironic theme in the novel. The conspiratorial secrecy with which he and his colleagues circulate "The Book" suggests that they are treating it like some kind of secular scripture, and in one of the last references to Pavlov in the novel a character compares the behaviorists' laboratory to a maze as if they have become their own self-mystified experimental subjects. As Thomas H. Schaub has argued about cause and effect, "the entire weight of *Gravity's Rainbow* calls the absoluteness of that idea into question, and moves both characters and readers into the uncertain ground between the distinctness of successive events and the timeless complementarities of meaning."[11]

Counterpointed against Pavlovian behaviorism Pynchon deploys a complex range of symbolism drawn from the Freudian writings of Norman O. Brown, particularly *Life Against Death: The Psychoanalytic Meaning of History* (1959), but also *Love's Body* (1966). In an important essay, Lawrence Wolfley has shown in detail how Pynchon incorporates into *Gravity's Rainbow* Brown's view of society as collectively repressed.[12] Drawing on the later writings of Freud, Brown explores the pathology of modern society and identifies a neurosis so severe that humans seem to be swayed by a death instinct. Where Pavlov clung to mechanistic explanations of behavior (he compares the cerebral cortex to a switchboard, for instance), Brown sees behavior as motivated by unconscious drives. In Pynchon's novel the latter view emerges through the recurrence of sadomasochistic acts and the multiple symbolism of blackness. *Gravity's Rainbow* repeatedly embeds its quotations from Pavlov within contexts of farce. The first time we encounter Pointsman his foot gets stuck in a toilet bowl, a slapstick image recalling film comedy but one which also glances towards the excremental symbolism described by Brown. In addition to Pavlov and Brown, a third element enters the novel when we learn that Pointsman's favorite fiction is the Fu Manchu novels, and at this point Manichean melodrama connects with behavioral analysis in a shared mindset dependent again on "ideas of the opposite."

Pynchon's allusive method works laterally. The juxtaposition of apparently diverse information invites the reader to compare and cross-relate. The publication of a letter which he wrote to a graduate student while working on *Gravity's Rainbow* sheds detailed light on those areas of that novel and of *V.* which relate to the South-West African Herero people. Initially Pynchon stumbled across this material while searching for a pamphlet on Malta but his interest grew and he consulted a range of German reports, anthropological studies and Herero dictionaries for incorporation into *Gravity's Rainbow*. In his letter, which was written at the height of the Vietnam War, Pynchon draws analogies which relate directly to the symbolic oppositions in his novel. He explains:

I was thinking of the 1904 campaign [by the Germans against the Herero] as a sort of dress rehearsal for what later happened to the Jews in the 30's and 40's [...] I feel personally that the number done on the Herero head by the Germans is the same number done on the American Indian head by our own colonists and what is now being done on the Buddhist head in Vietnam by the Christian minority in Saigon and their advisers: the imposition of a culture valuing analysis and differentiation on a culture that valued unity and integration.[13]

Pynchon here identifies an imperial theme running through most of his novels: the imposition of literacy on non-literate peoples like the Yurok in *Vineland* (1990) or of a new alphabet in the Central Asian section of *Gravity's Rainbow*. In his letter Pynchon acknowledges McLuhan and recognizes the inevitable filtering and possible distortion of Herero culture by its Western analysts. Not only does *Gravity's Rainbow* contain sections of commentary on the circular holistic structure of Herero villages; it also includes brief quotations in the Herero language, sometimes with a gloss, sometimes without. Since the Herero characters are exiles, as some commentators suggest, symbolizing the return of the Western repressed, these words function as the lexical traces of their lost culture, incomprehensible to the vast majority of readers.

In *Mason & Dixon* (1996) Pynchon extends these power themes to include the process of mapping. The famous 1763–67 survey by Mason and Dixon established the border between the proprietary colonies of Pennsylvania and Maryland, and between what became known as the Northern and Southern states. In other words, their lines mapped out property boundaries. Pynchon's novel not only narrates their survey; it also imitates the locutions, spelling and abbreviations common to the period so that the reader receives the action refracted through a pastiche text, which includes excerpts from nationalistic poetry (by Timothy Tox, Pynchon's own version of Joel Barlow), diaries and religious histories.[14] Pynchon draws, too, on Mason and Dixon's journal for many details of their survey, quoting one of the most striking passages describing a cave near South Mountain, which seems to contain designs "drawn by the Pencil of Time."[15] This is clearly one of the "engaging details" which Pynchon describes in his letter quoted at the opening of this essay. The journal account presents the cave as a solemn memento mori, but Pynchon uses the occasion to highlight a difference between Mason and Dixon. From an early point in the novel he presents Mason as a cryptologist, obsessed by hidden signs which might be directing their work. Dixon is more of a rationalist, used by Pynchon to demonstrate how mapping is a kind of discursive practice, as when he recognizes analogies between their own lines and the layout of Roman Roads in Britain. "Line" is the most overdetermined term in the novel, signifying variously an inscription on the landscape, a boundary, a direction, or the spatial figure embedded in the metaphor of orthodoxy (i.e., straight thinking). In an essay of 1993 Pynchon describes the construction of a business network in one of the key cities in *Mason & Dixon*: "Philadelphia, by Franklin's time, answered less and less to the religious vision that William Penn had started off with. The city was becoming a kind of high-output machine [...] The urban mazework of London [...] was here all rectified, orthogonal."[16] Pynchon's linkage between business and a rectangular structure recurs in the novel, which traces out the diminution of religion in America. The pastiche sermon which is "quoted" as an epigraph to chapter 53 thus already belongs to the past. When the surveyors reach the Allegheny Mountains, they record a pious visual panorama: "From the solitary tops of these mountains, the Eye gazes round with pleasure; filling the mind with adoration to that prevailing spirit that made them." In the novel the appropriation of space is secularized when a character tells Mason and Dixon that "ye may stand and look either way [...] and from your Eminence pretend that you own it."[17] The novel's use of different verbal registers and multiple perspectives problematizes the central act of surveying and relates it to a complex set of political, racial and economic tensions – especially to the process of appropriation.

Against the Day (2006) articulates its historical concerns from 1893, the year of the Chicago World's Fair, to the 1920s through references to the popular narratives of this period, in particular to dime novels. These brief tales, which were popular from 1860 up to the Second World War, marked a revolution in publishing and shared a number of characteristics. Their action was swift-moving, often with very short paragraphing and rapid dialogue. Although westerns were popular, the subjects also included new inventions, crime and the course of empire. Predominantly targeting young male readers, typical series were *Beadle's Boy's Library of Sport, Story and Adventure*; *The Boy's Star Library*; and the adventures of plucky heroes like Nick Carter and Frank Merriwell. By the 1890s, the starting period of *Against the Day*, the detective had become the most popular hero. The series which bears most closely on Pynchon's novel is that centering on Frank Reade Jr., a young inventor who constructs a number of airships held in the air by propellers and umbrella-like devices. The series carried titles like *Frank Reade on Government Service* and *Frank Reade in Siberia*. In *Against the Day*, dime novels form part of the collective consciousness of the young male characters. Pynchon invents his own pastiche series tracing the adventures of the Chums of Chance, his group protagonist. By referring his readers to different novels in this series (*The Chums of Chance and the Evil Halfwit* is the first example), he evokes a hinterland of other undisclosed narratives, linking his own novel with the narrative and publishing practices of the period. He implies a cyclical process whereby the experiences of the Chums of Chance are rapidly converted into fiction, which in turn inspires its readers with a desire for adventure. Adventure and travel in fact form the twin supports of the imperial theme in Pynchon's novel, as can be seen in his use of hollow earth narratives. Section One of the novel concludes with the Chums sailing through an opening in the Antarctic into the Earth's interior and emerging from the North Pole. At the turn of the century hollow earth stories enjoyed considerable popularity from their ability to combine exploration, fantasy and even spiritual themes. Willis George Emerson's *The Smoky God* (1908) was one of the very few to describe such a voyage through one polar opening to the other, but Pynchon is also drawing on William R. Bradshaw's *The Goddess of Atvatabar* (1892). This novel is more explicitly concerned with conquest and describes the discovery of a lost race in the interior presided over by a beautiful ruler. At the end of his adventures the narrator exclaims over the potential riches in "Plutusia" ("Plutonia" in Pynchon), ripe for American picking. In *Against the Day* Pynchon privileges science fiction, as well as boys' adventure stories, including H. G. Wells's *The Time Machine* (1895), which has been "adulterated to profitable effect" by dime novels.[18] Pynchon then proceeds to give his own comic pastiche of *The Time Machine* in his account of a ramshackle evil-smelling device worked by one Dr. Zoot. The imperial themes of *Against the Day* are repeatedly linked to contemporary adventure stories in such a way that it becomes unclear which is shaping which.

Here we can see the true richness of Pynchon's intertextuality. Identifying the materials he incorporates into his fiction involves far more than filiation or source-spotting. The variety of his narrative textures grows out of the complex interplay between startlingly diverse materials. *Vineland* (1990), for instance, deploys allusions to *Star Trek*, Lombroso, Native American mythology and even to Pynchon's own fiction in order to evoke the emergence of fascism in Reagan's America. Typically Pynchon tries to throw the reader off the pursuit of thematic concerns by a facetious reference to Deleuze and Guattari, whose *Anti-Oedipus* (1972) actually sheds useful light on the cultural processes described in *Vineland*. Pynchon demonstrates again and again how historically determined systems of ordering are applied in his fiction, and the ruptures within his texts between conflicting registers alert the reader to considering the human cost of these systems.

NOTES

1 Sarah Lyall, "Novelists Defend One of Their Own Against a Plagiarism Charge," *New York Times* (7 December 2006), www.nytimes.com/2006/12/07/books/07pync.html

2 Julia Kristeva, "Revolution in Poetic Language," in Toril Moi (ed.), *The Kristeva Reader* (Oxford: Basil Blackwell, 1986), p. 111.

3 Linda Hutcheon, *A Poetics of Postmodernism: History, Theory, Fiction* (New York and London: Routledge, 1988), pp. 105–23.

4 On Baedeker, see Edward Mendelson, "Baedeker's Universe," *Yale Review*, 74.III (Spring 1985), 386–403.

5 Thomas Pynchon, *V.* (Philadelphia: Lippincott, 1963), pp. 408–9. For a valuable discussion of Pynchon's use of Baedeker, see William M. Plater, *The Grim Phoenix: Reconstructing Thomas Pynchon* (Bloomington: Indiana University Press, 1980), chapter 2.

6 Marshall McLuhan, *Understanding Media: The Extensions of Man* (London: Routledge and Kegan Paul, 1964), p. 26; McLuhan's emphasis.

7 M. McLuhan, *Understanding Media*, p. 80.

8 Thomas Pynchon, *The Crying of Lot 49* (Philadelphia: Lippincott, 1966), p. 67.

9 Ivan Petrovitch Pavlov, *Lectures on Conditioned Reflexes* (London: Lawrence & Wishart, 1941), vol. II, p. 149.

10 Thomas Pynchon, "Foreword," George Orwell, *Nineteen Eighty-Four* (New York: Penguin, 2003), pp. viii–ix.

11 Thomas H. Schaub, *Pynchon: The Voice of Ambiguity* (Urbana: University of Illinois Press, 1981), p. 92.

12 Lawrence Wolfley, "Repression's Rainbow: The Presence of Norman O. Brown in Pynchon's Big Novel," in Richard Pearce (ed.), *Critical Essays on Thomas Pynchon* (Boston, G. K. Hall, 1981), pp. 99–123.

13 David Seed, *The Fictional Labyrinths of Thomas Pynchon* (Iowa City: University of Iowa Press, 1988), pp. 240, 241.

14 For Pynchon's sources, see David Foreman, "Historical Documents Relating to *Mason & Dixon*," in Brooke Horvath and Irving Malin (eds.), *Pynchon and Mason & Dixon* (Newark: University of Delaware Press, 2000), pp. 143–66.

15 A. Hughlett Mason (ed.), *The Journal of Charles Mason and Jeremiah Dixon* (Philadelphia: American Philosophical Society, 1969), p. 111; quoted in Pynchon, *Mason & Dixon* (New York: Henry Holt and Co, 1997), p. 497.

16 Pynchon, "Nearer, My Couch, to Thee," *New York Times Book Review*, June 6, 1993, p. 3.

17 A. H. Mason (ed.), *The Journal of Charles Mason*, p. 129; Pynchon, *Mason & Dixon*, p. 587.

18 Thomas Pynchon, *Against the Day* (New York: Penguin Press, 2006), p. 398.

PART III

Issues

9

AMY J. ELIAS

History

In a heated discussion about the value of historical novels, Ives LeSpark says to his son in *Mason & Dixon* (1997), "Facts are Facts, and to believe otherwise is not only to behave perversely, but also to step in imminent peril of being grounded, young Pup."[1] LeSpark is an arms dealer, and his profession, his threat and his assumptions about history are not linked by accident: for Pynchon, the Western military-industrial complex has always advocated a common sense view of things that tends to stifle dissent and sanctions business as usual. To believe that history is a series of inevitable and indisputable facts that add up to a narrative of Western progress is, for Pynchon, both to standardize and to colonize history and to make it congenial to totalitarian, or just oppressively uniform, world views and seemingly determined ends.

In the same passage in *Mason & Dixon*, however, LeSpark's son Ethelmer pronounces judgment on this theory about the facticity of history:

> Who claims Truth, Truth abandons. History is hir'd, or coerc'd, only in Interests that must ever prove base. She is too innocent, to be left within the reach of anyone in Power,— who need but touch her, and all her Credit is in the instant vanish'd, as if it had never been. She needs rather to be tended lovingly and honorably by fabulists and counterfeiters, Ballad-Mongers and Cranks of ev'ry Radius, Masters of Disguise to provide her the Costume, Toilette, and Bearing, and Speech nimble enough to keep her beyond the Desires, or even the Curiosity, of Government.[2]

Ethelmer counters his father's argument with an opposite narrative of how history works, one equally dependent on the language of the free market. Only the fabulist or storyteller, who seeks to examine the complexities of human history rather than use history didactically as indoctrination, is to be trusted with its handling and care. Since both views seem partial rather than full explanations of what history is, in this novel, the narrativization of history remains suspect, seemingly always partisan and always within the purview of power.

Situated somewhere between these views (or to their Left, perhaps) is that of their author. In relation to history, Thomas Pynchon behaves perversely; he is a master Crank, an ingenious fabulator, a crafty counterfeiter. Sometimes with glee and sometimes with fury, he repeatedly attacks the Gradgrindian belief that "facts are facts" and that they add up to a predictable and universally acceptable version of history. Yet his novels are saturated with historical facts; they are some of the best-researched literature produced in the twentieth century. Especially in the long, overtly historical novels (*Gravity's Rainbow* [1973], *Mason & Dixon*, *Against the Day* [2006]), Pynchon's goal, however, seems not to produce historical realism but rather to imply a philosophy of history, or meditations on the nature of history itself. Because of this, his novels are prototypes of what has been termed "historiographic metafiction" and "metahistorical romance."

The following discussion briefly examines Pynchon as a historiographer and suggests that he shares three assumptions with contemporary philosophy of history: the ideas that history is polyvocal; that history is produced by event; and that history is tropological narrative. What is extraordinary about Thomas Pynchon's novels is that they incorporate not one, but nearly all, of the major critiques of history debated in late twentieth-century philosophy of history. These three specific ways of understanding, or redefining, history lead, I believe, to specific presentations of past and present reality in Pynchon's work. A notion of polyvocal history leads Pynchon to advocate paranoia as a form of cognitive mapping; a notion of history as "event" leads him to construct history as sublime or "subjunctive" history; a notion of history as tropological narrative leads him to mythopoesis.

Polyvocal history

In *A Poetics of Postmodernism* (1988), Linda Hutcheon defended mid-twentieth-century experimental fiction and theory against many charges of ahistoricism and self-indulgent metafictional play leveled by liberal and Marxist critics alike. Derived from coterminous insights in the field of architecture, Hutcheon's definitions of postmodernism have been extremely influential and have allowed critics to see a new relationship between formalist experimentalism and historical inquiry in late twentieth-century fiction. In contrast to a high modernism she defines primarily as formalist and aestheticist, postmodernist fiction returns to history in a more vehemently interrogative manner: she claims that postmodernist fiction "reinstalls historical contexts as significant and even determining, but in doing so, it problematizes the entire notion of historical knowledge."[3] This fiction renders unstable the unity of the self/subject, elevates irony as the mode of provisional assertion, incorporates poststructuralism's semiotic awareness, and challenges narrative unity in the interests of multiplicity and disparity. Most importantly, postmodernist fiction questions the assumption that the writing of history is transparent and neutral by asserting that all values are context dependent and ideologically inflected, contests notions of history's teleological closure and developmental continuity, and tries to demonstrate that all historical accounts are emplotted in the manner of fiction rather than merely recorded in the manner of science. Postmodernist fiction advances these claims by contaminating the "neutral" voice of seemingly transparent historical narrative with metafictional narrative elements such as didacticism and jarringly opaque, anachronistic or allegorical story components that highlight the artificiality or constructedness of history in that historical narrative. Referencing the work of Jacques Derrida, Michel Foucault, Hayden White, Catherine Belsey, Dominick LaCapra, Paul Ricoeur and others, she shows how in this fiction "the formalist and the historical live side by side, but there is no dialectic," only paradox: in postmodernist fiction, the primary goal is to question our assumptions about what history is and how it has been recorded, and to what ends, and to make apparent how limited and limiting a single perspective on history may be.[4] Moreover, concurring with Hayden White that historians need to expose the historically conditioned character of the historical discipline itself, Hutcheon argues that the metafictional strategies in postmodernist fiction enable it to advocate a pluralist view of historiography "consisting of different but equally meaningful constructions of past reality."[5] As a result, she concludes, postmodernist fiction advocates a pluralized, polyvocal approach to history and culture.

Hutcheon's theory of historiographic metafiction elucidates Pynchon's historical fictions, which similarly interrogate the assumptions of "common sense" approaches to history and which value multiplicity over universalism. Moreover, when her insights are combined with those of Fredric Jameson, whose Althusserian Marxist poetics at first seem very different from her own, one sees how Pynchon's polyvocal approach to history is related to a central theme in his novels: paranoia. Jameson, like Hutcheon, defines postmodernism as a feature of the period of late capitalism, understood as a global economic system, and he claims that this system produces its own arts and aesthetic responses. For Jameson, however, the primary hermeneutic arising from this economic formation is "cognitive mapping." He derives this term from Kevin Lynch, who in *The Image of the City* (1960) had argued that today's cities are alienating and dehumanizing spaces (one thinks of Los Angeles). Jameson agrees, but argues that this is the state of global capitalism itself. Understood as a global economic system, capitalism succeeds by disorienting us – keeping its CEOs hidden, separating us from one another (and thus unable to form collectives of resistance), and convincing us that buying goods will give us a sense of place and belonging in the world. "Cognitive mapping" is a historicized resistance to this; it enables "a situational representation on the part of the individual subject to that vaster and properly unrepresentable totality which is the ensemble of society's structure as a whole."[6] In other words, the absent presence of global capitalism is the true, monocultural space beneath all appearances, and any art that attempts to make it visible will need to approach it necessarily through indirection. Any political art in the era of postmodernity will be able only to *gesture* toward this non-site-specific, always circulating, and centrally organizing principle of world culture. "The political form of postmodernism, if there ever is any," writes Jameson, "will have as its vocation the invention and projection of a global cognitive mapping, on a social as well as a spatial scale."[7] This means, as I have argued elsewhere, that the central logic of postmodernist art is paranoia.[8] We strongly intuit that the global market system is in place, gather clues that we can find about its domination over us, and gesture in our art whenever we can toward this system in order to reveal its omnipresence and dominion.

Hutcheon's polyvocal postmodernist history and Jameson's cognitive mapping intersect in the theme of paranoia that runs throughout Pynchon's fiction. There has been more published on Pynchon's paranoid vision of history and culture than perhaps on any other subject related to his work; all of his novels offer paranoia as the only hermeneutic compatible with a world in which social systems are run by powerful but protected and secretive global tycoons, multinational corporations and military-industrial conglomerates. These are all invoked in Pynchon's novels by the collective pronoun "Them." Paranoids strive to unmask the logic of history in which they move; they are people who believe that "They" run the world and that "everything is connected."[9] They understand "connectedness," however, in two ways. The "connectedness" that is desired by the Elect and which must be resisted by the Preterite is the monovocal, universalist connectiveness of totalitarian control. The "connectedness" that Pynchon's characters pursue as an act of resistance, however, is a polyvocal connectedness of persons and ideas and even time zones and spatial dimensions, the connectedness of association and community that resists standardization. For Pynchon's characters, paranoia is thus *creative* in two ways, as a hermeneutic that unmasks totalitarian control that wishes to remain invisible and box life into rigid, limiting, and controllable categories, and conversely as an open, polyvocal approach to the world that allows one to see connections, associations and creative difference.[10]

Particularly in Pynchon's long historical novels, paranoia serves as a way for his characters to locate themselves in historical time because they understand that history is "at best a conspiracy, not always among gentlemen, to defraud."[11] It is now an accepted critical commonplace that Pynchon's novels promote a conspiratorial view of history. In *Against the Day*, the Traverse family is intent upon piercing the plot of Scarsdale Vibe and the multinational politicos who will soon set the world on fire with World War I, while the Chums of Chance and the brothers Traverse become increasingly paranoid as they begin to suspect linkages between dimensions of reality, systems of knowledge and political conspiracies on a global scale. In *Mason & Dixon* the title characters start off rather forthrightly on a science expedition, and then through their travels to the Cape of Good Hope and America increasingly suspect that they are being used in an international game of power and intrigue that will cement the power of colonialism, erase the differences of indigenous cultures and remake North America in the image of Europe. In *The Crying of Lot 49* (1966), Oedipa shakes herself free from suburban isolation and political hibernation and awakens to Trystero's "plot" of history by cultivating a paranoia that connects her to others living and interacting in the space of the postmodern city. Against a "monovocal" or one-dimensional version of history that They want to institutionalize to consolidate Their own power, Pynchon's paranoid characters assert a Preterite multiculture whose history is open, unpredictable, and polyvocal.

History as "event"

Generally speaking, Anglo-European philosophy of history offers at least three dominant ways of understanding the movement of historical time. The first, exemplified in Christian eschatology or the historical tropology of Vico, figures history as a circle: the model associated with many religious and pre-modern societies, it emphasizes eternal return or a movement from harmony through disorder back to harmony. Exemplified in different degrees by the Scottish Enlightenment historians' stadialism (belief in progressively advancing stages of civilization) or Hegelian dialectic, the second model figures history as an arrow (the time line) from the past to the future; this model emphasizes incremental progress (in knowledge, human civilization) from one stage of history to another and is often seen as the model foundational to secular modernity. Both of these models can be teleological in nature, the second in particular constructing a positive (utopian) or negative (apocalyptic) endpoint to lived human history.

These two models have dominated Western historiography, but a third spatial model came to prominence in the mid twentieth century. Martin

Heidegger, Michel Foucault, Jean-François Lyotard, Gilles Deleuze, and Alain Badiou, for example, emphasized a different model of historical time: history as a series of discontinuous and unpredictable disruptions or radical epistemic shifts provoked by "events." The "event" is not just something that happens in everyday life: it is on the order of a cataclysmic explosion, revelation or singularity that reconfigures the social, epistemological and political landscape from that time forward. While Heidegger puts this in phenomenological terms (death, for instance, is an event), Foucault and Lyotard resituate the event in history (for Lyotard, the French Revolution is an event). The event is so disruptive and powerful precisely because even though it emerges from a specific set of historical conditions, it is not anticipated within the social and ideological matrix from which it springs and which it then radically disrupts. This view is similar to that articulated in philosophy of science by Thomas Kuhn, who in *The Structure of Scientific Revolutions* (1962) attacked the idea that science advanced teleologically or in accord with positivist principles and claimed instead that science advanced by non-teleological "paradigm shifts," or periodic revolutions that radically change the cognitive frames of interpretation.[12]

Within philosophy of history, Hayden White in particular has emphasized that if one accepts the event as the motor of historical change, then history as a subject of study loses its framing logic and becomes more and more opaque to us. Understanding history as essentially without pattern or form makes us aware of its *sublimity* in a Kantian sense: history becomes something that exceeds our cognitive faculties and makes us aware of the limitations of our own thought. White asserted that totalitarianisms result when this truth is suppressed: an essentially formless history is subjected to the historian's explanatory systems, each of which imposes on it some kind of discursive plot (and, in the process, that plot's associated politics, whether utopian or conservative). However, a truly visionary politics, White argues, can only result when people realize that history is meaningless and beyond our control, for this leads to a kind of humility. That is, acknowledging that history eludes our explanations and teleologies – understanding history as the *historical sublime* – is an ethical imperative for the historical profession (obliging it to see all narrative histories as stories or versions of truth instead of truth itself) and also for societies in general (underscoring the futility of utopian schemas and the importance of grassroots, humane action in the world of lived experience). This recalls Paul Ricoeur's claims in "Christianity and the Meaning of History" (1951) that historical understanding should be located somewhere between the supra-rational schema of hope and the rational scheme of progress; for Ricoeur, historical understanding demands "the *courage* to believe in a profound significance of the most tragic history ... and a certain rejection of system and fanaticism, a sense of the *open*."[13]

In my own work, I have argued that this concept of the historical sublime (as the secular-sacred space of desire, a desire for history that can never be fulfilled) characterizes Pynchon's historical novels and is a form of the post-1960s historical novel that I call "metahistorical romance."[14] Revising rather than rejecting Hutcheon's "historiographic metafiction," which defines all postmodernist fiction as an uneasy mix of historicism and metafictionality, I understand metahistorical romance to be a specific category of post-1960s literature, a continuation of (rather than a break with) the historical romance tradition. Historical romance since the time of Sir Walter Scott has held historism and romance in uneasy relation and anticipated many of the thematic obsessions of Pynchon's metahistorical novels (such as the value of modernity, or the relation between indigenous and universalist knowledge).[15] Losing faith in empirical and teleological history, Pynchon in fact returns to a notion of history as sublime. The result is fiction that turns the time of history into the space of a perpetual present, returns obsessively to history as an irresolvable question, elevates romance over realism, values *openness* as an approach to the world, and self-reflexively undermines its own authority and pretense to revelation or historical truth. His novels tend to turn to the body rather than to abstract systems of knowledge as the locus of value and meaning, and they value ethical human relations over utopian political schemas.

Pynchon's vision of history provides its own term for the historical sublime: the subjunctive. The subjunctive is a state of openness or Derridian undecidability in which multiple possibilities of interpretation coexist simultaneously. It is therefore an unsettling, uncanny, but also liberating space; evading definition and control, it disrupts the laws of consensus reality and normative, rational thinking, but it also opens up possibilities for alternative ways of being, thinking and acting, and tends to refocus attention on the here-and-now rather than on the utopian future. The sublime subjunctive is everywhere in Pynchon's work. It appears as history itself when Pynchon fictionalizes history and constructs alternate histories alongside his factual accounts. But most frequently, it characterizes the many "Zones" of Pynchon's fiction, particularly as these are historicized and take on the contradictions and uncanniness of specific periods in history.

Thus in *Lot 49*, the "zone" of the Infected City that Oedipa Maas traverses is a subjunctive space in which she must suspend possible interpretations of her reality and open herself to experience in the world. It is also, however, a metonymy of the 1960s psychedelic youth rebellion against the standardization of 1950s suburban middle-class life (a life that Oedipa flees by the end of the book). Such rebellion is carried over into *Vineland* (1990) and *Inherent Vice* (2009), in which hippie countercultures live on in California, and it counterposes an aggressive presentism against utopian futurisms of any kind. In *Mason & Dixon*, eighteenth-century America itself is a subjunctive Zone where proponents of sublimity (including Mason and Dixon in different ways, and the Mechanical Duck) and disciples of rationalization (for instance, the Royal Society) are undergoing a battle for dominance and will determine the future of the territory. Brian McHale has discussed America as "the subjunctive space of wish and desire" in *Mason & Dixon* and notes how the novel's subjunctive Zones challenge metanarratives of the time, such as the Great Chain of Being: "the orientation toward the horizontal corresponds to democracy in political philosophy and to a metaphysics of this-worldliness."[16] *Against the Day* presents the aftermath of this clash between forces of totalization and counterforces championing openness and improvisation in the period leading to World War I. The novel specifically aligns totalization with the emerging global dominance of capitalism and with science devoted to the technology of war, and resistance to it is found in the pursuit of the sublime in the form of alternative metaphysics and subjunctive geographical zones. *Gravity's Rainbow* likewise presents World War II as a pivotal moment in history, when forces of rationalization have achieved mastery. In this novel, the historical sublime emerges as a return of the repressed, the reality of chance, play and terrifying openness underneath all dogmas or empiricisms, and it is figured in the many war Zones in the novel. When Pointsman, the Pavlovian scientist at The White Visitation, queries Roger Mexico, a statistician, about patterns of rocket hits in London, he is increasingly frustrated that statistics will not give him definitive answers and fumes, "What if Mexico's whole generation have turned out like this? Will Postwar be nothing but 'events,' newly created one moment to the next? No links? Is it the end of history?"[17] Pynchon's answer seems to be, "yes," for good and for ill.

History as tropological narrative

The prominent historian R. G. Collingwood, in *The Idea of History* (published after his death in 1943), saw the historian's task as similar to that of the detective: historians should comb through the archives to find the facts relating to a historical event or moment, and then, by employing what he called "the constructive imagination," provide a plausible and reasonable narrative explanation for this evidence. He never claimed that this narrative was definitive, or even complete, only that it represented an ethical and honest attempt by the historian to approximate an accurate picture of what really happened in the past. In 1974, Hayden White published "The Historical Text as Literary Artifact," an implicit response to this view of historical work in what has become a classic essay in the field of postmodern philosophy of history. In this essay, White made a pronouncement that provoked the ire of historians – namely, that historical narratives are "verbal fictions, the contents of which are as much *invented* as *found* and the forms of which have more in common with their counterparts in literature than they have with those in the sciences."[18]

White was taking to a logical endpoint the fundamental truth of any narrative history: that history makes stories out of accumulated facts and chronological listings of events. The stories that history tells, like all stories, depend upon "emplotment," which turns facts and chronicles into historical narratives. How a specific historian understands the truth value of that narrative construction depends upon his or her philosophy of history and methodology. White observed that what was missing in definitions such as Collingwood's, however, was accounts of how this story of history was actually *made*: a recognition, that is, that something literary as well as something logical and sympathetic happens when facts, which are only the existents and actions of stories, are turned into narrative accounts. Working from the tropological history of Vico, the archetypal criticism of Northrop Frye, the insights of Russian Formalism and the perspective of semiotics, White claimed that while historical events – the elements of narrative – are value-neutral, the stories that we weave from them never are. In fact, he argued, all historical accounts must be emplotted *according to the tropes available to storytelling* – that is, as tragedy, comedy, romance or irony, depending upon how the historian understands these events.[19] The stories that history tells, like all stories, encode facts "as components of specific *kinds* of plot structures."[20] Significantly, a single historical event can be emplotted in a number of different ways: the French Revolution is an ideal case in point, often understood to be either a tragic fall (in the context of Edmund Burke's history) or a dark comedy (in the context of Michelet's history) depending upon the literary trope chosen to represent it by the historian.

Finally, White posited that these tropological frames for the telling of history actually *preceded* the facts, and that the historian went into the archive with her cultural moment's assumptions about those historical events already as a frame for them in her mind. Different stories about the French Revolution existed not, or not always, because historians found different facts about it in the archive, but because they "shared with their audiences certain preconceptions about how the Revolution might be emplotted."[21] According to White, then, a historian will emplot history based on what literary tropes culture makes available to her, which tropes tend to be associated with important historical events by that culture, and how she herself emplots the facts of the archives given these two preconditions for storytelling at her particular cultural moment. (Our own moment, White claimed, tends to plot history as irony.) Thus White does not deny that history gives us knowledge, or that this knowledge is culturally meaningful and important; he does, however, contest the idea that histories give us verifiably *factual* knowledge or any kind of knowledge unmediated by the frames of storytelling itself.

If history is a story that tells Truth through fabulation – that is, if it is essentially a fiction that attempts to tell the truth of the world from a specific cultural perspective – then it is more akin to myth than to chemistry. Myths are highly emplotted narratives that explain an absent ontological origin, provide a vision of reality in terms of human hopes and fears, lack rational tidiness, mutually reference and reinforce one another to form storytelling complexes, are rooted in a specific culture, are complex in structure and tend toward encyclopedism.[22] History, myth and fiction all attempt to narrate the logic of world events through the imposition of a hermeneutic frame, understood through White's theory as a tropological emplotment.

White, thus oddly defining history as the mythological narrative of the West, and Pynchon's critics, who discuss mythopoesis in Pynchon's fiction, all start from the tropological categories of myth established in literary criticism by Northrop Frye. Understanding Pynchon as a literary writer who conceives of history in White's terms (that is, as tropological narrative) allows us to see his historical fiction as akin to myth in many ways. But from this standpoint, Pynchon's historical fictions appear to be *doubly* emplotted: his historical novels trope as tragedy, romance or irony an already tropologically emplotted (mostly comic) Western historical narrative. If "factual" historical accounts repress the operation of tropological emplotment at their core, Pynchon's novels revel in and foreground it, turning history into overt explanatory myth, or fabulation. "Fabulation" is a literary term linked etymologically with fable, an explanatory legend about the values upon which the social world operates. On the one hand, Pynchon's double troping of history leads to a highly aestheticized, almost metafictional version of history that like White's historiography challenges the disciplinary assumptions of historians by rewriting historical "fact" as a set of cultural fictions. On the other hand, Pynchon's "double troping" of history causes his own historical fictions to reverse the dominant of historical narrative, from epistemological to ontological questioning – in the manner of myth.[23]

A number of critics have discussed Pynchon's presentation of history as mythopoesis. Kathryn Hume, for instance, has identified a mythic pattern in *Gravity's Rainbow* consisting of an initial paradise (the North American

New World), a fall (the colonization of that world by Slothrop's forebears, serpents in the Garden), a central symbolic action (immachination, which creates a symbolic marriage between human beings and the gods defined as machines and thereby creates a "new order"), and a predicted apocalypse (either holocaust or paradise, depending how one evaluates this wedding of man and machine).[24] In *Pynchon's Mythography*, Hume illustrates how this general schema is filled by Pynchon with value-laden concepts drawn from numerous mythological systems, from ancient pagan myths, Greek and Christian mythos, and postsecular religions. Using a different schema, Catherine R. Stimpson interprets Pynchon's presentation of women in his novels as a variation of the "white goddess" myth elaborated by Robert Graves.[25] Jungian interpretations of Pynchon's mysticism or mythopoesis, such as that by Thomas Moore, are variants of this kind of reading; from this perspective, the Jungian "archetype" would provide the tropes by which reality is organized.[26] Furthermore, Debra Moddelmog has discussed the significance of Oedipus myth elements in *Lot 49*, while John McClure has discussed syncretic myth as postsecularity in Pynchon's work.[27] These and other critics take pains to understand the odd mysticism, spirituality and religious allusions that are always a part of Pynchon's fiction. Pynchon's novels include symbolic references to Judaism and Christianity as well as pantheism, animism, Tarot and Blavatsky-like channeling, Orphism, Kabbalah, Hinduism, Buddhism, various scientific mysticisms, metempsychosis, gnosticisms, Native American dream-vision and Intelligent Design. These do not appear as ornamental images in his novels but rather as integral to Pynchon's historical vision, a mystical counter-history to the rationalistic, monovocal Anglo-European history of technocratic capitalism.

Pynchon seems repeatedly to assert that history *is* mythopoesis, and vice versa. His goal seems to be to attack and complicate mainstream belief in history as fact, and open readers to the idea that facts

> are but the Play-things of lawyers [...] Alas, the Historian may indulge no
> such idle Rotating. History is not Chronology, for that is left to lawyers,— nor
> is it Remembrance, for Remembrance belongs to the People. History can as
> little pretend to the Veracity of the one, as claim the Power of the other,— her
> Practitioners, to survive, must soon learn the arts of the quidnunc, spy, and
> Taproom Wit,— that there may ever continue more than one life-line back
> into a Past we risk, each day, losing our forebears in forever— [28]

History in Thomas Pynchon's novels is a complicated affair, but it is never reduced to fact. Perversely he asserts, with postmodern philosophers of history and literary theorists, that history is multi-voiced rather than monologic, chance and event rather than deterministic time, mythic rather than legalistic, openness and improvisation rather than a closed book of facts. History for Pynchon is a plot orchestrated by power. But this history is in dialectical relation with a "history from below," the unrecorded, accumulated force of preterite, everyday life. Stuffed to the brim with historical facts, his novels nonetheless provide history with "the Costume, Toilette, and Bearing, and Speech nimble enough to keep her beyond the Desires, or even the Curiosity, of Government."[29]

NOTES

1 Thomas Pynchon, *Mason & Dixon* (New York: Henry Holt, 1997), p. 350.
2 *Ibid.*, p. 350.
3 Linda Hutcheon, *A Poetics of Postmodernism* (New York and London: Routledge, 1988), p. 89.
4 *Ibid.*, pp. 87–105.
5 Hayden White, *Tropics of Discourse: Essays in Cultural Criticism* (Baltimore and London: Johns Hopkins University Press, 1978), p. 29.
6 Fredric Jameson, *Postmodernism, or, The Cultural Logic of Late Capitalism* (Durham: Duke University Press, 1991), p. 51.
7 *Ibid.*, p. 54.
8 Amy J. Elias, "Paranoia, Theology, and Inductive Style," *Soundings: An Interdisciplinary Journal*, 86.3–4 (2003), 281–313.
9 Thomas Pynchon, *Gravity's Rainbow* (New York: Viking, 1973), p. 703.
10 Mark Richard Siegel, *Pynchon: Creative Paranoia in* Gravity's Rainbow (Port Washington: Kennikat Press, 1978).
11 Pynchon, *Gravity's Rainbow*, p. 164.
12 Thomas Kuhn, *The Structure of Scientific Revolutions*, 3rd edn. (Chicago: University of Chicago Press, 1996).
13 Paul Ricoeur, "Christianity and the Meaning of History," in Ricoeur, *History and Truth* (Evanston: Northwestern University Press, 1965), p. 94.
14 Amy J. Elias, *Sublime Desire: History and Post-1960s Fiction* (Baltimore and London: Johns Hopkins University Press, 2001).
15 Historism (vs. historicity) rejects the notion that history operates by predictable laws and yet assumes that social and political life are products of historical action; a non-teleological perspective akin to social constructivism, it is represented by the historiography of Ranke, and was defined in contradistinction to historicism by Karl Popper in *The Poverty of Historicism* (1957).
16 Brian McHale, "*Mason & Dixon* in the Zone, or, A Brief Poetics of Pynchon-Space," in Brooke Horvath and Irving Malin (eds.), *Pynchon and* Mason & Dixon (Newark: University of Delaware Press, 2000), pp. 44, 59.
17 Pynchon, *Gravity's Rainbow*, p. 57.
18 Hayden White, "The Historical Text As Literary Artifact," in White, *Tropics of Discourse: Essays in Cultural Criticism* (Baltimore and London: Johns Hopkins University Press, 1978), p. 82.
19 Hayden White, *Metahistory: The Historical Imagination in Nineteenth-Century Europe* (Baltimore and London: Johns Hopkins University Press, 1975).
20 White, "The Historical Text," p. 83.

21 *Ibid.*, p. 85.
22 Kathryn Hume, *Pynchon's Mythography: An Approach to* Gravity's Rainbow (Carbondale: Southern Illinois University Press, 1987), pp. 1–30.
23 See Brian McHale, *Postmodernist Fiction* (New York and London: Methuen, 1987).
24 Kathryn Hume, "Pynchon's Mythological Histories," in Harold Bloom (ed.), *Thomas Pynchon* (Broomall: Chelsea House Publishers, 2003), pp. 131–44.
25 Catherine R. Stimpson, "Pre-Apocalyptic Atavism: Thomas Pynchon's Early Fiction," in George Levine and David Leverenz (eds.), *Mindful Pleasures: Essays on Thomas Pynchon* (Boston: Little, Brown and Company, 1976), pp. 15–30.
26 See, for example, Thomas Moore, "The Gods of *Gravity's Rainbow*," in Moore, *The Style of Connectedness:* Gravity's Rainbow *and Thomas Pynchon* (Columbia: University of Missouri Press, 1987), pp. 219–92.
27 Debra A. Moddelmog, "The Oedipus Myth and Reader Response in *The Crying of Lot 49*," *Papers on Language and Literature: A Journal for Scholars and Critics of Language and Literature*, 23.2 (1987), 240–49; John McClure, *Partial Faiths: Postsecular Fiction in the Age of Pynchon and Morrison* (Athens: University of Georgia Press, 2007).
28 Pynchon, *Mason & Dixon*, p. 349.
29 *Ibid.*, p. 350.

10

JEFF BAKER

Politics

Along with their encyclopedic scope and vast collective commentary upon modern history, Pynchon's novels also share Tyrone Slothrop's preoccupation with America, or, more precisely, two distinct Americas: one that embodies what Pynchon has called a "Christian Capitalist" dominant culture, and the other a subjunctive, communitarian America that could, or should, exist.[1] The politics of his fiction play out in the space between as various forms of resistance, and if (to invert Von Clausewitz) politics is war waged by other means, then the locus of this battle is the individual self. This reading locates Pynchon's politics within, first, a broader Emersonian conversation about the presumption of America's singular dispensation; and, second, an oppositional discourse surrounding "Emersonian self-reliance" characterized either as the rugged individualism of laissez-faire capitalism, or as democratic communitarianism. The stark political differences between these two Emersonian selves, and how each in turn might come to define the nature of America's singularity, stand at the heart of Pynchon's politics.

Yet much of what is characterized as Emerson's politics – his American exceptionalism, resistance to authority, antipathy toward capital, and turn toward self as the seat of cultural rejuvenation – emerges out of an "Emerson" variously re-formulated and re-inscribed.[2] It is thus useful to locate Pynchon's voice in this Emersonian conversation within an appropriate chronological and political context – one filtered through the 1960s American resistance movement whose politics embody ideals associated with that decade's counterculture. Students for a Democratic Society (SDS), for example, based their political philosophy on the work of American pragmatists C. Wright Mills, John Dewey and Emerson himself, and Pynchon's enthusiastic 1973 blurb for Kirkpatrick Sale's scholarly and sympathetic *SDS* stands as evidence that Pynchon was conversant in, and presumably influenced by, this intellectual and philosophical backdrop.[3]

In this context the formulation of the Emersonian individual as a communitarian political activist – standing in opposition to a model of the rugged laissez-faire individualist – arises principally from Dewey and Mills's re-inscription of Emerson's individual as an agent of radical democracy. For Dewey, Emerson's "evasion" of philosophy via a sidestepping of the epistemological orientation of Western idealism re-situates "philosophical reflection … in the midst of quotidian struggles for meaning, status, power, wealth, and selfhood."[4] That is, in "dethroning" age-worn essentialist debates in favor of an emergent new world, experience-privileging approach, Emerson politicizes intellectual inquiry, leading Dewey to "misread" Emerson as the "philosopher of democracy."[5] Mills takes this misreading a step further by personalizing the responsibility for such inquiry, suggesting that "it is our own personal style of life and reflection we are thinking about when we think about politics."[6] For West, this reading of Emerson "deeply influenced young activists in the sixties."[7] Thus, Pynchon's infamous aversion to direct political statement aligns with a countercultural pragmatism that emphasizes personal responsibility and rejects politics as rhetorical gamesmanship (as in Jerry Rubin's affirmation that "writing a novel isn't much of a revolutionary action" and Abbie Hoffman's assertion that in "Woodstock Nation there are no writers – only poet-warriors").[8] The common critical assessment that Pynchon's politics tend toward the "oblique" echoes this countercultural aversion to the polemical, and emphasizes the inherently political importance of individual characters' decisions and actions.[9]

For example, in *The Crying of Lot 49* Oedipa Maas is leaving her "one-dimensional life of Tupperware and fondue parties" to discover a reality her self-centeredness (and self-identification with Inverarity's capitalist culture) has prevented her from seeing, one where "alienation, waste, and death" characterize America's disenfranchised poor.[10] In her journey Patell sees a critique of Emersonian individualism wherein Oedipa becomes a "satire" of rugged individualism whose hard-fought journey ends, nonetheless, in indeterminacy.[11] Yet it is also true that this journey through America's waste, and her persistent need to continually re-orient herself within it, allows Oedipa to escape her solipsism and empathically connect with a homeless sailor suffering DTs toward the novel's end.[12] This passage embodies the culmination of Oedipa's journey out of self-concern into a communitarianism that is the antithesis of a personal past heretofore identified with Inverarity's laissez-faire culture (thus completing her "political re-education" away from "economic libertarianism").[13] Her dawning awareness, expanded now to acknowledge her connection with such waste, resembles philosopher George Kateb's Emersonianism, wherein "the development of individuality leads, not to egoism, but to a sense of connectedness."[14] Her awakening also raises what will become an ongoing concern in Pynchon's fiction: an exceptionalism postulating a hypothetical America (where the "chances [were] once so good for diversity") that ought to represent a way out of class differences, away from capital as the highest value (in Emerson's words) of a culture "taught to aim at low objects [that then] eats upon itself."[15]

In the broadest terms, *Gravity's Rainbow* is a pragmatic critique of North Atlantic idealism and the death culture it perpetuates, even as America is both its progeny and principle purveyor at the end of the twentieth century. Paradoxically, the novel also reaffirms the exceptionalist imperative of *The Crying of Lot 49*, wherein the superiority of precedent culture is repudiated and a hypothetical America ought to have represented Europe's second chance.[16] Thus Slothrop's ancestor, William, who writes a banned tract arguing for a spiritually democratic church eliminating the Puritanical distinction between elect and preterite, inspires Slothrop to ask: "Could he have been the fork in the road America never took, the singular point she jumped the wrong way from?"[17] This subjunctive America becomes a moral telos in Pynchon's fiction, against the measure of which all lesser "Americas" become occasions for lamenting opportunities squandered, resistances foregone. The discrepancy between the two versions of America is measured in the construction of self – in this case, Slothrop's.

Literally and figuratively, the Slothropian self is constructed by Their dominant culture. Physically, the Infant Tyrone's co-optation by Jamf's behavioral experimentation (on the Penis He Thought Was His Own) may account for adult Tyrone's prescient erections foretelling London's V-2 rocket strikes, but it also illustrates capitalist Lyle Bland's interest in Jamf's human control experiments and "the Capitalist's" manifold historical influence.[18] Figuratively too, Slothrop's Hawaiian shirts, zoot suits and clipped, noire-esque repartee represent the mindlessness of American consumer culture. In trying to escape repression by almost passively "riding their kind underground" through the Raketenstadt, Slothrop, somewhat anachronistically, symbolizes the "glozing neuters" whose brains have been "ravaged by antisocial and mindless pleasures."[19]

This vacuous self-concern is emphasized when Slothrop, just prior to his apparent disintegration, achieves a kind of empty-headed, hippie nirvana, "just feeling natural." Such a Romantic transcendence is reminiscent of Emerson's "Transparent Eyeball" passage, but is subject to a critique of the rugged individualism implicit in Emerson's self-reliance as re-inscribed by Bercovitch and Howe.[20] In his "great heresy" reading of this "Eyeball" passage, Howe argues that Emerson repudiates all moral ground but individual experience and intuition, eliminating divine authority. Building on this reading, Bercovitch then condemns this separation of the individual from a broader moral discourse as affirming the rugged individualist's "dream vision of laissez-faire."[21] This interpretation marks Slothrop's own apotheosis as solipsistic: he has transcended, but the culmination of his self-centered quest for freedom has simultaneously rendered him heedless of others – not an effective mode for would-be communitarian revolutionaries.

Yet this self-centered apotheosis is among the reasons Slothrop becomes a dubious symbolic source of inspiration for the novel's Counterforce, a group of characters attempting to bring down the "They-system" of the novel. The Counterforce can be seen as analogous to 1960s and 1970s resistance movements, re-casting the novel's ostensible setting within Pynchon's more contemporaneous (i.e., anti-Nixonian) agenda.[22] Admitting this anachronistic reading, we can see that Pynchon's wry post-mortem of those failed resistance efforts reveals a co-optation similar to Slothrop's own. In the Counterforce's failure to create an effective alternative (and oppositional) We-system, Roger Mexico's crew must adopt Their "rationalist" methodology and are thus co-opted by the very system they would overthrow. The Man has "busted the sod prairies of their brains," as Slothrop himself had discovered, so that nothing of their own will grow there.[23] The Counterforce's inability to realize communitarian principles (such as Geli Tripping's personal, yet community-oriented, ad hoc arrangements) as an alternative to Their rationalized, rugged individualism, precisely matches Slothrop's conundrum. The culminating logic of these analogous critiques suggests that communitarianism, actualized at the individual level, is the only basis for successful *collective* cultural resistance. This conclusion is corroborated in *Vineland* by Frenesi's inability (or refusal) to move beyond co-optation and personal collusion.

On the one hand, Patell and Dickson find in *Vineland* examples of the sort of communitarianism under discussion. Patell reads in the preparations for and enactment of the Traverse-Becker reunion a "commitment to an alternative, communitarian idea of America" in which "Eula, Jess, and most of their progeny are examples of situated selves, whose individual identities are formed by work, social commitment, and family life."[24] Similarly, Dickson reads Prairie's journey as a representation of the way the novel constructs the encounter between self and world, concluding that Prairie's uncertain future at the novel's end opens a new hermeneutic space in which she is exempted "from creating her own role *within pre-existing* historical designs."[25] This in turn leaves her free to create a different and ameliorative world for herself. The relative optimism of these readings exemplifies what we have been calling communitarian Emersonian individualism.

Equally compelling, though, is the way Dickson reads Jess Traverse's quoting of Emerson during the reunion. Pynchon's distancing of this passage (Traverse quoting William James quoting Emerson), along with Jess's own narrow interpretation of Emerson's "divine retribution" as merely "personal justice," can be seen as an ironic, conflicted and ambivalent take on the duality of Emersonian individualism.[26] This two-sided individualism then emerges in Frenesi's own "double allegiances," causing her to be both a "revolutionary girl of the sixties" and "a handmaid of repression."[27] As sixties political activist, the daughter of Sasha Gates (and great great-granddaughter of *Against the Day*'s industrial terrorist Webb Traverse) is an embodiment of the American Left.[28] Yet her characterization becomes another examination of the failures of sixties-era resistance arising out of not only drug use and mindless hedonism, but also, more significantly, willful political co-optation and collusion springing from self-interest and individual pathology.[29]

Frenesi's attraction to men in uniform represents another sexual co-optation by the dominant culture (menacingly symbolized by Federal Prosecutor Brock Vond) which clearly corrupts her ability to navigate the self's re-orientation from rugged individual to communitarian revolutionary. Her "helpless turn toward images of authority" results, first, in her willingness to betray her sixties film collective comrades and cause the murder of her activist lover, Weed Atman, and will eventually have her literally working for The Man.[30] Her personal revolution becomes a servile form of freedom which allows her to "act outside warrants and charters, to ignore history and the dead," by working as a snitch for the federal government. Thus Booker's assessment, that "much of the transgressive energy of the sixties was ... escapist rather than activist," perfectly describes Frenesi's self-serving revolution, which becomes both circumscribed by and willfully supportive of Reagan-era rugged individualism.[31] Her refusal to forego selfishness symbolizes the defeat, not only of the American Left, but of a broader American culture willingly participating in its own subjugation.[32]

In "The Poet," Emerson anticipates an artist who will know, and can express, the "value of our incomparable [American] materials."[33] This mythic poet of Emerson's prophecy, who both embodies *and* expresses the national genius, becomes himself a kind of conflation, an "exhortative conception of the individual *as* America."[34] Where the characters of previous novels seem to represent this conflation, signifying America in some larger, symbolic way, *Mason & Dixon* reverses this pattern, moving instead from "self" as America, to America as "self." Straddling two decades, including the liminal events preceding the Revolution as well as the new nation's formative aftermath, the novel's excavation of America's beginnings reveals a "self" poisoned from its conception by capital, collusion and co-optation.

Of course *Mason & Dixon* continues to represent the possibility for American exceptionalism: Dixon says, "No matter where we go, shall we find all the World Tyrants and Slaves? America was the one place we should *not* have found them." Here, a potentially communitarian America is presented as a "Rubbish Tip for subjunctive Hopes."[35] Yet this subjunctive America is corrupt from its inception; indeed, by its inception. The novel's Captain Volcanoe passage reveals that the seeds of the American revolution, and of revolutionary groups such as the Sons of Liberty, were neither communitarian nor democratic, but clearly mercenary.[36] Moreover, the imperialistic and divisive nature of Mason and Dixon's line-making operation will be an everlasting canker upon the aborning nation's soul, betokening "Bad History," in Captain Zhang's words: "All else will follow as if predestin'd, unto War and Devastation."[37] Debunking any nostalgia for a democratic origin myth and uncovering the roots of the mercenary enterprise beneath, Pynchon's novel again examines the conspiratorial role of its individual characters as they are implicated in the construction of this broader American self.

Predominant themes across Pynchon's work, personal collusion and co-optation become more urgently accusatory in *Mason & Dixon*, from Cherrycoke's reliance on the good graces of arms dealer LeSpark's comfortable perch from which he spins his tale, to Dixon's own beseeching of Mason toward the novel's end: "Didn't we take the King's money, as here we're taking it again? whilst Slaves waited upon us, and we neither one objected."[38] Moreover, Pynchon makes it clear, through his anachronistic, hippie-ish, postmodernized portrayal of the American Revolution that we, his contemporaries, constitute the principal target of this indictment.[39] Washington's penchant for pot-smoking and Franklin's rock star persona (complete with tinted granny glasses) imply a charge of collusion levied at both revolutionary generations.[40] This contemporaneous indictment is yet another critique of failed sixties resistance efforts, and also reinforces Emerson's exhortation to self-examination (and self-incrimination) as remedy for the impotence of wider social, political or cultural resistance in the absence of such self-reflection.

In *Against the Day*, Hume sees Webb Traverse's martyrdom as an endorsement of the politics of violence reflecting Pynchon's "increasing desperation over the direction America is taking."[41] Indeed, the novel's cynicism regarding the efficacy of collective lawful political resistance has become so complete that Reef Traverse's son will sum up "being American as meaning 'do what they tell you and take what they give you and don't go on strike or their soldiers will shoot you down.'"[42] The novel's rejection of *Vineland's* hippie aversion to "pick[ing] up the gun" demonstrates an increasingly desperate moral imperative in Pynchon's examination of the politics of individual responsibility.[43]

Transpiring in the end-of-the-nineteenth-century America of anarchistic murderers, antiterrorist security, scabs, strikers and Pinkertons, *Against the*

Day's battle for America is no longer metaphoric: here dynamite is both the "audible sign" of the miner's curse of "enslavement to mineral extraction," as well as "the American workingman's equalizer, his agent of deliverance."[44] A young Webb Traverse takes Reverend Moss Gatlin's exhortation to destroy "those who slaughter the innocent as easy as signing a check" to heart, becoming a violent anarchist, perhaps even the notorious dynamiter the Kieselguhr Kid himself.[45] He will be murdered for his efforts, yet his martyrdom is un-heroic: most of the Traverse family's terrible pathology (including daughter Lake's excruciating self-loathing) is clearly attributed to the smoldering rage associated with Webb's violence toward the "plutes," while the brooding secretiveness of his anarchism guarantees his absence from filial responsibilities whether home or away.[46] The isolated nature of Traverse's resistance to capital is symbolized by the fact that not one member of the miner's union attends his funeral or even sends flowers, and the harm he causes those on whose behalf he believes himself to be working becomes another negative example of resistance not informed by a communitarian ethos.[47] In a familiar inversion, Traverse's attempt at radical resistance becomes simply another form of rugged individualism.

Still, the novel's assertion that "the secret backlands of wealth" sooner or later "always depend on some act of murder" is borne out by capitalist Scarsdale Vibe's view of labor, in which the sole remedy for anarchists like Traverse is class genocide.[48] This view is revealed to Foley Walker, a working man who gains access to the capitalist's privileged world by serving as Vibe's Civil War surrogate, where a wound renders him presciently useful to Vibe's bottom line. Yet, as we learn of Walker's wound-derived "communications from far, far away," we also learn that there is one voice "unlike the others" reminding Foley to restrain himself "from escaping into the freedom of bloodletting unrestrained."[49] This voice, representing some higher value opposed to Vibe's monomania, interferes with Walker's devotion to Vibe to the point that, when ordered to kill would-be assassins Frank Traverse and Ewball Oust, Foley instead kills the capitalist, invoking an authority above even Vibe's pay grade.[50] Walker's act symbolizes a form of class warfare fought within the individual himself, between the communitarian and rugged individual selves implicit in Emerson's self-reliance. Significantly, the most "rugged" individual in the novel repudiates the spoils of laissez-faire and embraces a communitarianism opposing the "tyrants and [...] monopolists of the world."[51]

If Walker's repentance is salutary, *Inherent Vice*'s Mickey Wolfmann's subverted attempt to repent his "greedy-ass ways" is darkly pessimistic.[52] Wolfmann is a real estate mogul whose intake of certain alkaloids awakens in him the desire to atone for spending his "whole life making people pay for shelter, when it ought to've been free." In his effort to "make the money start to flow in a different direction," he begins constructing Arrepentimiento ("Spanish for 'sorry about that,'" as Puck Beaverton informs us), a new housing development where anyone who wants to can live rent free.[53] This turn toward philanthropy, however, results in Mickey's disappearance and, as the story unfolds thanks to private investigator Larry "Doc" Sportello's sleuthing, we begin to understand that this kidnapping may involve any number of governmental, mob-related and interested private parties.

By the time Doc's trail leads him to Vegas, he runs into "big trouble in brown shoes" at the Kismet Lounge in the form of FBI agents manhandling a heavily tranquilized Mickey: as Beaverton later explains, "Suddenly no more acid-head philanthropist. They did something to him." As usual, the paranoid question here is "which They?"[54] While we're offered a number of plausible explanations for Mickey's reprogramming, the most likely turns out to be the good old unseen agencies of "command and control" we've known for so long in Pynchon's fiction. By the time Doc meets up with well-heeled Orange County citizen Crocker Fenway (acting as a fixer between Doc and the shadowy Golden Fang), we discover the real interests behind the FBI's kidnapping of Wolfmann. Though Fenway's haughty disdain for anybody who has ever paid rent raises Doc's ire, he nevertheless straightens Sportello out on capital's unassailable pecking order, and why a traitor to capital like Wolfmann had to be stopped: "'It's about *being in place* [...] We've been in place forever. Look around. Real estate, water rights, oil, cheap labor – all of that's ours, it's always been ours.'"[55] This revelation of capital protecting its own interests might lull us into believing that *Inherent Vice* is merely a sequel to *Against the Day*'s unequivocal class warfare. Yet there is also a direct and bitter accusation levied here at a middle class "'eager to be bought off with a car of a certain make, model and year, a blonde in a bikini [...] a chili dog, for Christ's sake.'" Ruthlessly, Fenway concludes, "'We will never run out of you people. The supply is inexhaustible.'"[56]

NOTES

1 Thomas Pynchon, *Gravity's Rainbow* (New York: Viking, 1973), p. 623.
2 Cornel West, *The American Evasion of Philosophy* (Madison: University of Wisconsin Press, 1989); also see Cyrus Patell, *Negative Liberties* (Durham: Duke University Press, 2001).
3 Stewart Burns, *Social Movements of the 1960s* (Boston: Twayne, 1990), p. 57; Frederick Ashe, "Anachronism Intended: *Gravity's Rainbow* in the Sociopolitical Sixties," *Pynchon Notes*, 28–29 (1991), 63.
4 West, *American Evasion*, p. 73.

5   *Ibid.*, pp. 75, 89.
6   C. Wright Mills, "The Social Role of the Intellectual," in Irving L. Horowitz (ed.), *Power, Politics, and People: The Collected Essays of C. Wright Mills* (New York: Oxford University Press, 1963), p. 299.
7   West, *American Evasion*, p. 131.
8   Charles Hollander, "Pynchon's Politics: The Presence of an Absence," *Pynchon Notes*, 26–27 (1990), 5–59; F. Ashe, "Anachronism Intended," 59.
9   Samuel Thomas, *Pynchon and the Political* (New York: Routledge, 2007), p. 109.
10 Lois Tyson, "Existential Subjectivity on Trial: *The Crying of Lot 49* and the Politics of Despair," *Pynchon Notes*, 28–29 (1991), 5, 8; Mark Decker, "A Proliferation of Bad Shit: Informational Entropy, Politics, and *The Crying of Lot 49*," *Pynchon Notes*, 46–49 (2000–2001), 142.
11 Patell, *Negative Liberties*, p. 11.
12 Steven Weisenburger, "Reading Race: *The Crying of Lot 49* and Early Pynchon," in Thomas Schaub (ed.), *Approaches to Teaching Pynchon's* The Crying of Lot 49 *and Other Works* (New York: MLA, 2008), p. 53.
13 Jerry Varsava, "Teaching the Epochal Oedipa: *The Crying of Lot 49* as Political Dialogue," in Schaub (ed.), *Approaches to Teaching*, pp. 60–61.
14 Patell, *Negative Liberties*, p. 78.
15 Thomas Pynchon, *The Crying of Lot 49* (Philadelphia: Lippincott, 1966), 181; Ralph Waldo Emerson, "The American Scholar," in Nina Baym (ed.), *The Norton Anthology of American Literature*, Shorter 7th edn. (New York: Norton, 2008), vol. 1, p. 532.
16 Pynchon, *Gravity's Rainbow*, p. 722.
17 *Ibid.*, p. 556.
18 Jeffrey S. Baker, "Amerikkka Uber Alles: German Nationalism, American Imperialism, and the 1960s Anti-War Movement in *Gravity's Rainbow*." *Critique*, 40.4 (Summer 1999), 323–41.
19 Pynchon, *Gravity's Rainbow*, pp. 603, 681.
20 *Ibid.*, p. 626; David Dickson, *The Utterance of America* (Göteborg, Sweden: Acta Universitatis Gothoburgensis, 1998), pp. 22–23.
21 Sacvan Bercovitch, "Emerson, Individualism, and the Ambiguities of Dissent," *South Atlantic Quarterly*, 89.3 (1990), 629–30.
22 Jeffrey S. Baker, "A Democratic Pynchon: Counterculture, Counterforce and Participatory Democracy," *Pynchon Notes*, 32–33 (1993), 99–131.
23 Pynchon, *Gravity's Rainbow*, p. 210.
24 Patell, *Negative Liberties*, pp. 171–72.
25 Dickson, *Utterance*, pp. 182, 184.
26 *Ibid.*, pp. 163–64.
27 *Ibid.*, p. 164.
28 M. Keith Booker, "America and Its Discontents: The Failure of Leftist Politics in *Vineland*," *Literature, Interpretation, Theory*, 4.2 (1993), 89.
29 Molly Hite, "Feminist Theory and the Politics of *Vineland*," in Geoffrey Green, Donald J. Greiner, and Larry McCaffery (eds.), *The Vineland Papers* (Normal, IL: Dalkey Archive, 1994), p. 140.
30 Thomas Pynchon, *Vineland* (New York: Little Brown, 1990), p. 83.
31 *Ibid.*, pp. 71–72; Booker, "America," 97.

32 Barbara L. Pittman, "'Dangerously Absent Dreamers': Genealogy, History and the Political Left in *Vineland*," *Pynchon Notes*, 30–31 (1992), 39–51.

33 Ralph Waldo Emerson, "The Poet," in Baym (ed.), *Norton Anthology*, p. 563.

34 West, *American Evasion*, p. 13.

35 Thomas Pynchon, *Mason & Dixon* (New York: Henry Holt & Co., 1997), p. 693; Tony Tanner, "'The Rubbish-Tip for Subjunctive Hopes': Thomas Pynchon's *Mason & Dixon*," in Tanner, *The American Mystery* (Cambridge University Press, 2000), pp. 225–26.

36 Pynchon, *Mason & Dixon*, p. 403; Jeff Baker, "Plucking the American Albatross: Pynchon's Irrealism in *Mason & Dixon*," in Brooke Horvath and Irving Malin (eds.), *Pynchon and* Mason & Dixon (Newark: University of Delaware Press, 2000), pp. 168–72.

37 Pynchon, *Mason & Dixon*, p. 615.

38 *Ibid.*, pp. 411, 693.

39 Brian McHale, "Mason and Dixon in the Zone," in Horvath and Malin (eds.), *Pynchon and* Mason & Dixon, p. 48; Brian Thill, "The Sweetness of Immorality: *Mason & Dixon* and the American Sins of Consumption," in Elizabeth Jane Wall Hinds (ed.), *The Multiple Worlds of Pynchon's* Mason & Dixon: *Eighteenth-Century Contexts, Postmodern Observations* (Rochester: Camden House, 2005), pp. 55–56.

40 J. Baker, "Plucking the American Albatross," p. 183.

41 Kathryn Hume, "The Religious and Political Vision of Thomas Pynchon's *Against the Day*," *Philological Quarterly*, 86.1–2 (Winter 2007), 164.

42 *Ibid.*, p. 166.

43 Pynchon, *Vineland*, p. 229.

44 Thomas Pynchon, *Against the Day* (New York: Penguin Press, 2006), pp. 25, 86–87.

45 *Ibid.*, p. 171.

46 *Ibid.*, p. 95.

47 *Ibid.*, pp. 215–16.

48 *Ibid.*, pp. 170, 333.

49 *Ibid.*, pp. 100, 335.

50 *Ibid.*, p. 1006.

51 Pynchon, *Vineland*, p. 369.

52 Thomas Pynchon, *Inherent Vice* (New York: Penguin Press, 2009), p. 334.

53 *Ibid.*, pp. 244, 150.

54 *Ibid.*, p. 252.

55 *Ibid.*, pp. 346–47.

56 *Ibid.*, p. 347.

11

DEBORAH L. MADSEN

Alterity

Pynchon's engagement with alterity is thematized psychologically through paranoia, schizophrenia, and narcissism; politically through systems of control that attempt to destroy otherness; economically through monopolistic transnational corporations and cartels that supplant national governments; scientifically through determinism and theories of entropy; aesthetically through film and photography, storytelling and the "routinization" of language. Pynchon thematizes these various aspects of culture as the effort to substitute the randomness of nature with a perfectly controlled, and controllable, version of reality: what, in *Gravity's Rainbow* (1973), Pointsman describes as "a rather strictly defined, clinical version of truth."[1] This chapter considers how Pynchon's work has represented and complicated diverse contested understandings of identity and alterity by variously undermining and legitimizing them. Pynchon's narrative engagement with liberal humanist ideas of essentialized identities gives rise to much of his narratological innovation and complexity, particularly when his exploration of ontological identity categories takes place within the context of European colonialism and its New World legacies.

Alterity names the process by which an "Other" is constructed. It carries the double sense of both the subject position of "Otherness" in which someone is placed and also the adoption of that subject position as the Other's perspective. Alterity is then a double process of placement and perception. In narrative, consequently, alterity affects the construction of character and also the treatment of narrative perspective or focalization, spatiality, temporality, causality, and truth or authenticity. Thematically, alterity represents an ontological distinction between self and Other where the Other is marked according to categorical differences of gender, race, class, ethnicity, sexuality, religion and the like.

Alterity is less a thing or noun than it is a process or verb, a process of "Othering." Cultural anthropologist Michael Taussig writes that "alterity is every inch a relationship, not a thing in itself, and is in this case [of the indigenous Cuna people] an actively mediated colonial relationship meeting contradictory and conflicting European expectations of what constitutes Indianness."[2] I will turn to the issue of colonialism below; here, it is Taussig's characterization of alterity as an interpersonal process that I want to highlight. For in Pynchon's narratives also, alterity is a multidirectional process. The binary oppositions explored in Pynchon's fiction (ones and zeroes, in *The Crying of Lot 49* [1966]; "Them" versus the "Counterforce" in *Gravity's Rainbow*) sketch the contours of this dialogism but do not mark its limits. Characters like "Pirate" Prentice or, in *Against the Day* (2006), Madame Eskimoff both do and do not "change sides" – as she tells Lew Basnight – and yet they are defined by both. Pynchon's characterization relies on what characters say about themselves and their values, what is said about them and their behavior, and the actions witnessed by the reader in the course of the narrative. As a consequence, characters appear to acquire subjectivity and, for some, a significant degree of personal experience even while they are paranoically speculating about the extent to which their selfhood is a construction directed by powerful external cultural interests. Such speculations are contextualized by the interpretive efforts of other characters, narrators and the reader, all of whom are engaged dialogically in the construction of identity and alterity, sameness and Otherness.

One of the most baffling episodes in contemporary literature is the sequence in *Gravity's Rainbow* when Tyrone Slothrop, the ostensible protagonist of the novel, disintegrates or disseminates into multiple distinct personae. The fragmentation of Slothrop's character is referenced in a number of separate episodes. In the course of narrating Roger Mexico's experience of Frau Utgarthaloki's cannibalistic dinner party, the narrator remarks of Slothrop: "It's doubtful if he can ever be 'found' again, in the conventional sense of 'positively identified and detained.'"[3] This remark is presented as an aside; the narrator's primary subject in this scene is Roger Mexico and his realization that he must act: to do nothing would be to accept life on Their terms though his alternative is to die. Thus, Slothrop's disintegration is presented to the reader as the dialogical context within which the characters of both Slothrop and Mexico are developed.

In this aside, the narrator returns to the earlier image of Slothrop as a plucked albatross; living alone in the mountains, he is described as "changing, plucking the albatross of self now and then" but still hoping for a way to return home, to America.[4] At this point in the narrative, Slothrop is still pursuing the sense of an authentic self by puzzling out his relation to Laszlo Jamf and the conditioning of his infant self even while he is reading for further clues all the phenomena that surround him: from flights of birds to graffiti written amid the ruins of bombed buildings. On the wall of a public toilet he has not visited before he discovers the message "ROCKETMAN WAS HERE" and the narrator reports that "his first thought was that he had written it himself and forgot [...] Might be he was starting to implicate himself, some yesterday version of himself, in the Combination against who he was right then. In its sluggish coma, the albatross stirred."[5] There are a number of points here worth noting. The first is the fragmentation of Slothrop into "versions" of himself that are separate in time and space. Secondly, these putative disparate selves have no awareness of each other and so do not represent any kind of unifying convergence of identities into a singular and authoritative "Slothrop." Further, this entire account of Slothrop's early dissemination takes place within the discourse of the extra-diegetic narrator. Slothrop occupies the third-person pronominal position; Slothrop is always "he" and never "me." Thus the narrator places Slothrop in a position of Otherness or alterity and then adopts that "Othered" point of view, though in the subjunctive mode of what might be – not what unquestionably is – the case. Other characters besides the narrator express their uncertainty concerning Slothrop's identity, as he appears in various disguises such as Rocketman, then the pig-hero Plechazunga. That other characters refer to Slothrop as fragmenting into alternative identities encourages the reader to adopt the narrator's interpretation of Slothrop's fate as a character. The recurring albatross metaphor, which alludes intertextually to Coleridge's "Rime of the Ancient Mariner" (1798), belongs to the narrator's discursive lexicon (not Slothrop's) and is used pejoratively to evoke the image of selfhood as a source of anxiety, a burden of responsibility and also a liability: the narrator remarks late in the novel that "The Man has a branch office in each of our brains, his corporate emblem is a white albatross, each local rep has a cover known as the Ego, and their mission in this world is Bad Shit."[6]

Slothrop's final mountaintop appearance as a seemingly unified character prefigures elements of the episode that follows the explosion in the Transvestites' Toilet, when the narrator reports that, although he doesn't remember it, Slothrop studies a newspaper image of the nuclear bombing of Hiroshima: "a giant white cock, dangling in the sky straight downward out of a white pubic bush,"[7] an image that echoes the narrator's description of Slothrop's transformation into a "crossroad," when he "sees a very thick rainbow here, a stout rainbow cock driven down out of pubic clouds into Earth, green wet valleyed Earth, and his chest fills and he stands crying, not a thing in his head, just feeling natural...."[8] This narrative linking of the Rocket that Slothrop seeks with the devastation of Hiroshima is anticipated later by the narrator in a predictive aside, with the reference to "the Hafenstrasse in Greifswald, where Slothrop in early August may see a particular newspaper photo."⁹ Again, these anticipations and echoes are located in the third-person narrator's descriptions of Slothrop, expressed in the subjunctive mode.

So when the narrator turns explicitly to the story of Slothrop's disassembly, not only the narrative fate of this character but also the character of the narrator is brought into question:

> There is also the story about Tyrone Slothrop, who was sent into the Zone to be present at his own assembly—perhaps, heavily paranoid voices have whispered, his time's assembly—and there ought to be a punch line to it, but there isn't. The plan went wrong. He is being broken down instead, and scattered. His cards have been laid down [...] laid out and read, but they are the cards of a tanker and feeb: they point only to a long and scuffling future, to mediocrity (not only in his life but also, heh, heh, in his chroniclers too [...]—to no clear happiness or redeeming cataclysm.¹⁰

This much-quoted passage, which appears on first reading to define Slothrop's fragmentation, tells the reader more about the narrator than about the character. Through the motif of the Tarot, the narrator offers an interpretation of an interpretation of Slothrop's future that is further undermined by the prediction of future "mediocrity" for Slothrop's "chroniclers," which must include the narrator as well as the reader. Thus, at the moment when readers could expect an authoritative narrative statement concerning the protagonist, the narrative undermines the possibility of such epistemological authority. An unbridgeable Otherness is evoked among narrator, character and reader, an alterity that denies the possibility of knowing identity, experience and history as stable, external objects of knowledge. The narrator suggests that reality is the artifact or consequence of symbolic signifying systems, whether they be linguistic or iconographic like the Tarot. If Slothrop's reality is the product of language and he has effectively evaded language, then his reality is rendered unknowable, irretrievably Other, to the speculating narrator and reader alike.

To read Slothrop's narrative dissemination in terms of the deconstruction of objective reality is, of course, to offer an interpretation of this narrative scene that it would seem to resist. A number of prominent commentators interpret as a strategy of resistance to "Their" ever-encompassing networks of control Slothrop's disintegration as a humanistic subject, in possession of an essential and unchanging core of identity, which moves through a unified and knowable linear history, and occupies a stable position within an objective physical environment. Critics like Molly Hite, David Seed and Tony Tanner interpret Slothrop's character as an instance of a provisional, fluid, postmodern subjectivity that may be capable of resisting the globalizing hegemony of the military-industrial complex.[11] The determinism that underpins "Their" strategies of analysis and control could be eluded by the randomness and multidimensionality of the postmodern subject that is characterized by unpredictable change, the refusal of memory (and so of history) and constant movement. Indeed, Leo Bersani sees the denial of humanistic ontological privilege as characteristic of Pynchon's representation of "Them" as well.[12] Like the novel itself, which defies analysis, characters who refuse the unified categories of identity or subjectivity potentially represent a strategy by which to elude conditioning and control.

Slothrop is not the only character to be "[s]cattered all over the Zone"; while the narrator observes quite late in the novel that "fragments of Slothrop have grown into consistent personae of their own," much earlier the reader is told that "[s]eparations are proceeding. Each alternative Zone speeds away from all the others, in fated acceleration, red-shifting, fleeing the Center. Each day the mythical return Enzian dreamed of seems less possible [...] Each bird has his branch now, and each one is the Zone."[13] These separations, like the retreat of Mucho Maas in *The Crying of Lot 49* into musical frequencies only he can hear, are thematized variously as narcissism or solipsism, a narrowing of communicative possibilities to the individual consciousness. However, as Thomas Schaub has noted, the intersection of two or more isolated subjectivities, as happens for example during the deaf mutes' dance in *The Crying of Lot 49*, creates the impression of an external reality independent of individual human consciousness.[14] In such instances, where order spontaneously occurs in place of the chaos that is anticipated, Pynchon appears to contest the entropic interpretation of communication – according to which increasing amounts of information become available in systems with decreasing structure so that more structure results in less usable information – and the valorization of alterity that such an interpretation promotes.

The fragmentation of Slothrop into distinct personae involves the dispersal of his position within a unified linear time, memory or history. This temporality is not only the diegetic time of the narrative world but also the temporal component of the narrative experienced by the reader. In this way, Slothrop can be said to elude the confines of the narrative itself by escaping the reader's efforts to discover continuity of meaning within a stable, self-identical character. As Leo Bersani remarks, "he is of course on the run from us too, from the interpretative babbling that he sets off and never satisfies and that is so hard to stop."[15] Slothrop eludes the kind of singular history which Wicks Cherrycoke in *Mason & Dixon* (1997) describes as "hir'd, or coerc'd, only in Interests that must ever prove base."[16] If official "History" is written by those who dominate and win in historical conflicts, then, as

Michael Bérubé observes, Pynchon "constructs histories within History," to which we might add characters within "Character," plots within "Plots."[17]

These characters resist classification according to narratological categories such as E. M. Forster's "flat" versus "round" characters, though David Witzling refers correctly to "the tendency among Pynchon's critics to treat characters as metonyms for ideas rather than as simulations of real people."[18] Pynchon's characters are thematized as artifacts of larger discursive systems that enact patterns of control, power and ownership. That is, characters do not possess the innate selves assumed by liberal humanism: rather, they are spoken by powerful cultural agents like governments, popular culture or, more often, corporations. Slothrop's quest for selfhood is a search for an alternative way of interpreting his personal history. He learns, gradually, the extent to which he has been co-opted by "Them": sold as a baby by his family as an experimental subject and psychologically conditioned by Laszlo Jamf. The erection that is his conditioned behavioral response is described by the narrator as "an instrument installed, wired by Them into his body as a colonial outpost here in our raw and clamorous world, another office representing Their white Metropolis far away...."[19]

Pynchon's use of the metaphor of colonialism to signify corporate surveillance and control echoes Anne McClintock's description of imperialism not as "something that happened elsewhere – a disagreeable fact of history external to Western identity. Rather, imperialism and the invention of race were fundamental aspects of Western, industrial modernity."[20] This imperial modernity, both at home and abroad, depended upon the categorization of individuals according to race, gender, ethnicity, class, religion, in ways that facilitated their dehumanization and availability for economic exploitation and political domination. Slothrop describes his experience of having been "sold to IG Farben like a side of beef," using the trope of dead meat to underline his dehumanization.[21] However, more than imperial economics, Pynchon's novels explore the psychology of colonialism from the eighteenth-century slave trade in *Mason & Dixon*, through the nineteenth-century era of European expansionism in *V.* (1963), *Gravity's Rainbow* and *Against the Day*, to contemporary discourses of colonizing space. Much of Pynchon's treatment of colonialism focuses upon the opposition between savagery and civilization: in *Gravity's Rainbow* the narrator, addressing Karl Marx, denies that colonialism is "nothing but Cheap Labor and Overseas Markets.... Oh, no. Colonies are much, much more. Colonies are the outhouses of the European soul, where a fellow can let his pants down and relax, enjoy the smell of his own shit," where the constraints of civilization no longer apply.[22]

Slothrop is manipulated in his quest for the *Schwarzgerät* or "black-thing" through his ambivalent fear of all things black. The network of signifying relations among blackness, eroticism and death is engaged in such narrative episodes as Slothrop's descent into the toilet at the Roseland Ballroom, which is immediately motivated by his fear of being buggered by the black washroom attendant; Gavin Trefoil's attempt to persuade his colleagues at PISCES that "their feelings about blackness were tied to feelings about shit, and feelings about shit to feelings about putrefaction and death";[23] Brigadier Pudding's experience of coprophagia, which is eroticized as part of his sadomasochistic encounter with Katje but is also linked to his traumatization in the trenches of World War I; Gottfried's speculation that, like Enzian with Weissmann/Blicero, they are "lovers whose genitals are consecrated to shit"; and Foppl's Siege Party in *V.* where Mondaugen encounters white men exercising extreme physical brutality over their black slaves in the midst of sexual decadence.[24] Mondaugen's story raises the question of the extent to which those perpetrators of genocide like Foppl, who continues to celebrate von Trotha's 1904 campaign of extermination against the Hereros and Hottentots, are manipulated and conditioned into their savage behavior by the forces of colonialism. Foppl confesses to Mondaugen the sense of relief he experienced as part of an impersonal killing machine, freed from individual moral restraints into the systematic nature of the killing. Foppl's alienation from himself as the artifact of a system of domination echoes Slothrop's, but the very different contexts in which these characters are placed raise disturbing issues of alterity and co-optation.

This highly conflicted mix of alienation and complicity could include all those characters who, in *The Crying of Lot 49*, are described as performing "a calculated withdrawal from the life of the Republic" though, as Steven Weisenburger has pointed out, this withdrawal is always potentially complicit with what he calls "a segregationist and colonialist regime of power."[25] The deliberate, genocidal self-annihilation practiced by the Hereros known as the Empty Ones suggests this kind of complicity. Co-optation by "Them" is suggested by the "Zone-Hereros" who are described in *Gravity's Rainbow* as now living "in [their] step-father's house" and by Enzian's ironic confession that he may have "gone a bit native" in the Zone.[26] He "goes native" not in Germany generally but specifically in the space of the Raketen-Stadt where, as Michael Harris reminds us, "colonialism still remains alive and well in the form of a multinational corporate empire [...] that knows no boundaries and touches every sphere of life."[27]

Harris references here the global arena in which Pynchon's critique of colonialism takes place. The narrator observes, late in *Gravity's Rainbow*, that in America "Europe came and established its order of Analysis and

Death. What it could not use, it killed or altered. In time the death-colonies grew strong enough to break away. But the impulse to empire, the mission to propagate death, the structure of it, kept on."[28] Colonialism is represented as a will to control, dominate and possess. When Weissmann brings Enzian to Europe, to involve him in the building of the Rocket and the control of nature through technology, this gesture is a complex expression of love, patriarchal power and colonial domination. And this imperial power is most fully realized when the colonized become complicit in the conditions of their own servitude. The slave girl Austra in *Mason & Dixon* appears paradigmatically to embrace the decadent values of her owners, the Vroom family, who hope to breed her with Dixon and sell the fair-skinned babies that result. Austra escapes the worst excesses of colonial violence, which Mason and Dixon encounter elsewhere in the Dutch Cape Colony, but at the cost of alienation from herself and co-optation into the economics and psychology of colonialism.

Mason & Dixon explores the power of global colonialism at the moment of US independence, but Pynchon's fiction exhibits a sustained interest in colonial relations between Europe and America. Weisenburger, reading *The Crying of Lot 49* as Oedipa's "quest into an American space of colonial oppression and racial alterity," points to a little-noticed connection between the characters of Dr Hilarius and Winthrop Tremain.[29] Hilarius's history as a concentration camp psychiatrist and Tremaine's business selling swastikas link European and American fascism through the image of systematized racial hatred. Together they evoke "a mid-twentieth-century fascist white supremacy in its (anti-semitic) German and (anti-black) United States versions, thus also stipulating a historical link or inheritance joining American to European imperial and racial desires."[30] A similar link between European colonial experience and US domestic racism is made in *Gravity's Rainbow* when Sir Marcus Scammony tells Clive Mossmoon that the Americans will want "to see how we do with *our* lovely black animals [...] before they try it on their own, ah, target groups."[31] Dehumanizing and "Othering" racial classification is here explicitly brought into relation with colonial strategies of social control.

David Witzling argues that throughout his writing Pynchon "dramatizes mainstream American culture's inability to acknowledge the legitimacy of racially distinct experience and cultural expression."[32] This observation can be generalized to include what Pynchon calls the Western culture of "Analysis and Death." The postmodern ontological instability of identity categories in Pynchon's writing is generated in large part by the discourses of alterity that the narratives use to dramatize and engage issues of racial legitimacy. While the liberal humanist conception of identity as a stable, inherent core of self is deconstructed as an illusion and strategy of control in these narratives, still Pynchon's work suggests that resistance is a necessary struggle, that even in the midst of empire "[t]he savages of other continents, corrupted but still resisting in the name of life, have gone on despite everything ..."[33]

NOTES

1 Thomas Pynchon, *Gravity's Rainbow* (New York: Viking, 1973), p. 272.
2 Michael Taussig, *Mimesis and Alterity: A Particular History of the Senses* (New York: Routledge, 1993), p. 130.
3 Pynchon, *Gravity's Rainbow*, p. 712.
4 *Ibid.*, p. 623.
5 *Ibid.*, p. 624.
6 *Ibid.*, pp. 712–13.
7 *Ibid.*, p. 693.
8 *Ibid.*, pp. 693, 626.
9 *Ibid.*, p. 681.
10 *Ibid.*, p. 738.
11 Molly Hite, *Ideas of Order in the Novels of Thomas Pynchon* (Columbus: Ohio State University Press, 1983); David Seed, *The Fictional Labyrinths of Thomas Pynchon* (Iowa City: University of Iowa Press, 1988); Tony Tanner, *Thomas Pynchon* (London: Methuen, 1982).
12 Leo Bersani, "Pynchon, Paranoia, and Literature," *Representations*, 25 (1989), 112.
13 Pynchon, *Gravity's Rainbow*, pp. 712, 742, 519.
14 Thomas H. Schaub, *Pynchon: The Voice of Ambiguity* (Urbana: University of Illinois Press, 1981), pp. 49–50.
15 Bersani, "Pynchon," 118.
16 Thomas Pynchon, *Mason & Dixon* (New York: Henry Holt and Co, 1997), p. 350.
17 Michael Bérubé, *Marginal Forces/Cultural Centers: Tolson, Pynchon, and the Politics of the Canon* (Ithaca: Cornell University Press, 1992), p. 225.
18 David Witzling, "The Sensibility of Postmodern Whiteness in *V.*, or Thomas Pynchon's Identity Problem," *Contemporary Literature*, 47.3 (2006), 394.
19 Pynchon, *Gravity's Rainbow*, p. 285.
20 Anne McClintock, *Imperial Leather: Race, Gender, and Sexuality in the Colonial Context* (New York: Routledge, 1995), p. 5.
21 Pynchon, *Gravity's Rainbow*, p. 286.
22 *Ibid.*, p. 317.
23 *Ibid.*, p. 276.
24 *Ibid.*, pp. 276, 722.
25 Thomas Pynchon, *The Crying of Lot 49* (Philadelphia: Lippincott, 1966), p. 124; Steven Weisenburger, "Reading Race: *The Crying of Lot 49* and Early Pynchon," in Thomas H. Schaub (ed.), *Approaches to Teaching Pynchon's* The Crying of Lot 49 *and Other Works* (New York: Modern Language Association, 2008), p. 57.
26 Pynchon, *Gravity's Rainbow*, pp. 74–75, 362.

27 Michael Harris, "To Historicize is to Colonize: Colonialism in *V.* and *Gravity's Rainbow*" in Schaub (ed.), *Approaches*, p. 104.

28 Pynchon, *Gravity's Rainbow*, p. 722.

29 Weisenburger, "Reading Race," p. 55.

30 *Ibid.*, p. 53.

31 Pynchon, *Gravity's Rainbow*, p. 616.

32 Witzling, "Sensibility," 384.

33 Pynchon, *Gravity's Rainbow*, p. 722.

12

INGER H. DALSGAARD

Science and technology

Though the presence of both science and technology in his fiction is often considerable, Thomas Pynchon is rarely classified as a science fiction writer. This may prompt consideration of both the nature of his writing and workable definitions of the genre. There are certainly examples and elements of science fiction in his work, ranging from "Minstrel Island" (1958), his unpublished co-authored musical, to *Against the Day* (2006), with its time machine theme.[1] Yet there are also Pynchon texts – among them several early short stories collected in *Slow Learner* (1984) and his latest novel, *Inherent Vice* (2009) – which scarcely concern themselves with science or technology at all, either as overall themes or as props. Such fictions may appear as exceptions to a body of work almost defined by its preoccupation with the parameters and paraphernalia of science and technology: from the way it relates to and defines the very nature of power structures, industrialization or capitalism to its occasional, seemingly self-indulgent, nerdish romps around the material and technical details of some imagined gadget or piece of electronic equipment or machinery. As this Companion shows, however, applying a label such as "science fiction" would be reductive when trying to describe the many layers, strategies and effects of Pynchon's writing. Instead, this chapter explores a variety of the ways in which science and technology appear, and suggests a few overall strategies useful in the interpretation of Pynchon's fiction.

The scholarly texts

A reading of Pynchon's work readily confirms the extent of his references to science and technology. A brief review of secondary texts can serve to indicate not only the nature and range of uses to which Pynchon puts science and technology, but also the variety of scholarly interpretations of their significance and meaning.

One prominent critical focal point concerns how Pynchon's texts may be read at different levels as scientific metaphors. "Science," of course, can cover a potentially wide range of disciplines including the social sciences; yet it is Pynchon's use of ideas and images from the hard or natural sciences that has garnered most attention (as Susan Strehle remarks, there are "more general discussions of relativity theory and quantum mechanics in the criticism of Thomas Pynchon's fiction than anywhere else in the literature section of the library").[2] Different novels invoke various fields: for example, *Gravity's Rainbow* (1973) invokes ballistics, chemistry and geology, *Mason & Dixon* (1997) astronomy, and *Against the Day* mathematics, geometry and physics. Yet literary scholars naturally tend to look less at what natural sciences described in fiction say themselves about the real world or reality than at what fictional texts or literary strategies which include or mirror scientific fields, theories or methods say about the world.

Brian McHale associated a shift from modernist to postmodernist fiction with a movement from asking epistemological questions of the world to ontological ones – from asking (as Dick Higgins formulated it) how to interpret the world of which you are a part to asking which "world" and which "you" are relevant and (inter)acting.[3] Taking a point of departure from twentieth-century physics, it is possible to identify a parallel line of questioning or, rather, parallel answers arising from within the natural sciences. While Einstein's theories of relativity seemed to upset the stable reality of Newtonian physics (a challenge congruent to modernist experiments with new artistic perspectives on reality), it was quantum mechanics that heralded the real departure, after which the physical world could no longer be understood as a stable reality subject to a single set of identifiable laws. Quantum physicists have proven that there are other worlds than the Newtonian, that these are not answerable to the laws of nature once assumed to be fixed, and that the observer does not occupy a privileged, godlike position outside and separate from the "world" he or she observes. This scientific perspective may be viewed as a strong metaphor *transposed* (less rigorously) to literature, which accommodates Heisenberg's uncertainty principle or the Many-Worlds theory better than our classical view of reality.[4] Alternatively, it may be understood as a *parallel* approach whose congruence in relation to literature became manifest as twentieth- and twenty-first-century fiction cut some of its moorings to realism, if not reality, and the rules that once applied. Such a paradigm shift in science provides a plausible interpretive framework for literature. Thus while theorists have struggled to accept the two as covalent and coexisting, quantum mechanics can properly be said to have supplemented rather than supplanted classical and relative physics. Similarly, postmodernist, modernist and realist approaches to literature also continue to live alongside one another, if not within any given work of fiction then certainly within contemporary literature as a whole.

A second prominent focus in scholarly examinations of Pynchon's works is material rather than conceptual and revolves around technology. Such an approach is best exemplified by treatments of the rocket that is central to *Gravity's Rainbow*. The 00000 and the engineers, real and imagined, who surround it have prompted a number of different readings: the fictional text is taken to articulate postwar history and the US manned space program; the historical and fictional engineers of the Third Reich's V-2 rocket program who populate *Gravity's Rainbow* challenge notions of the nature of narrative and the relationship between novel and history; the unstable sense of self and ontology evinced by an engineer such as Franz Pökler provides an analogy with the position of a reader of postmodern literature, while his autobiographical strategies compare to the apologias of Nazi weapons designers.[5]

Scholarly readings of Pynchon do not, however, divide solely along thematic lines between hard science as an influence on or inspiration for his writing on the one hand, and his use of technologies (objects as well as engineering or technological systems) on the other. They may also be distinguished in terms of their narratological and historical approaches. To a greater or lesser degree, scholars focusing on science and technology in Pynchon's writing seek a balance, attending to the reality of those technologies or scientific fields on which his texts rely and acknowledging that they raise substantive issues or concerns, while also addressing their poetic significance or the literary strategies they imply.[6] It may well be that correspondences are more readily discerned between literary theory and scientific discourse than between literary theory and technology, industry and engineering. Consequently, Pynchon criticism preoccupied with science tends to explore poetics whereas technology in his writing is understood more often in relation to historical or political issues than simply as paraphernalia or props for the story. What makes Pynchon's use of science and technology so compelling is that, in part through their elaborations upon science and technology, his novels combine an exploration of the limits of narrative structure with thematic approaches and (implicit) social commentary and critique.

An appreciation of these qualities is enhanced by a familiarity with some of the many ways in which science and technology have themselves been interpreted by theorists and critics of particular relevance to Pynchon's writing. One critical tradition leads back to Marx's observations concerning "Machinery and Large-Scale Industry'" in the first volume of *Capital* (1867), wherein science and technology constitute elements of the means of production developed in relation to the laws of capital accumulation and in the interests of property. A second, closely related and equally long-standing perspective, exemplified by Jacques Ellul's *The Technological Society* (1954), understands its subject in terms of *technique*, an expansive concept referring not only to specific technologies but also to the methods, assumptions, beliefs and discourses they call forth; their tendency to integrate, extend, bolster and legitimate one another; and the increasing autonomy and authority that the resulting system exhibits. Less materialist than the first, less technologically determinist than the second, yet owing something to both, a third approach elaborated in a series of works by Lewis Mumford highlights the intimate relationship between scientific and technological advance and the exigencies of power, militarism and war.[7]

All three interpretive frameworks offer fruitful ways of approaching Pynchon's fictions, not least where they interrogate the intersections among those frameworks (as in *Gravity's Rainbow*, for example). Yet if his work engaged science and technology solely in terms of these frameworks then our readings might easily tend towards the dystopian. One of the attractions in studying Pynchon's fiction, though, is its propensity *not* to observe the terms of any set of concepts applied to it. Thus in its dealings with science and technology his work also entertains liberatory and utopian visions of and perspectives on science and technology. One might juxtapose to Ellul, for instance, the influential work of Marshall McLuhan, itself tending towards technological determinism, perhaps, yet also elaborating (via its matrices of typography and electronic circuitry, physical and sensory extensions, fragmentation and implosion) a progressive vision of a global humane order – one surely influential in the writing of *The Crying of Lot 49* (1966). Likewise, alongside Mumford's anxieties about invention, knowledge and humanity subordinated to what he dubs "megatechnics" one might usefully read Martin Heidegger's philosophical reflections on the essence of technology as a potential locus of challenge, revelation and truth, of salvation as much as risk. Here again, the "stellar course" (to use Heidegger's phrase) of *Gravity's Rainbow* invites readings in terms of Mumford's and Heidegger's related but distinctive understandings of mankind's quest, through science and technology, to analyze, manipulate and engineer the living world.[8]

Pynchon's texts

Most Pynchon texts yield plentiful examples of the distinctive and prominent place that science and technology occupy in his work. One of the earliest examples is Pynchon's short story "Entropy" (1960). The story has been reprinted for teaching purposes in a number of prominent literary anthologies, and is therefore probably one of the most widely read Pynchon texts (along with *The Crying of Lot 49*).[9] It was included in *Slow Learner* in spite of Pynchon's apparent disdain for his own early efforts as a writer: "It is simply wrong to begin with a theme, symbol or other abstract unifying agent, and then to try to force characters and events to conform to it," he writes in the introduction to the collection.[10] The story's title certainly announces the scientific theories (of thermodynamics and communications) to which plot and characters are bound; even the setting of the story in two neighboring apartments illustrates the concept of open versus closed systems; and when Meatball Mulligan downstairs decides to "try and keep his lease-breaking party from deteriorating into total chaos" he becomes a thinly veiled "sorting demon" who attempts to lower entropy in defiance of the second law of thermodynamics and in keeping with the thought experiment of physicist James Clerk Maxwell.[11] The fact that the mechanics of the text are comparatively visible contributes to its pedagogic appeal.

That readers can readily observe the workings of the text also renders visible another narrative feature. As you seek out and identify elements of the fiction which illustrate the second law of thermodynamics, the very attempt to "sort" is likely to make your interpretive efforts comply with the theory of entropy in the communications theory sense: the more information you gather, that is, the more noise is produced, and the less clear is the meaning of the text. A reader of Pynchon – not simply of "Entropy" but more broadly – often ends up enacting the very substance of the text itself, and this seems particularly true of some of the scientific ideas his writing appropriates (as this chapter will explore further). Thus a metaphor, allegory or allusion in the text becomes a description of how we approach it. Towards the end of *V.* (1963), for example, a character who seems to be the eponymous V. herself, is disassembled by inquisitive and mercilessly acquisitive children and discovered to be a collection of disparate mechanical and prosthetic elements: a clockwork glass eye, an artificial foot, false teeth, an ivory comb and so forth – all apparently significant and symbolic of her "life" throughout the text. It is easy to see "the disassembly of the Bad Priest" as an image of how readers themselves pick apart a text, which in the case of *V.* also seems to be made up of disparate parts under the covers.[12]

The potential futility of such sorting is famously shared by the detective/reader Oedipa Maas in *The Crying of Lot 49*, a text in which more overt attention is given to James Clark Maxwell. Maxwell's face adorns the perpetual motion machine which the inventor John Nefastis has conceived on the basis of Maxwell's thought experiment (the Nefastis Machine is itself a thought experiment). Oedipa tries, on the one hand, to move a piston by the power of mental suggestion; on the other, she questions the relationship between the reality of the machine (and demon) in front of her and the scientific metaphor into which she is becoming subsumed. Nefastis elaborates on the theories of communication and thermodynamics introduced in "Entropy": the sorting demon is the point at which the two distinct forms of entropy become connected rather than merely coincidentally alike; entropy consequently becomes a metaphor made "objectively true" by that demon. Oedipa wonders whether it is not the metaphor which engenders the demon.[13] As coincidences blossom, so Oedipa comes to describe her own quest as a "metaphor of God knew how many parts," an assertion which might lead the reader to adopt her own earlier question and to ask whether she is not a product of the metaphor herself. Is Oedipa a character created by the necessity of coincidences, by the strength of the metaphor, by Pynchon's thought experiment (in writing *The Crying of Lot 49*); or did she exist for him "long before the days of the metaphor," as Nefastis claims the demon did for Maxwell?[14] This passage raises the question of the true ontology of characters, and opens for debate the relationship between literary and scientific metaphors.

The physical, material and technological realities of incidental objects, like the Nefastis Machine, the printed circuit card inside her first transistor radio or the matrices of a "digital computer" which spring to Oedipa's mind as she views the hieroglyphic streetscape of San Narciso and reviews the plot she inhabits, all become metaphors or images in *The Crying of Lot 49*.[15] By comparison, the presence and function of the rocket in *Gravity's Rainbow* transcend this movement from technological object to narrative device, in part because of the central position and proliferation of references to rocketry in the novel.

The search for the rocket certainly propels the plot of *Gravity's Rainbow*. In Part One, for example, the relationship between Tyrone Slothrop's chart of amorous conquests and a map of V-2 rocket strikes on London is the central subject of investigation; in Part Two, likewise, the protagonist and the novel lose themselves in technical specifications – a "pornography of blueprints" – and in fantastic fabulations about a Rocket City (including obscene "rocket limericks") at Mittelwerke, the underground production site of the weapon.[16] The historical reality of V-2 strikes and the physical, technical reality of their construction are thus integral to the book, both as factual underpinnings or settings and as a platform for free creative imagination which is at once exuberant entertainment and serious commentary on present situations as much as past events. In addition to Pynchon's own use of the historical rockets of the Second World War, the novel also spawns its own rockets, the mysterious 00000 and 00001, the pursuit of which (by various characters) drives much of the rest of *Gravity's Rainbow*. The historical V-2 theme, in other words, has the ability to refer beyond the novel – to the history of World War II, to the future of Third Reich weapons programs in the Cold War United States – whereas the 00000 rocket is more readily seen as a narrative device within the fiction. The rocket is an object and an objective, indeed a fetish, because both characters in the novel and readers of it may pursue or follow it through the text, just as (for example) Tchitcherine tracks the 00000 or as British, American and Russian technical troops pursued historical V-2s when they scrambled around the zone at the end of the war securing blueprints, parts and people pertaining to this breakthrough in the machinery of war. In this case, fictional and historical rockets both seem emblematic of one aspect of the reading process: the desire to gather the pieces in order to construct meaning, allegiance, purpose or power, all or any of which may ultimately be somewhat frustrated or incomplete projects.

The rocket is also more than an object insofar as Pynchon has chosen a specific kind of technology, rocketry, as a focus of the novel. Seen as a technological form, rocketry, whether manifested in the historical V-2 or the imagined 00000, is also part of a process and a system which *Gravity's Rainbow* shows involve everything from the extraction of coal tar, the global significance of the oil industry and the impact of colonialism on the European mindset, to the humanity and culpability of an individual rocket scientist. At all levels, from implications for geology, through economics and politics, to psychology and morality, the engineering of a rocket in the novel is thus also a story about the engineering of the kind of postwar world we have inhabited since 1945.

Skipping ahead to Pynchon's latest metahistorical epic, *Against the Day*, we find a novel which charts scientific advances as well as blind alleys during a thirty-year period from the early 1890s to the beginning of the 1920s: one whose central vehicle is not a rocket but, perhaps, a time machine. Unlike the rocket which hangs over *Gravity's Rainbow* from beginning to end, the time machine in *Against the Day* appears in a manifest form quite suddenly some 400 pages into the narrative. Subsequently, the idea of time travel – mechanical, scientific or spiritual – recurs on occasion throughout the remainder of the novel. Significantly, the machine's materialization also has the retroactive effect of highlighting allusions to the time-travel theme when the first third of the novel is re-read.

In *Against the Day* the imagined workings of the time machine call attention to the reading process itself. Much as a time machine might, the act of reading a book allows one to go back in time and re-evaluate (and thereby change one's interpretation of) what has been read and what has already taken place within the story chronologically prior to the point at which the time machine enters the text of *Against the Day* by way of another text, H. G. Wells's 1895 novel *The Time Machine*. Though a complicated concept both in its own right and when transposed to the idea of how one reads the novel, time travel offers a relatively straightforward entry point compared to the often abstruse way in which this novel plays with the burgeoning thoughts and thought experiments associated with early twentieth-century physics and mathematics.[17] In fact, just at the point when Yashmeen Halfcourt, who has been talking at some length about complex mathematical and stochastic problems, begins to doubt that her lover Reef has "been following this," she finds herself "interrupted by the thud of Reef's head on the table, where it remained."[18] This passage might just as well describe humorously the effect Pynchon has on readers when they fail to share his nerdish enthusiasms or to follow allusions to the Riemann problem, the real difference between vectors and quaternions, or the precise relevance of the Michelson-Morley Experiment. Reef nonetheless appears subconsciously to have absorbed Yashmeen's lessons, which is emblematic, perhaps, of the way a text encompassing so many intricate references to science could affect the reader: cumulatively or indirectly.

The recurring science-based discussion of the relationship between space and time (and the possibility that alternative, refracted worlds and doubled people exist) groups *Against the Day* thematically with other texts – "Is It O.K. to Be a Luddite?" (1984), "Nearer, My Couch, to Thee" (1993) and *Mason & Dixon* – in which Pynchon concerns himself not solely with science and technology per se, but with the way they (and ultimately reason itself) become a handmaiden of the capitalist potentials latent within the Enlightenment project. The figure of the rationalist Benjamin Franklin, the standardization of time, and the regularization of space through mapping recur in these texts as means of exposing a mechanized mindset which has become a threat to spirituality. By the Age of Reason magic had "degenerated into mere machinery," but desire for magic had not.[19] In *Mason & Dixon* the main characters are involved in a rational project of geographical surveying or cartography which contributes symbolically to the "orthogonal" fate of America. Yet they are still prone to run into or seek out "evidence of magic and the supernatural."[20]

When scientists who theorized new relations between space and time, such as Hermann Minkowski, Bernhard Riemann, and Albert Einstein, appear briefly in *Against the Day*, their presence suggests a more complex idea of space and time (as a continuum, as manifold or relative, for example) than the industrial clock-time for which Franklin stands in the earlier texts. New geometries opening up in the field of science in the twentieth century might promise liberation from the orthogonal strictures of capitalist production imposed in the nineteenth century. However, the Trespassers, who use this freedom to travel through time in *Against the Day*, seem to illustrate how any scientific knowledge and any technological process may enable or permit – and even constitute – new levels of exploitation. In *Gravity's Rainbow* the narrator had asserted that "[t]he War has been reconfiguring time and space into its own image" and that "[t]he true war is a celebration of markets"; in *Against the Day* capitalism and colonialism permeate the fourth dimension and beyond.[21] Knowledge is power, and Pynchon asserts that there is "a pretty straightforward conversion between money and information."[22] In the process he may bring into question scientific pursuits; he certainly indicts the factory system, a concrete manifestation of the Industrial Revolution and the locus of its most destructive expressions: nuclear weaponry, long range missiles and death camps.

Here as elsewhere, then, in its treatment of science and technology Pynchon's fiction shows how they may be used and abused, particularly to control those who see the "virtues and attractions" of a technological world.[23] It also indicates how the disinterested or idealized pursuit of knowledge, such as star-gazing, may have negative consequences in the real world: for example when drawing a straight line, as do Mason and Dixon on the map of colonial America, yields "Bad History," directly and brutally.[24] Technology may be the root of the problem yet also part of its solution. Truly revolutionary ideas, such as the free distribution of electricity attributed to Nikola Tesla, may be thwarted; but at least inventors such as Roswell Bounce and Merle Rideout in *Against the Day* use their scientific curiosity and technological know-how to foster local resistance to the tyranny of business mogul Scarsdale Vibe, developing their strangely plausible desert diving gear, the Hypops apparatus, and putting Hollywood on edge with the possibilities inherent in their Integroscope, which reconstitutes the motion implicit in a still photograph.

Strategies for interpretation

Thomas Pynchon is an author who both experiments with the poetics of science and technology and offers commentary on the substantive issues they raise. As this chapter suggests, science and technology may function as intrinsic organizing principles, as in *The Crying of Lot 49* "with its invocation of Maxwell's Demon both as part of the plot and an image for plotting," or the short story "Entropy."[25] Pynchon's fiction may parody scientific exploration, as is the case with *Lot 49*, or work as a kind of machine or engine, following certain mechanisms or principles or testing them to the breaking point, whether that be the difference in propulsion between the narrative and ballistic rocket-parabolas in *Gravity's Rainbow* or the possibility that a novel like *Against the Day* may be read in non-linear fashion, in keeping with the operations of a time machine. In these and other ways Pynchon's work invites analysis and classification according to how he experiments with narrative structure, from the strategic to the detailed level, in ways which draw on examples and methods from science and technology.

Science and technology simultaneously provide countless occasions for Pynchon to comment on historical, political and social issues. They are intimately connected to some of the major concerns threaded through his fiction – sex, death, power, time, consciousness, rationalism, systems, war, business and capitalism, the environment, relationships between man and machine, and many other variations on these themes – as well as to specific issues which have shaped the western world in recent centuries: from the history of mining to economic policies, from the identity and role of engineers vis-à-vis corporate responsibility to the difference between theoretical and practical applications of science. The checkered histories of science and technology, placed in their proper, wider historical contexts, invite critical scrutiny by the reader.

If all this sounds slightly forbidding, it is worth remembering one of the joys of reading Pynchon: that his *jeux d'esprit* readily leaven a text heavy with serious issues and complex poetics. To paraphrase his own text, reading Pynchon can be "like riding across the country in a bus driven by a maniac bent on suicide ... though he's amiable enough, keeps cracking jokes back through the loudspeaker."[26] The outlook of the "engineer" in charge of the vehicle may be utopian or dystopian and his humor light-hearted or as black as coal tar. The reader, however, is by no means a helpless passenger and may find his or her own balance among amusement, instruction and warning in the process of reading a Pynchon text.

NOTES

1 Rodney Gibbs, "A Portrait of the Luddite as a Young Man," *Denver Quarterly*, 39 (2004), 35–42 at 35. For details see Luc Herman's chapter in the present volume.

2 Susan Strehle, *Fiction in the Quantum Universe* (Chapel Hill: University of North Carolina Press, 1992), p. 24. Strehle lists scholars whose work has included discussions of Pynchon's use of physics. A pioneer in this field is N. Katherine Hayles, *The Cosmic Web: Scientific Field Models and Literary Strategies in the Twentieth Century* (Ithaca: Cornell University Press, 1984).

3 Brian McHale, *Constructing Postmodernism* (London and New York: Routledge, 1992), pp. 147–57; Dick Higgins quoted in McHale, p. 33.

4 Roger Penrose, *The Road to Reality: A Complete Guide to the Laws of the Universe* (London: Jonathan Cape, 2004), pp. 782–85; see Inger H. Dalsgaard, "Readers and Trespassers: Time Travel, Orthogonal Time, and Alternative Figurations

of Time in *Against the Day*," in Jeffrey Severs and Christopher Leise (eds.), *Pynchon's* Against the Day: *A Corrupted Pilgrim's Guide* (Newark: University of Delaware Press, 2011), pp. 115–37; and Inger H. Dalsgaard, "Something to Compare It to Then," *Pynchon Notes*, 54–55 (2008), 85–98. See also S. Strehle, *Fiction*, pp. 7–26 on relations between new physics, fiction and reality.

5 Dale Carter, *The Final Frontier: The Rise and Fall of the American Rocket State* (London: Verso, 1988); Inger H. Dalsgaard, "*Gravity's Rainbow*: A Historical Novel of a Whole New Sort," *Pynchon Notes*, 50–51 (2002), 35–50; Robert L. McLaughlin, "Franz P: Narrative and Self in *Gravity's Rainbow*," *Pynchon Notes*, 40–41 (1997), 159–75; Joseph Tabbi, *Postmodern Sublime: Technology and American Writing from Mailer to Cyberpunk* (Ithaca: Cornell University Press, 1995).

6 Terry Reilly and Stephen Tomaske, "Hard Science and the Paranormal in *Gravity's Rainbow*: Precognition Machines, Cockroaches, and Not *That* Helmut Schmidt," *Pynchon Notes*, 54–55 (2008), 39–53; Terry Reilly, "Narrating Tesla in *Against the Day*" in J. Severs and C. Leise (eds.), *Pynchon's* Against the Day, pp. 139–63; Inger H. Dalsgaard, "Terrifying Technology: Pynchon's Warning Myth of Today," *Pynchon Notes*, 42–43 (1998), 91–110.

7 Karl Marx, *Capital* (Harmondsworth: Penguin, 2004), vol. I, pp. 455–599; Jacques Ellul, *The Technological Society* (1954; New York: Vintage, 1964); Lewis Mumford, *Technics and Human Civilization* (1934; New York: Harcourt, Brace and World, 1963); Lewis Mumford, *The Myth of the Machine*, I: *Technics and Human Development* (New York: Harcourt, Brace, Jovanovich, 1967); II: *The Pentagon of Power* (New York: Harcourt, Brace, Jovanovich, 1970).

8 Marshall McLuhan, *The Gutenberg Galaxy: The Making of Typographic Man* (University of Toronto Press, 1962); Marshall McLuhan, *Understanding Media: The Extensions of Man* (New York: McGraw Hill, 1964); Marshall McLuhan (with Jerome Agel and Quentin Fiore) *War and Peace in the Global Village* (New York: Bantam, 1968); Martin Heidegger, *The Question Concerning Technology and Other Essays* (New York: Harper and Row, 1977).

9 See, for example, Nina Baym (ed.), *The Norton Anthology of American Literature*, 7th edn. (New York: Norton, 2007), vol. E.; Paul Lauter (ed.), *The Heath Anthology of American Literature*, 6th edn. (Florence: Cengage 2009), vol. E.; and George McMichael (ed.), *The Concise Anthology of American Literature*, 7th edn. (Old Tappan: Longman, 2010).

10 Thomas Pynchon, *Slow Learner: Early Stories* (Boston: Little, Brown, 1984), p. 12.

11 *Ibid.*, p. 97.

12 Thomas Pynchon, *V.* (Philadelphia: Lippincott, 1963), pp. 237, 342–43.

13 Thomas Pynchon, *The Crying of Lot 49* (Philadelphia: Lippincott, 1966), pp. 105–6.

14 *Ibid.*, pp. 109, 106.

15 *Ibid.*, pp. 24, 180.

16 Thomas Pynchon, *Gravity's Rainbow* (New York: Viking, 1973), pp. 224, 305–11.

17 Inger H. Dalsgaard, "Clock Time and Creative Resistance in *Against the Day*," in Sascha Pöhlmann (ed.), *Against the Grain: Reading Pynchon's Counternarratives* (Amsterdam and New York: Rodopi, 2010), pp. 81–96 at p. 90.

18 Thomas Pynchon, *Against the Day* (New York: Penguin Press, 2006), p. 863.

19 Thomas Pynchon, "Is It O.K. to Be a Luddite?" *New York Times Book Review*, October 28, 1984: 1, 40–41 at p. 41.

20 David Cowart, "The Luddite Vision: *Mason & Dixon*," *American Literature*, 71, 2 (1999), 341–63 at 347.

21 Pynchon, *Gravity's Rainbow*, pp. 257, 105.

22 Pynchon, "Is It O.K." 41.

23 Kathryn Hume, "Pynchon's Mythological Histories" in Harold Bloom (ed.), *Bloom's Modern Critical Views: Thomas Pynchon* (Broomall: Chelsea House Publishers, 2003), pp. 131–44 at p. 142.

24 Thomas Pynchon, *Mason & Dixon* (New York: Henry Holt & Co., 1997), p. 615.

25 Gillian Beer, "Translation or Transformation? The Relations of Literature and Science," *Notes and Records of the Royal Society of London*, 44, 1 (1990), 81–99 at 94.

26 Pynchon, *Gravity's Rainbow*, p. 412.

Coda

HANJO BERRESSEM

How to read Pynchon

Reading Pynchon, or, how to make sense of a notoriously difficult writer

The promotional video clip for Thomas Pynchon's *Inherent Vice* (2009) opens up to a screaming guitar solo that catapults the viewer back into the 1960s. Pynchon, in the mildly self-ironic voice he reserves for his auto-biographical texts, both introduces and endorses the book. To his mock-noir voice-over narrative, the video shows images of Manhattan Beach in Los Angeles, which is transformed in the novel into the fictional "Gordita Beach." The video, which followed a number of earlier semi-public, mostly tongue-in-cheek appearances, is the latest indication that Pynchon has mellowed out some, become more laid back and less paranoid. Maybe the next time around, he will actually explain to us what it all means.

Critical flashback

Until then, however, we're left to wonder. In fact, since the publication of his first novel *V.* in 1963, word has been out that Pynchon is a notoriously difficult writer. What exactly does "difficult" mean in this context? First, Pynchon injects an incredible amount of often extremely arcane cultural knowledge into his novels. Second, Pynchon constantly modulates narrative voices and stylistic registers, which makes his texts eminently heteroglossic.[1] Rhetorical modes move from his signature bad lyrics for imaginary songs to highly poetic descriptions, such as that of a Christmas Mass during World War II in *Gravity's Rainbow* (1973). Often, stylistic shifts are as fluid as the modulation of the "night's sonorous score" that Oedipa senses while drifting through San Francisco in *The Crying of Lot 49* (1966).[2] Third, the novels' narratives are labyrinthine, with countless characters, and pages crammed with irredeemably diverging plots and sub-plots, many of which go off on tangents or simply dribble away. It doesn't help that the novels' chronological structures are equally complicated, with flashbacks within flashbacks and flashforwards within flashforwards. Pynchon *aficionados* love him precisely for this intricacy and his stylistic mannerisms; for the sheer exuberance of his imagination, the novels' horror vacui, the "high magic" of his "low puns," and his lovingly detailed descriptions of paranoid landscapes – which is how Pynchon became a cult writer.[3]

Early critical responses to Pynchon's work attempted to come to terms with these difficulties by clarifying – to themselves as much as to the critical community – some of the central concepts Pynchon uses to organize his texts. That was difficult, as many of these were taken from the hard sciences, and few critics could bridge the divide between the "two cultures" with the ease and the grace with which Pynchon did. In fact, some of the early criticism functioned also as readers' guides – a role that has now been taken over by electronic forums.[4] The growing "Pyndustry" developed centripetal conceptual figures that functioned as hermeneutical guides and promised to somehow contain Pynchon's exceptional writing. In particular, Pynchon's references to entropy, information theory and paranoia – all of which were already central to his early short story programmatically titled "Entropy" (1960) – became the focus of critical scrutiny.

In this phase, Pynchon was read as a prophet of doom and miscommunication who brought ideas from science, technology, politics, history, philosophy and art into resonance in order to orchestrate the gradual decline of Western civilization. His complex discursive assemblages were inclined slopes slanted towards the inanimate. They slouched towards universal disorder, heat-death, noise and, ultimately, to pure static. *V.* presented a panorama of growing cultural despair, ennui and the decline from individual to mass culture: from the "prince" to "the bureaucrat." *The Crying of Lot 49* unveiled, for Oedipa Maas as much as for the reader, a counterculture operating in the interstices of official power and lines of information – a counterculture made up of preterites and losers, a group for whom Pynchon reserves, throughout his work, most of his sympathy. The novel's historical diagnosis was a massive, "calculated withdrawal from the life of the Republic" – a move echoed, just maybe, in Pynchon's own personal withdrawal.[5] Beyond the historical and the political, critics noted Pynchon's interest in the tragic logic of a seemingly immutable human condition: the universal sadomasochism of master and slave; or, less philosophically, of "fuckers and fuckees."[6] Despite their diversity, most critical analyses attempted to make sense of the novels by organizing their complexities and convolutions into meaningful patterns.

In a second phase of Pynchon criticism, which was inspired by post-structuralist theory, critics went violently centrifugal. Suddenly, Pynchon turned into a master deconstructionist whose immensely convoluted plots should make the reader aware of the futility of any search for order. The texts were about the endless dissemination of meaning; vast, sprawling allegories of the reign of the signifier and its materiality: complicated metafictional games. The characters were either Lacanian "barred subjects" caught in the prison house of language and looking for lost objects, or the novels became, if the critics inclined towards deconstruction, discursive sites where meaning was infinitely deferred: zones of grammatological *différance*.[7] Pynchon played with the reader's expectations and delighted in bringing these expectations down through texts resisting cognitive containment.

In the course of the 1990s, this critical game also became less exciting. Much as the image of the "prophet of doom" had lost its allure, Pynchon as prophet of pure play and as master of ironical detachment became less interesting. Throughout the deconstructive phase, in fact, some critics had not stopped seeing something in Pynchon that exceeded pure play; a certain intensity, an affective urgency that concerned, among others, the question of whether art, such as the songs of The Paranoids in *The Crying of Lot 49*, could express the "luminous beauty" of a metaphysical truth, or whether their music expressed nothing but a physical "power spectrum."[8] Politically, this affective urgency concerned the fear, in *Vineland* (1990), that America's light was no longer the bright light of democracy, but a dim "prefascist twilight" or, even worse, the tubal glow from within an already realized and implemented fascism.[9]

The publication of *Vineland, Mason & Dixon* (1997) and *Against the Day* (2006) coincided conveniently with the rise of New Historicism. The complementary critical phase brought about a re-historicization, re-politicization and, most recently, an ecologization of Pynchon's writing.[10] It began to dawn on readers that Pynchon's project was to write a complete counter-history of America. *Mason & Dixon* showed how much this project had to do with the desire to save the realm of the fictional from the forces of relentless factualization and rationalization which, in moving westward across the American continent, changed "all from subjunctive to declarative, reducing Possibilities to Simplicities that serve the ends of Governments."[11] The difference between the fictional and the factual, which had permeated all of Pynchon's novels, was taken up in *Against the Day* in the conceit of the double refraction of light by Iceland spar.

In the course of his grand project Pynchon's writing had changed. It became less harsh and was often suffused with the atmosphere of magic realism. In parallel, Pynchon's poetics shifted from the logic of entropic decline to a negentropic logic of multiplicity; a shift that conveniently coincided with the first book-length study of his work that argued from a Deleuzian perspective.[12] *Inherent Vice* is Pynchon at his most accessible. Somewhat ironically, the author formerly known as notoriously difficult has become "easy reading," while many literary critics bemoan a certain lack of complexity.

What can one learn from this extremely rough and cursory panorama of critical responses, other than that we tend to refract Pynchon's texts through the latest academic fashions? How should one read Pynchon? How should one make sense of him? Should one even make sense of him? If his poetics oscillate between pure aesthetic play on the one hand and a deeply felt political and cultural concern on the other, should one choose sides? Or should one try to reconcile these two aspects? In addressing these questions, I want to circumvent an image that still lingers from the poststructuralist phase of reading Pynchon: that of Pynchon as a writer who is making things difficult, and who is actively and programmatically subverting and making fun of the reader's desire for meaning.

Radical readings

In *Inherent Vice*, Doc Sportello remembers how "in junior college, professors had pointed out" to him "the useful notion that the word is not the thing, the map is not the territory."[13] Alred Korzybski's statement shows that the metaphysical and the physical, or, in other words, mind and matter, are related but at the same time radically different. Why? Humans, just like other living beings – to which Pynchon sometimes refers, quite lovingly, as "critters" – are members of the set of bodies that make up the material world and as such in constant thermodynamic exchange with that world. Their minds, however, Pynchon maintains, are radically separated from this world; hence the dividing line between things and words, which are, as Slothrop feels in *Gravity's Rainbow*, always "Δt" – or also an "eye-twitch" – away "from the things they stand for."[14] As German scientist Erwin Schrödinger quotes Baruch de Spinoza in his article "Mind and Matter," "the body cannot determine mind to think, nor can the mind determine body to motion or rest."[15] In *The Crying of Lot 49*, Oedipa experiences precisely this when, hooked up to the Nefastis Machine, she cannot, purely by mental concentration, cause a physical action.

While Pynchon tends to lead his narratives to moments that promise a possible conjunction of the bodily and the spiritual – by means of telepathy, séances, ouija boards, psychic media, ghosts, sensitives or drugs – he invariably leaves the reader in suspension both about the validity of these conjunctions and about their possible extension into the transcendental. This, however, is not a cruel or cynical literary game. Rather, it is a form of realism.

Every living thing, from single cell to human being, is part and parcel of the physical *and* of the metaphysical. The faculty of the imagination negotiates between the two levels by turning the perception of recurrent material irritations coming from the environment into immaterial universes of meaning. It creates images of the world. As pattern-creating and pattern-recognition junkies, humans constantly project these images back onto the material world, which is why Oedipa's fictional problem – "*Shall I project a world?*" – is also the reader's factual problem.[16]

In a kind of perceptual pointillism, the imagination creates immaterial "surfaces of meaning" and "sheets of time" from the unconnected and instantaneous multiplicity of material matters-of-facts. It transfers a multiplicity of discrete, raw data into a "falsely continuous" and thus fictional history. The downside of this process of "natural integration" is that from immediate material movement the imagination retains only mediated, cut-up, discrete sections. As Pynchon notes in *Gravity's Rainbow*, both "film and calculus" are only "pornographies of flight," never the real flight.[17]

Pynchon might have added that historiography is only "the pornography of history" – a realization that underlines Pynchon's extremely critical take on näive historiography, and his deep investment in historiographic metafiction as a field where the human imagination and the literary imagination converge.[18] His way of redeeming history from within historiography is to show the complexity of history, the fictional character of all forms of historiography, and the ways in which history is hijacked and falsely factualized by the powers that be. The first two strategies explain some of his texts' difficulty; the third, their political urgency.

As historical meaning is constructed within the individual and cannot be transferred from one individual to the other directly, we are all ontologically paranoid. All that can be transferred is information, and even that is difficult. As Pynchon notes early on in "Entropy," even a simple sentence like "I love you" is shot through with "Ambiguity. Redundancy. Irrelevance, even [...] Noise screws up your signal, makes for disorganization in the circuit."[19] How, then, can we communicate at all? While his early writing deals with this question in terms of information theory, Pynchon's later writing shows that it is a much larger, both cultural and biological question. The construction of meaning is predicated upon systems of co-evolution and the development and the sharing of codes. We learn to project a communal world by comparing and contrasting notes and by probing, from within, the given world and the living things we share this world with.

The creation of meaning, therefore, is communal. If the elements of meaning are extracted from the material world by way of the "Daily Harvest" that the individual "Sensorium brings in," successful communication can only be based on good will.[20] This is why love – what Pynchon calls "Togetherness" – is an inherently and eminently evolutionary force. When successful communication is based on a not only imagined but also lived community, a calculated withdrawal from the life of the Republic is indeed tragic. If we construct meaning from comparing pattern recognition, we must rely less on a will to truth than on a will to community. Pynchon, I think, looks for this sense of community and resonance with his readers as well.

One of Pynchon's main concerns, indeed, is to show how terrifying it is when the will to resonance is overridden by bad vibes. In *Against the Day*, in fact, the "bad" family are literally called the Vibes – with members ranging from Scarsdale to R. Wilshire Vibe – while the "good" family's forefather is the much more connective Webb Traverse. The main reasons for bad vibes in Pynchon are always greed and the desire for power, which define both the bad guys and the good guys who turn bad because they are attracted by them. Mostly, the latter are women who fall for the allure of male power, like Frenesi Gates in *Vineland*, Lake Traverse in *Against the Day* or Shasta Fay Hepworth in *Inherent Vice*. Frenesi's mother Sasha actually feels that what she fears is "a fatality, a helpless turn toward images of authority [...] as if some Cosmic Fascist had spliced in a DNA sequence requiring this form of seduction and initiation into the dark joys of social control."[21] The virus of betrayal, however, does not attack women exclusively. Even Doc Sportello at some point wonders "who" or, even more frightening, "*what* was he working for anymore?"[22] Symptomatically, Pynchon's darkest figures, from Pierce Inverarity in *The Crying of Lot 49* to Crocker Fenway in *Inherent Vice*, all embody the founding fathers' curse. Beyond even the politics of real estate lurks the invisible presence of an elect group – grim and humorless – who are "*in place*" and who use their power to remain there.[23] Ultimately, *Inherent Vice* is about how this group "deals with" Mickey Z. Wolfmann, the real estate developer turned philanthropist.

The Pynchon vibe

Depending on one's aesthetic convictions, fictional narratives either mirror the world or they express it. In "The Art of Fiction," Henry James argues for the second option. If life is an infinitely complicated habitual multiplicity that does not follow clear-cut laws, a narrative that aims at creating the illusion of life must also be infinitely complicated and multiplicitous. Only if fiction "offers us ... life *without* rearrangement do we feel that we are touching the truth; in proportion as we see it *with* rearrangement do we feel that we are being put off with a substitute."[24]

Consider, however, that, in our daily lives as well as in literature, we generally ask of narratives precisely to reduce multiplicity, as I did in the critical panorama earlier, which also reduced an immensely complex field to a meaningful pattern. We love detective novels because they start with a multiplicity of possibilities which they slowly reduce to one certainty. This desire is almost inevitable: living beings constantly and invariably reduce an infinitely complex "given" to a finitely complex "given." Our mode of going through the world is to reduce its inherent complexity to perceptually and cognitively manageable portions. We focus on things and relations that are important to us, and exclude others. Through perceptual reduction and pattern recognition we gain agency. We obscure the world in order to clarify it and live within it.

Which brings me back to Pynchon's difficulty. It is when narratives provide us with smoothly patterned answers that we tend to say they are meaningful. We tend to like redundant narratives that are clear rather than obscure. It is the privilege of art, however, to eschew redundancy and the reduction of complexity, to create counter- and subjunctive complexities. In order to bring about the transformation of an experienced multiplicity into an artistic multiplicity, James notes, the artist must be a medium:

> Experience is never limited and it is never complete; it is an immense sensibility, a kind of huge spider-web, of the finest silken threads suspended in the chamber of consciousness and catching every air-borne particle in its tissue. It is the very atmosphere of the mind; and when the mind is imaginative … it takes to itself the faintest hints of life, it converts the very pulses of the air into revelations.[25]

For Pynchon, what James calls sensibility is directly related to the sensorium. This is why a political power set against the senses and "anything that could remotely please" them is particularly frightening.[26] To chronicle life's "Multiplexity" and transform the complex vibrations and James's "strange irregular rhythms of life" into a charged prose that charts the changing weather of life's karmic flow – such as the "karmic thermal" over Los Angeles that Doc feels in *Inherent Vice* – one needs to be, artistically, both extremely sensitive and conscious.[27] Politically, one needs to be both responsive and responsible.

Pynchon's worlds

As a human being, Pynchon is embedded in the world that he transforms into writing. *Gravity's Rainbow*, for example, presents an image of the world that originated in Pynchon's imagination while he lived in Manhattan Beach in the 1960s, while *Inherent Vice* is the retrospective image of the time and place from which he was writing *Gravity's Rainbow*. When we read the resulting texts, we initially might want to reconstruct from them specific material matters-of-fact and their meanings. Because they are all projected by Pynchon, however, all we can do is to construct from them our *own* images. The more we are cognitively and affectively in tune with Pynchon's projections, the more we will be able to engage with them. If there is a lesson about how to read Pynchon, then, it is that we should remember that Pynchon's texts project worlds. Some of these might seem more familiar than others. All of them, however, are constructed by a singular individual with a specific systemic history who lived and lives in very specific milieus; by someone who expresses his own perspective on the world from *within* this world and for a community of more or less comparable living beings. Someone who artistically expresses the world even while he himself is an expression of this world. Pynchon just happens to have the personal habit – in literary terms, the style – of constructing complex, and thus inherently difficult narratives. Or, maybe more accurately, if one starts with the notion of an infinitely complex world, Pynchon's habit is to not unduly reduce this complexity.

At the end of *Inherent Vice*, Doc Sportello is driving southbound on the 405. His Vibrasonic radio engulfs him in reverberant sound. Although there is the familiar hope of revelation – for the fog to "burn away, and for something else, this time, somehow, to be there, instead" – the mood is relatively mellow.[28] The fog creates a nomadic, automotive republic, a "temporary commune to help each other home through the fog."[29] The songs that reverberate from the novel into our own lives all stress vocal harmony: a politics of sound. The song Sportello listens to while the novel ends is "God Only Knows." Given the novel's surf philosophy and its love of the liminality of the beach, The Beach Boys are perfect carriers of "good vibrations," although they represent mainstream America rather than its subculture – being to the beach what The Carpenters are to the flatland – and although they are directly linked to one of the book's dark attractors, the Manson murders.

Despite, or maybe just because of this ambiguity, it seems that at this moment Pynchon stakes the countless plots and sub-plots he has imagined, all of the beautiful, convoluted sentences, all of the assembled knowledge, against the song's affective density. As if all of his work would, for a short moment, flow into its lyrics and melody. As if he and Brian Wilson had found, after their "missed encounter" in real life, an unexpected artistic resonance. As if they were aware that, although the sixties are long gone, it was their time.

When all seems said and sung, at the end of *Inherent Vice*, "God Only Knows," with its anonymous addressee, is about anybody or anything that holds the promises of the 1960s: Shasta Fay, the Beach, the Surf and, yes, maybe even America itself. In fact, maybe the multiplicity of Pynchon's worlds all add up to one highly ambiguous figure: if James has written *The Portrait of a Lady*, Pynchon, I would argue, has always been, and still is, writing *A Portrait of America*.

NOTES

1 Mikhail Bakhtin, *The Dialogic Imagination: Four Essays*, ed. Michael Holquist (Austin: University of Texas Press, 1981).
2 Thomas Pynchon, *The Crying of Lot 49* (Philadelphia: Lippincott, 1966), p. 117.
3 *Ibid.*, p. 129.
4 Steven Weisenburger, *A Gravity's Rainbow Companion: Sources and Contexts for Pynchon's Novel* (1988; Athens: University of Georgia Press, 2006).
5 Pynchon, *Lot 49*, p. 92.
6 Thomas Pynchon, *Vineland* (Boston: Little, Brown, 1990), p. 81.
7 Alec McHoul and David Wills, *Writing Pynchon: Strategies in Fictional Analysis* (Urbana: University of Illinois Press, 1990).
8 Pynchon, *Lot 49*, p. 136.
9 Pynchon, *Vineland*, p. 371.
10 Elizabeth Jane Wall Hinds (ed.), *The Multiple Worlds of Pynchon's "Mason & Dixon"* (Rochester: Camden House, 2005); Thomas H. Schaub, "The Environmental Pynchon: *Gravity's Rainbow* and the Ecological Context," *Pynchon Notes*, 42–43 (1998), 59–72.
11 Thomas Pynchon, *Mason & Dixon* (New York: Henry Holt & Co, 1997), p. 345.
12 Stefan Mattessich, *Lines of Flight: Discursive Time and Countercultural Desire in the Work of Thomas Pynchon* (Durham: Duke University Press, 2002).
13 Thomas Pynchon, *Inherent Vice* (New York: Penguin Press, 2009), p. 194.
14 Thomas Pynchon, *Gravity's Rainbow* (New York : Viking, 1973), pp. 100, 510.
15 Erwin Schrödinger, "Mind and Matter," in Schrödinger, *What Is Life?* (Cambridge University Press, 1992), pp. 93–164.
16 Pynchon, *Lot 49*, p. 82.
17 Pynchon, *Gravity's Rainbow*, p. 567.
18 Linda Hutcheon, "Historiographic Metafiction: Parody and the Intertextuality of History," in Patrick O'Donnell and Robert Con Davis (eds.), *Intertextuality and Contemporary American Fiction* (Baltimore: Johns Hopkins University Press, 1989), pp. 3–32; Linda Hutcheon, *A Poetics of Postmodernism: History, Theory, Fiction* (New York: Routledge, 1988).
19 Thomas Pynchon, *Slow Learner* (Boston: Little, Brown, 1984), pp. 90–91.
20 Pynchon, *Mason & Dixon*, p. 742.
21 Pynchon, *Vineland*, p. 83.
22 Pynchon, *Inherent Vice*, p. 314.
23 *Ibid.*, p. 347.

24 Henry James, "The Art of Fiction," in *Literary Criticism*, I: *Essays on Literature, Amerian Writers, English Writers*, ed. Leon Edel (Harmondsworth: Penguin, 1984), p. 58.

25 *Ibid.*, p. 52.

26 Pynchon, *Vineland*, p. 313.

27 Pynchon, *Mason & Dixon*, p. 523; James, "Art of Fiction," p. 58; Pynchon, *Inherent Vice*, p. 11.

28 Pynchon, *Inherent Vice*, p. 369.

29 *Ibid.*, p. 368.

SELECTED BIBLIOGRAPHY

Works by Thomas Pynchon

Novels

V. Philadelphia: Lippincott, 1963.
The Crying of Lot 49. Philadelphia: Lippincott, 1966.
Gravity's Rainbow. New York: Viking, 1973.
Vineland. Boston: Little, Brown, 1990.
Mason & Dixon. New York: Henry Holt, 1997.
Against the Day. New York: Penguin Press, 2006.
Inherent Vice. New York: Penguin Press, 2009.

Other fiction

"Appendix: Pynchon's Juvenilia." In Clifford Mead, *Thomas Pynchon: A Bibliography of Primary and Secondary Materials.* Elmwood Park: Dalkey Archive Press, 1989, pp. 155–67.
"Mortality and Mercy in Vienna." *Epoch* 9.4 (1959), 195–213.
Slow Learner. Boston: Little, Brown, 1984. (Includes an introduction by Pynchon, and the stories "The Small Rain," "Low-lands," "Entropy," "Under the Rose" and "The Secret Integration.")

Essays and reviews

"Togetherness." *Aerospace Safety* 16.12 (1960), 6–8.
"A Journey Into the Mind of Watts." *New York Times Magazine*, June 12, 1966, 34–35, 78, 80–82, 84.
"Is It O.K. to Be a Luddite?" *New York Times Book Review*, October 28, 1984, 1, 40–41.
"Introduction." In Richard Fariña, *Been Down So Long It Looks Like Up to Me.* Harmondsworth: Penguin, 1983, pp. v–xiv.
"The Heart's Eternal Vow." Review of *Love in the Time of Cholera* by Gabriel García Márquez. *New York Times Book Review*, April 10, 1988, 1, 47, 49.
"Introduction." In Donald Barthelme, *The Teachings of Don B.*, ed. Kim Herzinger. New York: Turtle Bay, 1992, pp. xv–xxii.
"Nearer, My Couch, to Thee." *New York Times Book Review*, June 6, 1993, 3, 57.
"Introduction." In Jim Dodge, *Stone Junction: An Alchemical Pot-Boiler.* Edinburgh: Rebel Inc., 1997, pp. vii–xii.

"Foreword." In George Orwell, *Nineteen Eighty-Four*. New York: Plume, 2003, pp. vii–xxvi.

Secondary sources

Journal

Pynchon Notes (1979–) Every issue of this academic journal exclusively devoted to Pynchon's work combines a set of essays with a bibliography of primary and secondary sources.

Essays, book chapters, essay collections and monographs

Abbas, Niran, ed. *Thomas Pynchon: Reading from the Margins*. Madison: Fairleigh Dickinson University Press, 2003.

Attewell, Nadine. "'Bouncy Little Tunes': Nostalgia, Sentimentality, and Narrative in *Gravity's Rainbow*." *Contemporary Literature*, 45.1 (2004), 22–48.

Baker, Jeffrey S. "*Amerikkka Über Alles*: German Nationalism, American Imperialism, and the 1960s Antiwar Movement in *Gravity's Rainbow*." *Critique*, 40.4 (1999), 323–41.

Baringer, Sandra. "Motherhood and Treason: Pynchon's *Vineland* and the New Left." *The Metanarrative of Suspicion in Late Twentieth Century America*. New York: Routledge, 2004, pp. 89–102.

Berger, James. "Nostalgia, Cultural Trauma, and the 'Timeless Burst' in *Vineland*." *After the End: Representations of Post-Apocalypse*. Minneapolis: University of Minnesota Press, 1999, pp. 169–88.

Bergh, Patricia A. "(De)constructing the Image: Thomas Pynchon's Postmodern Woman." *Journal of Popular Culture*, 30.4 (1997), 1–12.

Berressem, Hanjo. *Pynchon's Poetics: Interfacing Theory and Text*. Urbana: University of Illinois Press, 1993.

Bérubé, Michael. *Marginal Forces/Cultural Centers: Tolson, Pynchon, and the Politics of the Canon*. Ithaca: Cornell University Press, 1992.

Bersani, Leo. "Pynchon, Paranoia, and Literature." *Representations*, 25 (1989), 99–118.

Bloom, Harold, ed. *Thomas Pynchon* [Bloom's Major Novelists]. Broomall: Chelsea House Publishers, 2003.

  Thomas Pynchon [Bloom's Modern Critical Views]. Broomall: Chelsea House Publishers, 2003.

Booker, M. Keith. "America and Its Discontents: The Failure of Leftist Politics in *Vineland*." *Literature, Interpretation, Theory*, 4.2 (1993), 87–99.

Bové, Paul A. "History and Fiction: The Narrative Voices of Pynchon's *Gravity's Rainbow*." *Modern Fiction Studies*, 50.3 (2004), 657–80.

Brivic, Shelly. "Opposing Trajectories in *V*." *Tears of Rage: The Racial Interface of Modern American Fiction: Faulkner, Wright, Pynchon, Morrison*. Baton Rouge: Louisiana State University Press, 2008, pp. 108–43.

Brown, Donald. "A Pynchon for the Nineties." *Poetics Today*, 18.1 (1997), 95–112.

Brownlie, Alan W. *Thomas Pynchon's Narratives: Subjectivity and Problems of Knowing*. New York: Peter Lang, 2000.

Bulson, Eric. "Pynchon's Baedeker Trick." *Novels, Maps, Modernity: The Spatial Imagination, 1850–2000*. New York: Routledge, 2007, pp. 85–105.

Burns, Christy L. "Postmodern Historiography: Politics and the Parallactic Method in Thomas Pynchon's *Mason & Dixon.*" *Postmodern Culture*, 14 (2003), n.p.

Caesar, Terry and Takashi Aso. "Japan, Creative Masochism, and Transnationality in *Vineland.*" *Critique*, 44.4 (2003), 371–87.

Carter, Dale. *The Final Frontier: The Rise and Fall of the American Rocket State.* London: Verso, 1988.

Chambers, Judith. *Thomas Pynchon.* New York: Twayne, 1992.

Clerc, Charles, ed. *Approaches to* Gravity's Rainbow. Columbus: Ohio State University Press, 1983.

Cohen, Samuel. "*Mason & Dixon* & the Ampersand." *Twentieth-Century Literature*, 48.3 (2002), 264–91.

Collignon, Fabienne. "A Glimpse of Light." *Textual Practice*, 22.3 (2008), 547–62.

Colville, Georgiana M. *Beyond and Beneath the Mantle: On Thomas Pynchon's* The Crying of Lot 49. Amsterdam: Rodopi, 1988.

Conte, Joseph M. "The Excluded Middle: Complexity in Thomas Pynchon's *Gravity's Rainbow.*" *Design and Debris: A Chaotics of Postmodern American Fiction.* Tuscaloosa: University of Alabama Press, 2002, pp. 163–92.

Cooley, Ronald W. "The Hothouse or the Street: Imperialism and Narrative in Pynchon's *V.*" *Modern Fiction Studies*, 39.2 (1993), 307–25.

Copestake, Ian, ed. *American Postmodernity: Essays on the Recent Fiction of Thomas Pynchon.* Bern: Peter Lang, 2003.

Coughran, Chris. "Green Scripts in *Gravity's Rainbow*: Pynchon, Pastoral Ideology and the Performance of Ecological Self." *ISLE: Interdisciplinary Studies in Literature and Environment*, 16.2 (2009), 265–79.

"Plotting a 'Discourse of the Secluded': Pynchon's Literary Ecology." In *Reading America: New Perspectives on the American Novel.* Ed. Elizabeth Boyle and Anne-Marie Evans. Newcastle upon Tyne: Cambridge Scholars, 2008, pp. 201–20.

Cowart, David. "The Luddite Vision: *Mason & Dixon.*" *American Literature*, 71.2 (1999), 341–63.

"Pynchon and the Sixties." *Critique*, 41.1 (1999), 3–12.

Thomas Pynchon: The Art of Allusion. Carbondale: Southern Illinois University Press, 1980.

Dalsgaard, Inger H. "*Gravity's Rainbow*: 'A Historical Novel of a Whole New Sort.'" *Pynchon Notes*, 50–51 (2002), 35–50.

"Something to Compare It to Then: Rereading Terror in Coincidences Between Pynchon's Germany and America's 9/11." *Pynchon Notes*, 54–55 (2008), 85–98.

Dechand, Thomas. "Pynchon, Cohen, and the Crisis of Victorian Mathematics." *MLN*, 122.5 (2007), 1180–92.

Drake, Scott. "Resisting Totalizing Structures: An Aesthetic Shift in Thomas Pynchon's *The Crying of Lot 49* and *Gravity's Rainbow.*" *Critique*, 51.3 (2010), 223–40.

Dugdale, John. *Thomas Pynchon: Allusive Parables of Power.* London: Macmillan/ New York: St. Martin's Press, 1990.

Duyfhuizen, Bernard. "'A Suspension Forever at the Hinge of Doubt': The Reader-Trap of Bianca in *Gravity's Rainbow.*" *Postmodern Culture*, 2.1 (1991), n.p.

"Taking Stock: 26 Years since *V.*" *Novel*, 23.1 (1989), 75–88.

Eddins, Dwight. *The Gnostic Pynchon*. Bloomington: Indiana University Press, 1990.

Elias, Amy. "Coda: *The Sot-Weed Factor* and *Mason & Dixon*." *Sublime Desire: History and Post-1960s Fiction*. Baltimore: Johns Hopkins University Press, 2001, pp. 221–42.

Giles, Paul. "Virtual Englands: Pynchon's Transatlantic Heresies." *Virtual Americas: Transnational Fictions and the Transatlantic Imaginary*. Durham: Duke University Press, 2002, pp. 225–53.

Ghosh, Shubha, ed. *Thomas Pynchon and the Law*. Oklahoma City University Law Review, 24.3 (1999).

Gibbs, Rodney. "A Portrait of the Luddite as a Young Man." *Denver Quarterly*, 39.1 (2004), 35–42.

Grant, J. Kerry. *A Companion to* The Crying of Lot 49. 2nd edn. Athens: University of Georgia Press, 2008.

A Companion to V. Athens: University of Georgia Press, 2001.

Green, Geoffrey, Donald Greiner and Larry McCaffery, eds. *The "Vineland" Papers: Critical Takes on Pynchon's Novel*. Normal, IL: Dalkey Archive Press, 1994.

Gussow, Mel. "Pynchon's Letters Nudge His Mask." *New York Times*, March 4, 1998, E8.

Hägg, Samuli. *Narratologies of* Gravity's Rainbow. Joensuu: University of Joensuu, 2005.

Hamill, John. "Confronting the Monolith: Authority and the Cold War in *Gravity's Rainbow*." *Journal of American Studies*, 33.3 (1999), 417–36.

"Looking Back on Sodom: Sixties Sadomasochism in *Gravity's Rainbow*." *Critique*, 41.1 (1999), 53–70.

Hawthorne, Mark D. "Homoerotic Bonding as Escape from Heterosexual Responsibility in Pynchon's *Slow Learner*." *Style*, 34.3 (2000), 512–29.

"Pynchon's Early Labyrinths." *College Literature*, 25.2 (1998), 78–93.

Heise, Ursula. "Δt: Time's Assembly in *Gravity's Rainbow*." *Chronoschisms: Time, Narrative and Postmodernism*. Cambridge University Press, 1997, pp. 179–219.

Herman, Luc and John M. Krafft. "Fast Learner: The Typescript of Pynchon's V. at the Harry Ransom Center in Austin." *Texas Studies in Literature and Language*, 49.1 (2007), 1–20.

"Race in Early Pynchon: Rewriting Sphere in *V*." *Critique*, 52.1 (2011), 1–13.

Herman, Luc and Petrus van Ewijk. "Gravity's Encyclopedia Revisited: The Illusion of a Totalizing System in *Gravity's Rainbow*." *English Studies*, 90.2 (2009), 167–79.

Hinds, Elizabeth Jane Wall. "Animal, Vegetable, Mineral: The Play of Species in Pynchon's *Mason & Dixon*." In *Humans and Other Animals in Eighteenth-Century British Culture: Representation, Hybridity, Ethics*. Ed. Frank Palmeri. Burlington: Ashgate, 2006, pp. 179–99.

Hinds, Elizabeth Jane Wall, ed. *The Multiple Worlds of Pynchon's* Mason & Dixon: *Eighteenth-Century Contexts, Postmodern Observations*. Rochester: Camden House, 2005.

Hite, Molly. *Ideas of Order in the Novels of Thomas Pynchon*. Columbus: Ohio State University Press, 1983.

Hogue, W. Lawrence. "The Privileged, Sovereign, Euro-American (Male) Post/Modern Subject and Its Construction of the Other: Thomas Pynchon's V. and

Paul Auster's *The New York Trilogy.*" *Postmodern American Literature and Its Other.* Urbana: University of Illinois Press, 2008, pp. 42–93.

Hollander, Charles. "Pynchon's Juvenilia and *Against the Day.*" *GRAAT* 3 (2008), 38–55. www.graat.fr/5%20Hollander.pdf

Hohmann, Charles. *Thomas Pynchon's* Gravity's Rainbow: *A Study of Its Conceptual Structure and of Rilke's Influence.* New York: Peter Lang, 1986.

Holton, Robert. "In the Rathouse of History with Thomas Pynchon: Rereading *V.*" *Textual Practice,* 2.3 (1988), 324–44.

Horvath, Brooke and Irving P. Malin, eds. *Pynchon and* Mason & Dixon. Newark: University of Delaware Press, 2000.

Huehls, Mitchum. "Global Technologies: Thomas Pynchon's *Mason & Dixon.*" *Qualified Hope: A Postmodern Politics of Time.* Columbus: Ohio State University Press, 2009, pp. 57–78.

Hume, Kathryn. "The Perspectival Subtext in *Gravity's Rainbow.*" *American Literature,* 60.4 (1988), 625–42.

Pynchon's Mythography: An Approach to Gravity's Rainbow. Carbondale: Southern Illinois University Press, 1987.

"The Religious and Political Vision of Pynchon's *Against the Day.*" *Philological Quarterly,* 86.1–2 (2007), 163–87.

"Repetition and the Construction of Character in *Gravity's Rainbow.*" *Critique,* 33.4 (1992), 243–54.

Hurley, Patrick J. *Pynchon Character Names: A Dictionary.* Jefferson: McFarland, 2008.

Hutcheon, Linda. *A Poetics of Postmodernism: History, Theory, Fiction.* London: Routledge, 1988.

Johnston, John. "Pynchon's 'Zone': A Postmodern Multiplicity." *Arizona Quarterly Review,* 46.3 (1990), 91–122.

"Rocket-State Assemblage: *Gravity's Rainbow*" and "An American Book of the Dead: Media and Spectral Life in *Vineland.*" *Information Multiplicity: American Fiction in the Age of Media Saturation.* Baltimore: Johns Hopkins University Press, 1998, pp. 61–96, 206–32.

Kharpertian, Theodore. *A Hand to Turn the Time: The Menippean Satires of Thomas Pynchon.* Rutherford: Fairleigh Dickinson University Press, 1990.

Kim, Sue J. "Not Three Worlds But One: Thomas Pynchon and the Invisibility of Race." *Critiquing Postmodernism in Contemporary Discourses of Race.* New York: Palgrave Macmillan, 2009, 83–116.

King, Vincent. "Giving Destruction a Name and a Face: Thomas Pynchon's 'Mortality and Mercy in Vienna,'" *Studies in Short Fiction,* 35 (1998), 13–21.

Kolbuszewska, Zofia. *The Poetics of Chronotope in the Novels of Thomas Pynchon.* Lublin: Learned Society of the Catholic University of Lublin, 2000.

Kopp, Manfred. *Triangulating Thomas Pynchon's Eighteenth-Century World: Theory, Structure and Paranoia in* Mason & Dixon. Essen: Blaue Eule, 2004.

Lam, Melissa. *Disenfranchised from America: Reinventing Language and Love in Nabokov and Pynchon.* Lanham: University Press of America, 2009.

LeClair, Tom. "Prologue: Thomas Pynchon's *Gravity's Rainbow.*" *The Art of Excess: Mastery in Contemporary American Fiction.* Urbana: University of Illinois Press, 1989, pp. 36–72.

Levine, George and David Leverenz, eds. *Mindful Pleasures: Essays on Thomas Pynchon*. Boston: Little, Brown, 1976.

Liste Noya, José. "Mapping the 'Unmappable': Inhabiting the Fantastic Interface of *Gravity's Rainbow*." *Studies in the Novel*, 29.4 (1997), 512–37.

Lynd, Margaret. "Science, Narrative, and Agency in *Gravity's Rainbow*." *Critique*, 46.1 (2004), 63–80.

McClure, John. "Ontological Pluralism and Preterite Spiritualities: Thomas Pynchon." *Partial Faiths: Postsecular Fiction in the Age of Pynchon and Morrison*. Athens: University of Georgia Press, 2007, pp. 26–62.

"Resisting Romances: Pynchon's *V.* and *Gravity's Rainbow*." *Late Imperial Romance*. London: Verso, 1994, pp. 152–82.

McHale, Brian. *Postmodernist Fiction*. New York: Methuen, 1987.

"(Mis)Reading Pynchon." *Constructing Postmodernism*. New York: Routledge, 1992, pp. 59–141.

McHoul, Alec and David Wills. *Writing Pynchon: Strategies in Fictional Analysis*. London: Macmillan/Urbana: University of Illinois Press, 1990.

McHugh, Patrick. "Cultural Politics, Postmodernism, and White Guys: Affect in *Gravity's Rainbow*." *College Literature*, 28.2 (2001), 1–28.

Madsen, Deborah. *The Postmodernist Allegories of Thomas Pynchon*. New York: St. Martin's Press, 1991.

Maltby, Paul Leon. *Dissident Postmodernists: Barthelme, Coover, Pynchon*. Philadelphia: University of Pennsylvania Press, 1991.

Mangen, Anne and Rolf Gaasland, eds. *Blissful Bewilderment: Studies in the Fiction of Thomas Pynchon*. Oslo: Novus Press, 2002.

Martinez, M. Angeles. "From 'Under the Rose' to *V.*: A Linguistic Approach to Human Agency in Pynchon's Fiction." *Poetics Today*, 23.4 (2002), 633–56.

Mathijs, Ernest. "Reel to Real: Film History in Pynchon's *Vineland*." *Literature/Film Quarterly*, 29.1 (2001), 62–70.

Maxwell, Marilyn. "Thomas Pynchon." *Male Rage, Female Fury: Gender and Violence in Contemporary American Fiction*. Lanham: University Press of America, 2000, pp. 115–87.

Mattessich, Stefan. *Lines of Flight: Discursive Time and Countercultural Desire in the Work of Thomas Pynchon*. Durham: Duke University Press, 2002.

Mead, Clifford. *Thomas Pynchon: A Bibliography of Primary and Secondary Materials*. Elmwood Park: Dalkey Archive Press, 1989.

Medoro, Dana Elizabeth. *The Bleeding of America: Menstruation as Symbolic Economy in Pynchon, Faulkner and Morrison*. Westport: Greenwood Press, 2002.

Melley, Timothy. "Bodies Incorporated: Scenes of Agency Panic in *Gravity's Rainbow*." *Contemporary Literature*, 35.4 (1994), 709–38.

Mendelson, Edward, ed. *Pynchon: A Collection of Critical Essays*. Englewood Cliffs: Prentice Hall, 1978.

Moore, Thomas. *The Style of Connectedness: Gravity's Rainbow and Thomas Pynchon*. Columbia: University of Missouri Press, 1987.

Moraru, Christian. "'Zonal' Ethics: *Gravity's Rainbow*, Dislodged Subjects, and Infernal Technology." *Canadian Review of Comparative Literature*, 24.2 (1997), 263–81.

O'Donnell, Patrick, ed. *New Essays on* The Crying of Lot 49. Cambridge University Press, 1991.

Olster, Stacey. "A 'Patch of England, at a Three-Thousand-Mile Off-Set'? Representing America in *Mason & Dixon*." *Modern Fiction Studies*, 50.2 (2004), 283–302.

"Thomas Pynchon: An Interface of History and Science." *Reminiscence and Re-creation in Contemporary American Fiction*. Cambridge University Press, 1989, pp. 72–105.

Palmeri, Frank. "Parody and Paradigms in *The Crying of Lot 49*." *Satire in Narrative: Petronius, Swift, Gibbon, Melville, and Pynchon*. Austin: University of Texas Press, 1990, pp. 109–25.

Parrish, Timothy. "Pynchon's *Mason & Dixon*: Drawing a Line in the Sands of History." *From the Civil War to the Apocalypse: Postmodern History and American Fiction*. Amherst: University of Massachusetts Press, 2007, pp. 283–85.

Patell, Cyrus R. K. *Negative Liberties: Morrison, Pynchon, and the Problem of Liberal Ideology*. Durham: Duke University Press, 2001.

Pearce, Richard, ed. *Critical Essays on Thomas Pynchon*. Boston: G. K. Hall, 1981.

Plater, William. *The Grim Phoenix: Reconstructing Thomas Pynchon*. Bloomington: Indiana University Press, 1978.

Pöhlmann, Sascha, ed. *Against the Grain: Reading Pynchon's Counternarratives*. Amsterdam: Rodopi, 2010.

Pynchon's Postnational Imagination. Heidelberg: Universitätsverlag Winter, 2010.

Price, Victoria. *Christian Allusions in the Novels of Thomas Pynchon*. New York: Peter Lang, 1989.

Punday, Daniel. "Pynchon's Ghosts." *Contemporary Literature*, 44.2 (2003), 250–74.

"Pynchon from A to V." *Bookforum*, 12.2 (2005), 29–40.

Redfield, Marc. "Pynchon's Postmodern Sublime." *PMLA*, 104.2 (1989), 152–62.

Rosenfeld, Aaron. "The 'Scanty Plot': Orwell, Pynchon, and the Poetics of Paranoia." *Twentieth-Century Literature*, 50.4 (2004), 337–67.

Russell, Alison. "Travels in Baedeker Land: Thomas Pynchon's *V*." *Crossing Boundaries: Postmodern Travel Literature*. New York: Palgrave, 2000, pp. 51–82.

Schaub, Thomas H. ed. *Approaches to Teaching Pynchon's* The Crying of Lot 49 *and Other Works*. New York: Modern Language Association, 2008.

Pynchon: The Voice of Ambiguity. Urbana: University of Illinois Press, 1981.

Seed, David. *The Fictional Labyrinths of Thomas Pynchon*. Iowa City: University of Iowa Press, 1988.

Severs, Jeffrey and Christopher Leise, eds. *Pynchon's* Against the Day: A Corrupted Pilgrim's Guide. Newark: University of Delaware Press, 2011.

Siegel, Mark Richard. *Pynchon: Creative Paranoia in* Gravity's Rainbow. Port Washington: Kennikat Press, 1978.

Simons, John. "Postmodern Paranoia? Pynchon and Jameson." *Paragraph*, 23.2 (2000), 207–21.

Slade, Joseph. *Thomas Pynchon*. 1974. New York: Peter Lang, 1990.

Smith, Mack. "The Postmodern Subject in the Paracinematic Reality of *Gravity's Rainbow*." *Literary Realism and the Ekphrastic Tradition*. University Park: Pennsylvania State University Press, 1995, pp. 195–237.

Smith, Shawn. *Pynchon and History: Metahistorical Rhetoric and Postmodern Narrative Form in the Novels of Thomas Pynchon.* New York: Routledge, 2005.

Smith, Zak. *Pictures Showing What Happens on Each Page of Thomas Pynchon's Novel* Gravity's Rainbow. Portland: Tin House, 2006.

Spencer, Nicholas. "Realizing Abstract Space: Thomas Pynchon and William Gaddis." *After Utopia: The Rise of Critical Space in Twentieth-Century American Fiction.* Lincoln: University of Nebraska Press, 2006, pp. 139–78.

Staiger, Jeffrey. "James Wood's Case Against 'Hysterical Realism' and Thomas Pynchon." *Antioch Review*, 66.4 (2008), 634–54.

Stonehill, Brian. *The Self-Conscious Novel: Artifice in Fiction from Joyce to Pynchon.* Philadelphia: University of Pennsylvania Press, 1988.

Strehle, Susan. "Thomas Pynchon: *Gravity's Rainbow* and the Fiction of Quantum Continuity." *Fiction in the Quantum Universe.* Chapel Hill: University of North Carolina Press, 1992, pp. 27–65.

Tabbi, Joseph. "Mapping the Cor(e)tex(t): Thomas Pynchon." *Cognitive Fictions.* Minneapolis: University of Minnesota Press, 2002, pp. 23–53.

"Meteors of Style: *Gravity's Rainbow*" and "Technology and Identity in the Pökler Story, or the Uses of Uncertainty." *Postmodern Sublime: Technology and American Writing from Mailer to Cyberpunk.* Ithaca: Cornell University Press, 1995, pp. 74–126.

Tanner, Tony. "'The Rubbish-Tip for Subjunctive Hopes': Thomas Pynchon's *Mason & Dixon.*" *The American Mystery.* Cambridge University Press, 2000, pp. 222–38.

Thomas Pynchon. London: Methuen, 1982.

Thomas, Samuel. *Pynchon and the Political.* New York: Routledge, 2007.

Van Delden, Maarten. "Modernism, the New Criticism and Thomas Pynchon's *V.*" *Novel*, 23.2 (1990), 117–36.

Varsava, Jerry A. "Thomas Pynchon and Postmodern Liberalism." *Canadian Review of American Studies*, 25.3 (1995), 63–100.

Weisenburger, Steven. *A* Gravity's Rainbow *Companion: Sources and Contexts for Pynchon's Novel.* 2nd edn. Athens: University of Georgia Press, 2006.

"Thomas Pynchon at Twenty-Two: A Recovered Autobiographical Sketch." *American Literature*, 62.4 (1990), 692–97.

Willman, Skip. "Spectres of Marx in Thomas Pynchon's *Vineland.*" *Critique*, 51.3 (2010), 198–222.

Wilson, David L. and Zack Bowen. "Preparing for Pynchon: Thermodynamics, Maxwell's Demon, Information, and Meaning." *Science and Literature: Bridging the Two Cultures.* Gainesville, University of Florida Press, 2001, pp. 118–37.

Wilson, Rob. "On the Pacific Edge of Catastrophe, or Redemption: California Dreaming in Thomas Pynchon's *Inherent Vice.*" *Boundary* 2, 37.2 (2010), 217–25.

Witzling, David. *Everybody's America: Thomas Pynchon, Race, and the Cultures of Postmodernism.* New York: Routledge, 2008.

Wood, James. "Thomas Pynchon and the Problem of Allegory." *The Broken Estate: Essays on Literature and Belief.* New York: Random House, 1999, pp. 169–79.

Yerkes, Andrew. "*Against the Day* and the Prospects of Historiographic Metafiction." In *Remaking Literary History.* Ed. Helen Groth and Paul Sheehan. Newcastle upon Tyne: Cambridge Scholars, 2010, pp. 223–32.

Websites

pynchonwiki.com

www.themodernword.com/pynchon (includes an archive of Zak Smith's pictures for each page of *Gravity's Rainbow*)

www.thomaspynchon.com

www.vheissu.org

INDEX

Cambridge companions to ...

AUTHORS